America in Change

REFLECTIONS ON THE 60's AND 70's

Ronald Weber

EDITOR

UNIVERSITY OF NOTRE DAME PRESS
Notre Dame   London

INTERNATIONAL STUDIES OF THE
COMMITTEE ON INTERNATIONAL RELATIONS
UNIVERSITY OF NOTRE DAME

Contents

CONTRIBUTORS

All contributors are members of the faculty of the University of Notre Dame. DONALD P. COSTELLO is Professor of English and Director of Undergraduate Studies in English. MICHAEL J. CROWE is Associate Professor and Chairman of the General Program of Liberal Studies. WILLIAM I. DAVISSON is Professor of Economics. C. F. DELANEY is Associate Professor and Chairman of the Department of Philosophy. THOMAS S. FERN is Associate Professor and Chairman of the Department of Art. PHILIP GLEASON is Associate Professor and Chairman of the Department of History. STANLEY HAUERWAS is Assistant Professor of Theology. KEN JAMESON is Assistant Professor of Economics. RICHARD A. LAMANNA is Associate Professor of Sociology and Anthropology and Director of Graduate Studies in Sociology and Anthropology. THOMAS J. MUSIAL is Associate Director of the Collegiate Seminar. JULIAN R. PLEASANTS is Assistant Professor of Microbiology. JOHN ROOS is Assistant Professor of Government and International Studies. JOSEPH W. SCOTT is Associate Professor of Sociology and Anthropology and Director of the Black Studies Program. THOMAS STRITCH is Professor of American Studies. RONALD WEBER is Associate Professor and Chairman of the Program in American Studies. THOMAS WERGE is Assistant Professor of English and Chairman of the Committee on Academic Progress.

Introduction: Pursuing America

This ostentatiously simple and monolithic America is in fact a congeries of inner tensions. It has been so from the beginning; it is more so now than at the beginning. . . . Confronted with so gigantic a riddle, the analyst becomes wary of generalizations, though incessantly he strives to comprehend.
   —Perry Miller, *Errand into the Wilderness*

The analyst of America must surely be wary of generalizations, but in trying to comprehend its tangled riddles he can't very well do without them. Perry Miller himself offered us a durably suggestive one in the shape of a Puritan metaphor: the American experience as an "errand" into the New World "wilderness" and the consequent need to discover the point and purpose of the errand, the reason for which it was and is run. In its basic form the question is whether America has meaning and intention beyond itself or is simply its own end, an intense religious dilemma for New England Puritanism and felt by subsequent generations in various secular reformulations, and it has given rise, from *Magnalia Christi Americana* to *The Greening of America* and in mingled tones of brightest hope and the most abject despair, to a long and uniquely American tradition of national self-examination.

Numerous cultural analysts have suggested that at work in this critical tradition is not so much a need to know as a passion to be saved, not so much a need for understanding as a passion for judgment and redemption, a haunting passion, beyond the accumulation of trinkets and worldly powers, to be a true beacon to the world, the shining city upon a hill. In any case, the inclination to the deepest self-analysis and, as often as not, self-condemnation seems finally the most characteristic of American traits, a curious underlayment to our confident pragmatism and aggressive salesmanship but almost a definition in the eyes of sensitive observers of what it means to be an American. Stephen Spender, for example, in a recent *Partisan Review* (Spring, 1972) pictures Americans, far from being comfortable with themselves, as deeply critical of their motives and methods, "their own existence even." This fundamental unease, he adds, "seems entirely lacking in the rest of the world and enables America to retain its newness, its innocence and

5

even, at the end of the huge tunnel of the vulgar and factitious, its mystery."

Of late the pursuit of America's peculiar mystery has centered on an insistent question, hardly a new one in our national literature of self-examination but nonetheless treated with great urgency and in some cases with an apocalyptic rhetoric that Cotton Mather might have savored. Simply put, the question is this: Is America now experiencing—either just under way or already well along—a period of fundamental change? Or to vary it a bit: Is America now experiencing a transformation from a cultural situation that might be labeled "old" to one that is sharply "new"? Certainly there's no question that during the latter half of the decade of the 1960's and on into the 70's America has seen a floodtide of change—in life styles, race relations, urban living, sexual attitudes, schooling, the arts; the list seems endless. In these years change has swept over us so swiftly that more than ever it appears the only certainty in a society in which centuries are capsuled into decades; and ahead of us looms only more of the same, as Alvin Toffler informs us in *Future Shock* by characterizing what remains of the century in terms of "The Death of Permanence." But do all the present manifestations of change add up to a genuine cultural shift or radical turning point?

A number of recent books have argued that it does. In *The Greening of America* Charles Reich proclaims the beginning of a revolution in consciousness that is replacing plastic, dehumanized America with a "new head," a new way of living, a new man. In *The Pursuit of Loneliness* Philip Slater portrays us at the point of polarized choice between an old, individualistic, and humanly unsatisfying culture and a new culture geared to communal happiness, and warns that if the latter is not ushered in as gracefully as possible we must be prepared for a "bloodbath such as has not been seen in the United States since the Civil War. . . ." Zbigniew Brzezinski locates us, in the title of his book, *Between Two Ages,* caught in the process of transformation into a postindustrial, "tech—netronic" culture that will create a society as different from the old industrial order as it in turn was from the agrarian. And Norman Mailer, to take a last example, concludes the Pentagon confrontation between the forces of law and order and the legions of radical reform in *The Armies of the Night* with a meditation on an America poised at a decisive moment in history:

Brood on that country who expresses our will. She is America, once a beauty of magnificence unparalleled, now a beauty with a leprous skin. She is heavy with child—no one knows if legitimate —and languishes in a dungeon whose walls are never seen. Now the first contractions of her fearsome labor begin—it will go on: no doctor exists to tell the hour. It is only known that false labor is not likely on her now, no, she will probably give birth, and to what? . . .

Unlike Mailer, most turning-point commentators on America have tried to spell out the nature of the cultural shift that is or should be taking place in the country. But Mailer's questioning— "and to what?"—and the sense of being present at a period of deep change may be as significant in itself as the possible outlines of the brave new world we have entered upon. At any rate, it is with this mood of national questioning and the idea of cultural change in the 1960's and 70's as reflected in recent examples of our traditional literature of self-examination that this collection of topical essays is concerned, and of which it in turn is a modest part.

Each of the following writers looks at an area of interest and competence in light of current old culture-new culture thinking or possible shifts of attitude within the area. Taken together, we hope the essays form a larger reflection on the sense of change and transformation in contemporary America. Beyond this I won't try to characterize the essays except to underscore a few obvious things. First, the collection makes no claim to completeness; one can think of many areas that might have been dealt with—education, women's liberation, shifting sexual mores, the cult of youth, violence—if our effort were meant to be comprehensive rather than eclectic and suggestive. Second, there is considerable and intentional variation in the form, tone, and general approach of the essays. Some are done in broad summary fashion while others are sharply focused on a specific issue; some are detached overviews while others argue a position; in every case the writers worked independently and there was no editorial effort to meld their views into a consistent attitude. Lastly, the reader should no doubt keep in mind the period in which the essays were put in final form—the spring and early summer of 1972.

I mention this to emphasize the topicality of the essays and not to borrow the wonderfully specious argument of *Future Shock* that the obsolescence of much of its data verifies its thesis about the rapidity of change. I also mention it because it may have something

to do with the way in which the writers, myself included, responded to the problem we had set for ourselves. In 1972 the mood
of the country was one of relative calm after the dislocations of the
preceding years. Things seemed to be slipping back into old
grooves; old styles and attitudes, seemingly outdated and consigned
to history, reasserted themselves; idealism and urgency and new
communal feeling seemed to give way to depression, weariness, and
the old privatism; what had been new and even radical a few
months or years before tended in 1972 to seem just more of the
same. The reader can judge to what extent, if any, the mood of
1972 affected the essays. He also can judge to what extent that
mood might have been deceptive, merely a temporary lull or breath-
ing space in a period of continuous upheaval, one in which, as
Marshall McLuhan tells us, every man has come to be profoundly
alienated from his past image of himself and change is pervasive.

But that brings to mind another thing this collection is not—
futurology. Although some of the writers offer a prediction here and
there, most are content to struggle with comprehending past and
present, and I suspect they would agree with Samuel McCracken's
remark in *Commentary* (October, 1971) that there is some folk-
wisdom in the tense system of the English language, which recognizes only past and present. "For there can be no future," he notes,
"until it appears in the present, and the present disappears into the
past just as soon as we can perceive it. The present and the past,
then, are all we have, and we must make the most of them."

But while perhaps indicating a certain common-sense realism,
our limitation to past and present may be a mixed blessing. It may
be that the largest omission in this collection is the presence of a
full-blown futurologist, or at the very least a science fiction writer.
In *God Bless You, Mr. Rosewater* Kurt Vonnegut has his saintly
hero tell a gathering of science fiction writers that they are the only
ones really worth reading anymore:

You're the only ones who'll talk about the *really* terrific changes
going on, the only ones crazy enough to know that life is a space
voyage, and not a short one, either, but one that'll last for billions
of years. You're the only ones with guts enough to *really* care
about the future, who *really* notice what machines do to us, what
wars do to us, what cities do to us, what big, simple ideas do to
us. . . . You're the only ones zany enough to agonize over time and
distances without limit, over mysteries that will never die, over the

fact that we are right now determining whether the space voyage for the next billion years or so is going to Heaven or Hell.

For better or worse, the reflections that follow aren't in the science fiction league. But they do represent an effort, rooted in a particular moment of earthly time, to take notice of some of the things that have been happening to us, to offer some wary generalizations, to comprehend the riddle of America.

A conference held at the University of Notre Dame some 15 years ago resulted in a collection of essays, edited by Professors Stephen D. Kertesz and M. A. Fitzsimons and published in 1959, entitled *What America Stands For*. At the suggestion of Professor Kertesz, a similar two-day conference was held at Notre Dame in April, 1972, to discuss developments in American culture since that time, particularly the sense of radical change in recent years. The conference was jointly sponsored by the Program in American Studies, the Committee on International Relations, and the Student Academic Commission; the participants, those who prepared papers and those who gathered in discussion, were all students and faculty members at Notre Dame and represented a variety of ages, attitudes, and academic disciplines. The essays collected here are revisions of the conference papers.

I wish to offer grateful thanks to the contributors to the conference and to this volume; their cooperation was remarkable and enabled us all to have the rare academic experience of finding out what our immediate colleagues, rather than only those in other places, were thinking on a particular issue. Special thanks also are due to Professor Kertesz, not only for initiating the conference but for continued guidance leading to the publication of the papers; to Professor Fitzsimons, who took an active part in the conference, read and commented on all the papers, and kindly extended the pages of *The Review of Politics* for publication of the papers in a special issue of October, 1972; and to Professor Thomas Stritch for assistance and suggestions along the way as well as his conference paper.

Ronald Weber

Society

The Castle or the Tipi:
Rationalization or Irrationality in the
American Economy

Ken Jameson

DURING a 1957 Notre Dame conference entitled "What America Stands For," Karl De Schweinitz, Jr., examined the "contemporary problems of the American economy." His major themes should be familiar: the effect of concentration of power and production on the functioning of the economy; the instability which the economy exhibits from year to year; and the continuing tension in the economy between individual preferences and economic imperatives.

The writer of 1972 shares the same concerns. For a time in the 1960's, it appeared that some or all of these problems were in the process of solution. By 1972 they had reasserted their existence and importance. In addition, a new dimension had been added to our view of the problems of the economy. Since 1957 changes have taken place whose implications for the functioning of the economy would justify terming them "structural." In addition, these structural changes have called into question the global stability of the American economic system. Are such changes simply adaptations to new circumstances, which can be easily incorporated into the economic structure and which may actually be system-preserving? Or are these changes of a very different sort, autonomously generated and contradictory to the system; does their continuance threaten that economic system with breakdown and fundamental change? There are strong views on both sides of the question, but an approach to an answer can be made only by close examination of the structural changes and their interrelations.

The paper will focus on three institutions which played a role in that structural change: the growth and extension of the domestic conglomerate firms; the growth in size and importance of the United States multinational enterprises; and the persistence, and perhaps growth, of the "economic counterculture." Several considerations lead to their selection. First, in terms of increase in importance over the recent period, no other economic developments are at all comparable with these three. No one of them was considered important in the 1950's, and their growth was not at all foreseen. But by 1972

13

all of them play major roles in the functioning of the economy. Secondly, they appear to be autonomous changes which were not directly results of economic adjustments to maintain stability. Thus they seem most likely to provide the system with an internal contradiction. Finally, they and their interrelations embody the sense and feeling of contradiction which seems prevalent. Vine Deloria describes this well:

> The contest . . . is between a return to the castle or the tipi. The difference between the castle and the tipi is immense, yet there are such great similarities that it is difficult to distinguish between them. Each offers social identity and economic security within a definite communal system. But the leveling process of the tribal form prevents the hereditary control over a social pyramid, and the feudalistic form has the efficiency to create and control technology.[1]

In economic terms, the rationalization process represented by the conglomerates and the multinational firms is a movement toward greater concentration and hierarchical control, the castle of Deloria's quote. The economic counterculture is a movement in the opposite direction, toward the tipi, a type of economic existence which must seem irrational by our traditional economic standards. Does the continuation of these two tendencies provide the economy with a contradiction that will eventually result in fundamental change?

The Castle: Economic Rationalization

The conglomerate is not an entirely new phenomenon in the United States, but it was during the 1960's that the increase in number and importance of these firms brought them and their operations into the public eye. A conglomerate is a firm which is engaged in more than one line of activity and which operates with several distinct products and in several distinct geographical areas. By this general definition, all but the smallest firms are conglomerates. In technical usage the term refers to the new type of firm whose primary goal is expansion and whose primary mechanism for this expansion is not the traditional growth through internal investment, but growth through the acquisition of and merger with other companies already in operation. Examples of active acquirers

---

[1] Vine Deloria, *We Talk, You Listen* (New York: Macmillan, 1970), p. 16.

are Teledyne with 124 acquisitions between 1961 and 1968 and Litton Industries with 79 in the same period. An example of the resultant diversification is Gulf and Western; what started out as an auto supply company, through acquisitions now finds itself involved in motion-picture making, production of sugar, zinc, cigars, fertilizer, and paper, and operation of insurance, investment, publishing, and real estate companies.

The explanation offered for conglomerate growth is that they are involved in a process of rationalization of the economy. They claim to possess a special expertise in the management of firms and particularly in the management of their investment funds. They call this "synergism" or "asset management economies." Acquisition of existing firms allows improvement in these areas and thus rationalizes the economic process by allowing greater efficiency of operation. At the same time of course it results in further centralization of control and power and less direct control of individuals over their economic lives, a movement toward the castle.

To assess the impact of the conglomerate on the economy, it is necessary to describe their growth since 1950. The spate of acquisitions began around 1950. Until 1958 the number of acquisitions ran at less than 500 per year, a figure somewhat higher than the average over this century. The pace quickened after 1958 until it hit a historic high in 1968 when 2,400 acquisitions were consummated. The pace has slowed by about 100 per year, but by historical standards it remains quite high.

Seemingly the effects of this movement on the structure of the economy have not been extreme. The share of assets owned by the top 200 corporations has risen from 45 per cent in 1947 to 60.4 per cent in 1968, an average of about 7.5 per cent per decade. From 1958 to 1968 the rise was only 5.2 per cent, from 55.2 per cent to 60.4 per cent of total assets. So the conglomeration movement simply continued a tendency to concentration which existed in the economy. Examination of concentration in individual industries shows the same pattern. In some industries, concentration rose significantly, but in others it did not; conglomerates were active in both groups. Other measures would show similar patterns of continuity.

Behind these seemingly stable surface phenomena, conglomerates were causing significant change. The main structural effect which the conglomerates have fostered is a change in the pattern of "rationalization" which accompanies corporate growth and development. The contrast between the present conglomeration movement and previous merger movements in these terms will highlight this.

There were two periods of major merger activity prior to the present one. Around the turn of the century, there was a great consolidation of the production apparatus in the country, giving rise to such giants as Standard Oil. The economic basis of these mergers was rationalization of production through the implantation of better production techniques. The outcome in many cases was a growth in monopoly, but there were benefits to the entire economy since the rationalization of production increased the amount of goods and services which were available. This was "production rationalization." The second merger movement, in the 1920's, had the same type of result, in this case due to the utilization of large-scale plants. In the era of the assembly line, to compete with Henry Ford a company had to have the ability to produce on a large scale. This was the reason that a number of small auto companies joined together to form the General Motors Corporation. Other mergers were similarly motivated. Once again there was rationalization in terms of production, and the economy got more output for its resources.

Underlying the present conglomeration movement is an economic goal and effect of a somewhat different sort. To be sure, there are elements of the same type of rationalization that occurred before, but they are far less important. There are some gains in managerial efficiency, though in many cases of acquisition the actual managerial changes go little beyond letterheads. The dominant consideration in conglomeration behavior is financial, and acquisitions are carried out for their effect on the financial reports of the firm. In particular, the price/earnings ratio of the firm becomes a crucial variable in firm operation, for a high value is a key factor in the assessment of the firm by the financial market.

This concentration on financial considerations gave a particular character to much of the acquisition movement of the 1960's. Finances are quite affected by tax and accounting considerations, and it was to take advantage of their stipulations that the conglomeration movement took on its particular pattern, at times a bizarre pattern. For example, the Penn Central was quite a good merger partner because it had been chronically unprofitable and thus had significant tax losses which could be written off against profits of the merged company.

The economic effects of this type of expansion are interesting. In the first place, conglomeration did lead to some increase in monopoly power in various markets. Such power is rational from the standpoint of the firm which can much more completely determine the outcome of its operations. However, in the economy the major effect is the restriction of output and a consequent loss of jobs. The losses from all monopoly power have been variously estimated at from $15.6 billion to $100 billion per year. Earlier merger movements had the same type of effect, but their output rationalization offset the loss to the economy to a great extent. It allowed output to continue at a high rate at the same time as concentration and monopoly increased. But synergism has a somewhat different result. In the first place, it can be questioned whether such rationalization actually occurs. The Penn Central debacle and the recent poor performance of such conglomerates as LTV cast some doubt on its existence. Even if rationalization does occur, a prime difference remains. The effect of conglomerates is not to maintain output nor to improve production techniques, rather it is to generate a higher amount of financial profit from the firm and to distribute this to the stockholders of the firm. So the results of whatever rationalization there might be accrue not to the economy as a whole in terms of increases in output, but to the individual stockholders of the firms, that is, to those who own a piece of the castle. There is no direct gain in terms of output and jobs such as occurred in earlier merger movements.

The conglomeration movement may appear to be a quirk of the 1960's, having by now slowed because of the exhaustion of attractive opportunities and changes in some of the tax and accounting procedures which had facilitated it. But it continues, and even more importantly, it occurred; and the economy has changed in a significant way.

The second realm of rationalization contains the multinational firm, commonly defined as a firm which has subsidiaries in six or more countries. An examination of the top 500 firms in the United States in terms of asset size shows that by this definition 187 of them are multinationals.

The multinational firm has a long history also, but the growth in the number of multinationals and their foreign subsidiaries has been extremely rapid since 1955. Peter Drucker indicates that prior to 1955 all but a handful of American companies were that, *American* companies.[2] By 1967, 187 of the 500 largest firms were multinational; since 1955, the foreign manufacturing subsidiaries of these firms increased from 786 to 1,442; and from 1960-1970 their sales more than tripled, from $24 billion to $77 billion and the book value of their subsidiaries increased from $11 billion to $29 billion. This is a far higher rate of increase than occurred domestically where sales increased by only 69 per cent over the same period and the book value of assets by only 30 per cent. Once again, the growth of such firms must be accounted for in any treatment of the economy.

Again the explanation offered for the growth of the multinationals is economic rationalization. In this case the rationalization operates on two fronts. First is output rationalization brought about by the transfer of technology and technical expertise to the subsidiary country. Such implants allow greater output from the same resources and thus are output creating. The second effect is managerial and financial. There seem to be significant economies in managing several enterprises from one central point, and the ability to operate in the international capital market makes financial management rewarding as well.

When looked at in terms of their effect on the economy, however, the results of multinational operation are very similar to those of conglomeration. They have little effect on output in the United States. There may be some increase in exports of components by our manufacturers with resulting gains in scale economies. But the major effect is really in the opposite direction, output and jobs are exported from the country and are carried out in other parts of the world. The one domestic benefit is again the generation of higher money profits for stockholders of the multinational firm.

This brief examination of the impact of the development and growth of the multinational firms illustrates again the effect of the structural changes of the 1960's. While the castle is in the international realm, its effect on the economy and on economic lives is very similar to that of the conglomerate. Most importantly, the type of rationalization which occurred is very different from that which the economy has traditionally seen. No longer is the domi-

---

[2] Peter Drucker, "The New Markets and the New Capitalism," in Daniel Bell and Irving Kristol, eds., *Capitalism Today* (New York: Signet, 1971), p. 66.

nant motif output rationalization with gains in jobs and efficiency domestically, rather, the impact is financial and is limited to a relatively select segment of the country.

The Tipi: Irrationality

At the time that the corporate sector was undergoing a process of concentration and rationalization, a seemingly contradictory development was occurring in the private sector. The economic counterculture was developing, experimenting with new organizational and economic forms, failing, renewing, but always persisting and apparently growing. The dominant theme of this culture was a rejection of traditional economic forms and institutions and the search for alternatives, all of which would seem quite irrational by our traditional economic standards. The search for the tipi is an apt characterization.

The definition of the economic counterculture is difficult. However, several groups seem objectively important and their economic effects are of sufficient homogeneity to allow their aggregation. Among these are the hard-core alienated who reject the work culture and seek to return to some sort of subsistence existence; the urban or rural communal or cooperative group which endeavors to establish a separate economic base independent of the behavior structure of the dominant economic system; the ecologist who attempts to severely limit the amount of consumption carried out and particularly the resources expended in that consumption; and the ethnic or racial group which attempts to increase its self-sufficiency while existing in close involvement with the dominant society.

It is difficult to assess the impact of these groups in economic terms, though it is certain that their numbers are small and fluid and the viability of their institutions is unproven. But two types of influences on the economy seem likely nonetheless. The first is the possible effect on the cultural basis of the capitalist structure, best described by Daniel Bell:

> The social structure today is ruled by an economic principle of rationality, defined in terms of efficiency in the allocation of resources; the culture in contrast is prodigal, promiscuous, dominated by an anti-rational anti-intellectual temper. The character structure inherited from the nineteenth century—with its emphasis on self-discipline, delayed gratification, restraint—is still relevant to the

demands of the social structure; but it clashes sharply with the culture, where such bourgeois values have been completely rejected . . .[3]

So Bell finds a contradiction between the culture and the economy. He concludes that "culture has become supreme." In other words, the economic system will soon begin to dance to the tune of the counterculture. While such a likelihood cannot be dismissed, the case is not completely convincing. In the first place, it is equally plausible that the causal factor in these developments is the same rationalization that was mentioned before, that its effect on the work experience and the economic experience is affecting the culture in significant ways. A second objection is more fundamental. The economy, and particularly its corporate sector, has its own culture which shows very few signs of losing its viability. There have been examples of betrayals of that culture such as *Up the Organization,* but they are so few as to illustrate the point. More direct evidence comes from one major attempt to confront the corporate sector with the new cultural themes. This was an effort by the Los Angeles County Museum of Art to place contemporary artists with business firms for 12 weeks or more for an "encounter between art and technology." Spawned by the encounter were progeny such as the suggestion to the Rand Corporation that it shut off its phones for a day and have a picnic in the patio, or "Giant Icebag," a 16-foot sculpture resembling a salmon-colored icebag which does a 20-minute dance number. Perhaps the best expression of the impact of the experiment was by Herman Kahn of the Hudson Institute when he heard his artist's suggestion to produce an edible book with the world's 100 greatest quotations. Said Kahn, "Why are we bothering with Jim? After all, I want the organization to run right."[4] If this experiment is any indication, the corporate culture is hardly experiencing catatonia in reaction to the onslaught of the counterculture.

There is another level, however, on which the economic counterculture may definitely affect the overall economy. The members of this culture are in some sense a part of the economy and their

---

[3] Daniel Bell, "The Cultural Contradictions of Capitalism," *Capitalism Today,* p. 30.
[4] Earl Gottschalk, Jr., "What's That Thing Resembling a Giant, Salmon-Hued Ice Bag?," *The Wall Street Journal,* May 6, 1971, p. 1.

economic actions will affect its functioning. Looked at in this light there are two areas of behavior where the effect will be greatest. The first is the relation of the members to the economic labor market. In almost all of its manifestations, the economic counter-culture rejects the usual participation in the job market. Production line jobs are to be avoided at all costs, and if any labor beyond subsistence labor is required, it should be of a nonalienating sort. In economic terms, this reduces the effective supply of labor and our models suggest that consequently the rate of growth of the economy should slow with resultant tendencies toward stagnation and economic strain. Counterculturalists also play another role in the economy, that of consumers or nonconsumers. It is again a fairly uniform characteristic that traditional consumption patterns are rejected, partly out of the cultural norms themselves and partly as a result of the work attitude. Looked at in terms of usual economic concerns, such a fall in the aggregate demand of the economy could have very detrimental effects on its operation. The continually astounding success of the economy in avoiding "secular stagnation" has been largely a result of the growth of consumption demand. In a fundamental way the economy is a consumer economy, and disruptions at this level could lead to economic instability.

The thesis which Bell expounds is interesting and may eventually be important for the economy and its functioning. However, at this point it seems that the contradiction of rationalization and irrationality, of the castle and the tipi, could very well exist at a purely economic level. The rejection of the traditional participation in the labor market, coupled with the attempt to break the pattern of consumption which has traditionally buoyed the economy, could well place a severe strain on that economy and could indeed lead it to a fundamental transformation.

The Interrelations

While the above developments were individually notable in their rapidity and importance for the economy, it is their interrelations that reflect most directly on its overall stability.

The relation of conglomerates and multinationals is quite direct, for many of the conglomerates are also multinational firms. Of the 25 most active conglomerates in terms of their acquisitions from 1961-1968, nine would also be classified as multinational enterprises. This close relationship promises to become even closer in future

years. Evidence comes from the data on multinational expansion
through acquisition of existing firms in other countries. During the
first year that data were available, 1963, there were 228 such acquisitions. But by 1968 the number had risen to 800 and in 1969 it
reached 847 acquisitions, a number which is over one-third of the
acquisitions within the United States by the conglomerate firms.
Stronger evidence of the importance of this trend comes from ex-
amining the mode of institution of subsidiaries. For manufacturing
subsidiaries in foreign countries, we find that of those founded before
1946, 40 per cent were instituted through acquisitions; of those
beginning between 1946 and 1957, 44 per cent were through acquisitions; but 60 per cent of the foreign subsidiaries formed
between 1957 and 1967 came about by the acquisition route, a substantial increase. So what may be developing is a new form of
organization, the "multinational conglomerate."

Some recent occurrences may accelerate the tendency of overseas
expansion through acquisitions. ITT notwithstanding, there is
evidence that the Justice Department is discouraging domestic conglomeration efforts. Changes in tax and accounting practices have
had somewhat the same result. At the same time, there are recent
changes in accounting procedure that have made overseas involvement more attractive to firms seeking improvements in earnings.
This adds plausibility to the widespread prediction that by 1985
virtually all of the output of manufactured products will come from
some 300 multinational corporations, producing a wide variety of
products in a wide variety of locations.[5]

Some direct effects of these developments on the stability of the
economy may already be apparent. First, the dollar crisis of 1971
can be laid partially at the door of these enterprises. A major con-
stituent of the United States payments deficits has been the capital
funds flowing overseas, and a major reason for this flow has been
investment by our companies in other countries. Recently the situation has been made more acute by the United States trade position,
where our exports haven't kept pace with our imports. This again
is partly a function of business expansion overseas, for overseas
production can substitute for domestic production and subsequent
export. Also, many subsidiaries now actually ship goods to the
United States, increasing our imports. Thus on all of these fronts
the multinational conglomerate played an important role in our

---

[5] Drucker, *op. cit.*, p. 67.

dollar crisis and is likely to continue doing so. Secondly, growth of the conglomerates has led to an increase in the coordination of their activity with government policy. ITT can truthfully say that government restraints on its activity will upset the entire economy. It can also make a convincing case that actions taken by the government of Chile will have similar effects. Thus the pressure on policymakers is significant. The multinational conglomerates' need for government sanction is partly because they are at the frontier of the law, and developments in the law will affect their well-being more than they would the older, more established types of firms. But their dependence is also because of the nature of these firms whose involvements span several industries or countries and whose financial situation can be severely strained by disarray in any one of these. Thus general economic order is essential, and political power is the most effective means of obtaining it. Previously, cartel-like agreements might have been effective, but this is no longer true. Now government aid is necessary for stability.

Given this tendency to instability caused by the rationalization movement, the effect of the economic counterculture on the economy could indeed represent a basic contradiction through its effect on consumption and on the job market. The members of the economic counterculture are not good consumers, and the effect of its growth is to reduce aggregate demand. This would seem to be an added disruptive influence on the corporate sector, for such a decrease in final demand could cause a slowdown in economic growth and rationalization, with resulting pressure on the operation of business. However, the earlier analysis suggested an important reason for doubting a fundamental contradiction on the level of consumption. It was noted that the dominant consideration and effect of expansion by multinational conglomerates is financial and is divorced from the output questions of earlier years. As long as there are opportunities for financial gains through acquisition and merger, the process can continue. Of course stagnant aggregate demand would eventually limit financial maneuvers. However, the rapid growth of overseas sales indicates that this area may provide adequate growth in demand to forestall any such eventuality in the proximate future. Thus the conclusion is that in economic terms, the effect of the economic counterculture on consumption does not provide the system with a basic contradiction.

The second link is in the area of jobs. One implication of the relative independence of multinational conglomerates from domestic aggregate demand is that their interest in internal expansion and job creation is greatly lessened. Expansion of production facilities provides jobs, but the conglomerate mode of operation is primarily financial expansion. The multinational firm also operates in a fashion that will slow the creation of jobs domestically. This could be a source of extreme instability in the domestic economy, but it is here that the economic counterculture may have its most important effect. To the extent that the job becomes less important to a viable life style, the less need there is for the economy and its firms to create jobs. Thus in the extreme, the economy would not be damaged at all if there were no new jobs created, as long as enough persons were willing to leave the job market and to enter the economic counterculture. It is difficult to say how important this factor is at present, let alone how important it will be in the future; but suffice it to say that the present disarray in the labor market, best seen in the wage-price freeze, and the difficulties economic policy is having in that area suggest that such an outlet valve may be essential for the continued functioning of the economy. This may become even more the case as conglomerate expansion continues. So once again no contradiction is visible.

The Castle or the Tipi?

The dominant structural changes in the economy of the 1960's and beyond were the tendency to rationalization in the conglomerates and multinationals and the development of a viable economic counterculture, irrational by usual standards. The view is widespread that these were contradictory trends which might force fundamental change on the economy. An initial examination of these two tendencies seemed to support this view, but closer examination yields a different conclusion. The economy will not be forced to a new basic structure, the castle or the tipi. Rather, the operation of the economy may well depend on the continued coexistence of these two competing but basically complementary spheres. With the substitution of financial motives in expansion and the shift in concentration of energy to the multinational sphere, the ability of the economy to incorporate the entire populace seems severely hampered. Such a failure would have had severe repercussions in previous periods, but with an alternative approach to economic life now available and attractive, such is not the case. In the final analysis, castle and tipi interrelate in a fashion which yields stability to a system which would otherwise be unstable.

This does not imply, however, that there is complete consistency in the economy, only that the contradictions are not internal. The analysis suggests contradiction from a different side. If the possibilities of international expansion open to the multinational conglomerates were to be significantly narrowed, the effect of the economic counterculture would no longer be beneficial. Its effect on the consumption front and on the job front would quickly begin to cut into the dynamic of the corporate sector, forcing a type of adjustment that might be impossible for a multinational conglomerate. So it is in the international sphere that the potential for instability exists; it is there that the contradiction may lay. Changes internationally might finally force a decision between the castle and the tipi.

Change and Diversity in American Community Life

Richard A. Lamanna

Introduction

IN ANY DISCUSSION of American community life two beliefs are likely to quickly come to the fore. First, that we have over the last 50 years undergone a revolution in community settlement patterns and today we are an urban nation with more and more of our population crowding into our urban areas. Many now speak with disdain about the runaway urbanization and the emerging "ant-hill society." A second theme that almost always accompanies the first is that the quality of life in our urban communities is deteriorating rapidly. One can hardly read a daily metropolitan newspaper without spotting a headline which sounds the alarm. Not long ago, for example, the *New York Times* had a front-page spread with the startling headline, "Eleven Mayors Warn Here of Collapse of U.S. Cities."[1] Stewart Alsop, in a *Newsweek* column with the foreboding title "The Cities Are Finished," managed in the course of one page to inform his readers that the cities may be "finished" because they have become unlivable; that the net population of cities will continue to fall; that the future is statistically predictable—in another 10 years most of our cities will consist mostly of blacks; and that the cities will come to resemble reservations for the poor and the blacks surrounded by heavily guarded middle-class suburbs.[2] More recently, Sol Linowitz, Chairman of the National Urban Coalition, declared, "We have abandoned our cities . . . [and while they] are not on fire today, most of the conditions that caused the civil disorders in recent years have worsened."[3] Meanwhile, HUD Secretary George Romney estimated it would take $3,000 billion ($3 trillion) to bring all American metropolitan areas up to snuff.[4] Many intellectuals have joined in this chorus of doom. Book titles such as *A City Destroying Itself*,

---

[1] *New York Times*, April 22, 1971.
[2] *Newsweek*, April 5, 1971.
[3] "Saving the Cities," *New York Times*, April 11, 1972.
[4] *HUD Newsletter*, U.S. Dept. of Housing and Urban Development, Washington, D.C., June 12, 1972.

Sick Cities, The Withering Away of the City, Crisis in Our Cities, and *Metropolis in Crisis* further reflect the growing conviction that the nation is in the grip of an urban crisis.

In the words of one observer of the urban scene, "The approved way to talk about cities these days is to speak solemnly, sadly, ominously, and fearfully about their problems. You don't rate as an expert on the city unless you foresee its doom."[5] At the risk of destroying my credibility as an expert, I would like to examine in detail some of the evidence related to these beliefs so that we might get a better picture of the kinds of communities Americans live in, the changes in the settlement pattern that have occurred in recent decades, and are likely to occur in the next few decades, and finally the implications of these changes for the quality of life in American communities.

What Kinds of Communities Do Americans Live In?

Today, some 74 per cent of the American population resides in urban communities—an increase of 3.6 percentage points above the figure for 1960. It is estimated that without the rural-urban migration that took place from 1940 to 1970, some 50 million people, a quarter of the present national population, would have been living on farms instead of the urban areas where they now reside. In short, the change has been dramatic. It has transformed the society into an urban one. It is easy, however, to misinterpret these figures. "Urban" by the census definition is simply a place of 2,500 people or more. In other words, it includes everything from an isolated place of a few thousand to a metropolis of several million.[6] A review of the distribution of the population by size of place will give one a better idea of where Americans live. (See Table I) The census identifies almost 21,000 different incorporated and unincorporated places—almost 14,000 of them are not urban or in urbanized areas. Of the 7,000 urban places, less than 400 of them are 50,000 or larger. We must conclude then that

---

[5] Paul Ylvisaker quoted in Charles Silberman, "The City and the Negro," *Fortune,* March, 1962. This is, of course, by no means a universal view. Recent works by James Q. Wilson, Edward Banfield, Irving Kristol, Scott Greer, and Raymond Vernon have effectively challenged the apocalyptic view of the urban situation.

[6] A related concept used by the Census Bureau is "urbanized area," which refers to a city or twin cities of 50,000 or more plus its developed surrounding area (at least 1,000 people per square mile).

even now the typical American community is a fairly small place in terms of population.

On the other hand, it is apparent that the larger communities have a disproportionate amount of the total population. Nevertheless, only 36 per cent of the total population lives in cities of 50,000 or more. In other words, almost half of the urban population still lives in fairly small cities.

It is not too meaningful, however, to view urban places as isolated entities, that is, independent of their spatial and socioeconomic relationship to each other. Today 69 per cent of the American people live in what the Census Bureau calls Standard Metropolitan Statistical Areas, that is, cities of 50,000 or more and the surrounding county or counties economically integrated with the city. There are at the present time some 243 SMSA's and this represents an increase from 212 in 1960. Between 1960 and 1970 the population of the United States grew some 13 per cent while the metropolitan population grew 23 per cent. Nearly all the metropolitan growth took place with the growth of suburbs and territorial expansion into previously rural areas. The SMSA's also vary in size and other characteristics. It is apparent from an examination of Table II that there is a considerable amount of variation between metropolitan areas on each of the 35 variables presented. For example, population size varies from 52,000 for the Meriden, Connecticut SMSA to 10,695,000 for the New York SMSA; density from a low of 13 persons per square mile (Reno, Nevada) to a high of almost 13,000 persons per square mile (Jersey City, New Jersey); per cent Negro from zero (Fargo, North Dakota) to 43.5 per cent (Pine Bluff, Arkansas); median family income from under $3,000 (Laredo, Texas) to $8,700 (Stamford, Connecticut); per cent of population on public assistance from under one per cent (Anderson, Indiana) to almost 10 per cent (Fresno, California); per cent of housing that is sound with all plumbing facilities from 44 per cent (Laredo, Texas) to 93.2 per cent (Anaheim, California); violent crime rate per 100,000 persons from 19 (Green Bay, Wisconsin) to 1,023 (Baltimore, Maryland). In other words, on every dimension from population size and composition to socioeconomic and physical characteristics, economic resources, social disorganization, and government expenditures there are enormous differences and no basis for such a statement as that recently made by Mayor Lindsay of New York that small towns and big cities are fundamentally the same.[7] It is extremely difficult to generalize about metropolitan areas, never mind small towns.

Within metropolitan areas there is also a great deal of variation. The metropolitan areas are in reality a constellation of urban communities and their hinterlands. Although substantial portions are usually comprised of more or less continuous settlement, most SMSA's provide a variety of residential settings within the functional sphere of a single economy. This mosaic of living environments ranges from rural to highly urban. Such environments often coexist within a common functional framework without intruding spatially on each other. Even in "Megalopolis"—the region running along the Atlantic Coast from Maine to Virginia which has one out of every six Americans and is our most densely populated region—it is estimated that only one-fifth of the area is currently in urban use.

The most common comparison made within metropolitan areas involves comparing the central city with the remainder—which is often referred to as the suburban ring. Even this crude comparison defies easy generalization. For example, the report of the Advisory Commission on Intergovernmental Relations on *Metropolitan Social and Economic Disparities* concluded:

The strongest conclusion to be drawn from the analysis is that very few meaningful generalizations about economic, social, and racial disparities can be applied to all metropolitan areas. For a number of population characteristics the differences among metropolitan areas are far larger than the differences between central cities and their surrounding area. For most characteristics it is possible to generalize about disparities only for particular kinds of metropolitan areas.

The classic dichotomy of the poor, underprivileged, nonwhite central city contrasted with the comfortable white suburb is not revealed by these data. While racial disparities are large everywhere, the other elements of the dichotomy—education, income, employment, and housing—fit the stereotype consistently only in the largest metropolitan areas and those located in the Northeast. The Northeast includes only 41 of the 190 standard metropolitan statistical areas studied, however, and outside of that region there are only 39 metropolitan areas with population in excess of half a million. For the remaining 110 metropolitan areas the classic dichotomy does not generally apply.

[7] "Lindsay Stresses Mayoral Experience," *New York Times*, March 27, 1972.

In the small and medium sized metropolitan areas outside the Northeast some elements of both high and low socioeconomic status tend to be equally important in both central cities and suburbs, while other low status characteristics predominate in the suburbs and some high status characteristics are more important in the central city. In many metropolitan areas of the South and West, poverty, especially nonwhite poverty, and underprivileged are more typical of the suburbs; most central city dwellers are relatively well off.

These generalizations about region and metropolitan size must be further modified by considering population dispersal and relative size of the nonwhite population. Disparities in all regions and size groups tend to be exaggerated in metropolitan areas whose total populations are largely suburbanized. While central cities are more likely to represent underprivileged segments of the population, suburbs in highly suburbanized metropolitan areas, rather than being wealthy as in the large and Northeastern SMSA's, are likely to represent the large middle class. *Where nonwhites constitute an important element of the total metropolitan population, the classic disparity pattern occurs in the North, but in the South and West the pattern runs the other way—high socioeconomic status in the cities and lower status in the suburbs.*[8]

Trends and Projections

Between 1960 and 1970 the population of the United States increased some 24 million. This was the largest decennial gain in absolute numbers for any decade except that of the 1950's. However, in percentage terms the 13.3 per cent gain was the smallest for any decade in American history except that of the Depression 1930's. The growth in population was not evenly distributed. More than two-fifths of the counties had a net loss of population. Net out-migration in the 1960's was the experience of about 70 per cent of all counties.

More than four-fifths of the national growth took place in the SMSA's, and in these areas more than four-fifths of the total growth took place outside the cities designated as central cities. The areas within the SMSA's but outside the central cities, often called suburbs, now for the first time in our history include more population than the central cities themselves, or more than is found in the

---

[8] *Metropolitan Social and Economic Disparities: Implications for Intergovernmental Relations in Central Cities and Suburbs* (Washington, D.C.: U.S. Government Printing Office, 1965), pp. 11-12.

entire nonmetropolitan portion of the United States. (See Farm, City, and Suburban Population Chart[9])

Many of the large cities reported population losses during the 1960's, as had also been the case during the 1950's. Fifteen of the 21 central cities with a population of 500,000 or more had lost population by 1970. Of the 130 cities with a population of 100,000 or more in 1960, 62 had a decline in population during the 1960's. In fact, declining central cities lost more people in the 1960's than were lost by declining rural counties. The proportion of the total population living in cities of 100,000 or more actually declined between 1960 and 1970 from 28.3 to 27.6. This proportion has remained virtually unchanged over the last 50 years.

There also has been some decline in the proportion of the population living in towns and cities of less than 50,000. Yet the notion that the small towns are disappearing is not borne out by the data. More than half of the nonmetropolitan municipalities grew during each of the last three decades. A growing proportion of people are living in places over 10,000, and places closest to metropolitan areas were more likely to grow than those in more remote locations.

The decline of the central city populations coupled with the emergence of new SMSA's (from 212 in 1960 to 243 in 1970) and the rapid expansion of metropolitan boundaries have resulted in a decline in average metropolitan densities. In 1950, the average population density in all urbanized areas in the United States was 5,408 per square mile. By 1970 it was down to 3,376 per square mile—a decline of almost 38 per cent. For central cities, density fell from 7,786 per square mile in 1950 to 4,463 in 1970. During these same years, population densities in suburban areas fell from 3,167 per square mile to 2,627 per square mile. While comparable data are not available prior to 1950, it appears this is part of a long-term trend in American society. One study which reconstructed population densities in several urbanized areas as far back as 1880 has shown that in most metropolitan areas population density at the center of the primary city has been declining since at least 1910. This certainly has been the case in New York City, the nation's most densely populated city. For example, the population density of the Borough of Manhattan has declined almost continu-

---

[9] *Population Bulletin*, 27 (October, 1971), 9.

ously since 1910, from 102,711 per square mile in 1910 to 67,160
per square mile in 1970.[10] Nevertheless, even now (1970) metropolitan America still covers only a small proportion of the nation's
land area—about three-quarters of the population now lives on less
than two per cent of the land. In an ecological sense then we have
been witnessing a simultaneous process of concentration into metropolitan areas on a national scale and dispersion and expansion at
the local level. This trend reflects both the technology of the society
we live in and the values of the residents.[11]

The President's Commission on Population and the American
Future noted that when asked where they would prefer to live,
Americans show pronounced preferences for small towns and rural
areas. For example, 34 per cent indicate they would prefer to live
in open country but only 12 per cent of them are actually living
there. However, when you probe more deeply you find that they
really prefer to live in a smaller place but within commuting
distance of a metropolitan central city. A study in Wisconsin, for
example, found that 70 per cent would prefer to live near a metropolitan area but only 54 per cent now do.[12] It appears Americans
want the best of both worlds—the serene and clean environment of
rural areas and the opportunity and excitement of the metropolis.
It is not too surprising then that much metropolitan growth occurs
in peripheral areas with a semi-rural environment.

There is no reason to believe this trend will not continue. The
space is available, the automobile makes it possible, and the public
appears to want it. Anthony Downs is correct in assuming that
peripheral sprawl will be the dominant form of future urban growth
throughout the United States.[13] But even if this is the case, the

---

[10] *Report on National Growth, 1972* (Washington, D.C.: U.S. Government
Printing Office, 1972), pp. 19-20.

[11] It is interesting to note that the reduction in densities at the communal
level has been accompanied by a comparable change at the level of individual
dwelling units. There were fewer people per housing unit in 1970 than 10
years earlier—the average declining to 3.1 from 3.3 in 1960. The average
family's house is much better and larger. Fewer homes are crowded—the
number of housing units with more than one person per room dropped by ap-
proximately 900,000 in 10 years from 6.1 million to 5.2 million. Our average
of .54 persons per room is the lowest in the Western world.

[12] *Population and the American Future* (New York: New American Library,
1972), pp. 35-36.

[13] Anthony Downs, "Alternative Forms of Future Urban Growth in the
U.S.," *Journal of the American Institute of Planners* (January, 1970), pp. 3-11.

land area occupied by urban uses in the year 2000 will still be relatively minor. (See Urban Regions Map[14])

It appears moreover that there are strong advantages to continuing the present trend. The transition to a metropolitan society in many ways has been beneficial, at least in terms of living standards and enhancing personal opportunity. The residents of metropolitan areas, including those of central cities, have improved their status between 1960 and 1970 on virtually all dimensions of socioeconomic status. Income, education, employment, housing, and racial equality all show marked gains in the metropolitan areas and substantial advantages over the nonmetropolitan areas of the country.[15] The evidence does not at all support the image of deteriorating metropolitan communities so popular with the press, although to be sure such communities can be found. Moreover, this is not to say that all segments of the population have benefited equally from these gains. In fact, a close look at the data reported in the report on "Social and Economic Characteristics of the Population in Metropolitan and Nonmetropolitan Areas, 1970 and 1960" confirms what Daniel P. Moynihan calls the "up-and-down" phenomenon.[16] Changes in the per cent of black families living in the central cities of metropolitan areas who were below the poverty level in 1969 and 1959 illustrate the point. If you consider all black families without regard to the sex of the head of the family, it appears there has been a 20 per cent decline in the number below the poverty line. However, this total incorporates two sharply divergent experiences. For male-headed black families there was a 57 per cent *decline* but for female-headed black families there was a 40 per cent *increase*. The point is that it is entirely possible to have a situation of overall improvement coupled with serious decline or deterioration in the conditions of life in some localities and/or some components of the population.

---

[14] *Population Bulletin, op. cit.*, 14.

[15] "Social and Economic Characteristics of the Population in Metropolitan and Nonmetropolitan Areas, 1970 and 1960," *Current Population Reports,* P 23, No. 37, June 24, 1971. See also *The People Left Behind,* Report of the President's National Advisory Commission on Rural Poverty (Washington, D.C.: U.S. Government Printing Office, 1967); *Urban and Rural America: Policies for Future Growth,* Advisory Commission on Intergovernmental Relations (Washington, D.C.: U.S. Government Printing Office, 1965); and *Report on National Growth, 1972, op. cit.,* pp. 26-27.

[16] Daniel P. Moynihan, "The Schism in Black America," *The Public Interest,* 27 (Spring, 1972), 4-7.

Implications

At this point, we might ask ourselves what the likely consequences are for the quality of life in American society if the trends outlined above continue on their present course.

1. Given the fact that in terms of income, educational and health facilities, housing, and the incidence of poverty the rural sector of the population is consistently more disadvantaged and, given the clear advantages of the metropolitan areas over nonmetropolitan areas, it follows that the continued urbanization and metropolitanization of the population will result in a wider sharing of the social and material advantages of the modern world and an increase in the standard of living of the average American.

After reviewing the facts one cannot help but wonder what accounts for the purple prose of so many writers on the city and their insistence that things are not only bad but getting worse. I have no simple answer to this question but several factors seem to be of importance. First, it should be noted that a gloomy and disapproving view of urban life is an old American tradition. Over a half-century ago people like the industrialist Henry Ford felt sure that cities were doomed to extinction and that "we should solve the City problem by leaving the City."[17] Another reason is the common tendency to label all of the problems of American society as "the problems of the cities." As Scott Greer has noted, "Most of the 'problems of the cities' are the problems, conflicts and harsh dilemmas of the American soul."[18] A third source grows out of the failure to differentiate the part from the whole—to become so aware of and sensitive to some aspects of a situation that one concludes or assumes it represents the whole. Perhaps it is just our impatience to put an end to all problems. We speak of a crisis not because the problems are more acute than they have been, nor because we are failing to make progress toward their solution, but because the pace at which we are moving is slow when compared to our escalating expectations. My expectation is that we will continue to make impressive gains while simultaneously deploring the deterioration in the quality of life.

2. Part of the push-out to the periphery of the metropolitan areas

---

[17] Quoted in Morton and Lucia White, *The Intellectual Versus the City* (New York: New American Library, 1962), p. 201.

[18] Scott Greer, *The Urbane View: Life and Politics in Metropolitan America* (New York: Oxford University Press, 1972), p. 2.

will be an extensive sorting-out process. Suburbs typically are internally homogenous but differ from one another along social and economic lines, with the rich in some, the less affluent in others. This spatial differentiation and segregation is likely to create serious obstacles to the development of area-wide governments or planning authorities. With blacks increasingly concentrated in the central cities and only slowly penetrating the suburban ring, we are likely to have an extended but temporary period of strain and conflict based on the fragmented and racially and economically segregated pattern of settlement.

Some writers speak of the demise of "place" as an important factor in social differentiation and identification.[19] Although modern technology and the mobility of the population have undoubtedly had a profound effect on social relations, there is considerable evidence of the continuing importance of spatial and territorial factors. The roll of current community issues, including busing, community control, blockbusting, suburban exodus, property tax equalization, crime in the streets, annexation, and resistance to metropolitan government, that are essentially disputes over the character and control of local living environments, suggests that where one lives and whom one lives near will continue to be matters of the utmost importance to most Americans.

3. Developing effective alternatives to peripheral sprawl, or even mitigating some of its socially segregating effects, would require major changes in deeply rooted existing political and social institutions. These include local control over land use and zoning, local financing for schools, fragmented planning of new development, and the ability of individual landowners to engage in real estate speculation.

At the heart of these institutional practices is our commitment as a society to individualism—the belief that everyone should pursue autonomously his own destiny. The principle is so widely shared and uncritically accepted that neither suburbanites nor hippies see the role of the value they embrace so fervently in generating the phenomena they so detest.[20] The traumatic nature of any sub-

---

[19] Alvin Toffler, *Future Shock* (New York: Bantam Books, 1970), pp. 92-93; Melvin M. Webber, "Order in Diversity: Community Without Propinquity," in Lowdon Wingo, Jr., ed., *Cities and Space* (Baltimore: Johns Hopkins Press, 1963), pp. 23-54.

[20] Philip E. Slater, *The Pursuit of Loneliness* (Boston: Beacon Press, 1970), p. 25.

stantial changes in these practices can hardly be overestimated. In fact, they are likely to occur only if the failings of existing arrangements become far more pressing and obvious than they are now in most areas of the country or likely to be in the foreseeable future.

It is interesting to note how this philosophy is even reflected in the President's Report on National Growth, which grew out of the national debate over urban growth policy. The preface clearly states:

> One important source of our strength as a people has been our unwillingness to trust our destiny to the edicts of any government or the whims of any group. There is no place in our country for any policy which arbitrarily dictates where and how our citizens will live and work and spend their leisure time. Our plans for national growth must rather seek to help *individual* Americans develop their unique potentials and achieve their *personal* goals. [emphasis added][21]

Some have interpreted the emergence of the communal movement in recent years as a form of rebellion against modern urban-industrial society and our traditional ideas about community life. There may now be as many as 3,000 communes across the country, often filling in the urban interstices between city and suburb and more and more moving out to abandoned farmlands lying just beyond the farthest exurbias. They vary in population size from about 10 to a 100 or more. In contrast to groups formed by accident or propinquity, family, professional, or other ties, these are intentional communities—founded to realize and make manifest certain new and renewed intentions. Among the most important are: to be free, to live in harmony with nature, to live in the spirit of love, to escape from industrial society, to live in the here and now, to end the repression caused by civilization and recover instinctual life, to establish an alternative reality.[22]

---

[21] *Report on National Growth, 1972, op. cit.,* p. xi.

[22] The movement is only beginning to be studied in an objective manner. Among the more helpful descriptions and studies are: Sonya Rudikoff, "O Pioneers! Reflections on the Whole Earth People," *Commentary,* July, 1972, pp. 62-74; Ron Roberts, *The New Communes: Coming Together in America* (Englewood Cliffs: Prentice-Hall, 1971); Keith Melville, *Communes in the Counter Culture: Origins, Theories, Styles of Life* (New York: Morrow, 1972); David Bromwich, "Walden Is Alive Again," *Dissent* (Spring, 1972), pp. 326-336; Benjamin Zablocki, *The Joyful Community* (Baltimore: Penguin Books, 1971), chap. 7, "A Model for Utopia," pp. 286-326; Herbert A. Otto, "Communes: The Alternative Life Style," *Saturday Review,* May 15, 1971, pp. 16-

The import of the movement can be evaluated in several ways. First, one might ask how many people have embraced this alternative life style. No one really knows and estimates vary widely but something in the neighborhood of 150,000 people have probably been directly involved— a relatively small number if you are talking about the settlement patterns of a nation of over 200 million. The attention and publicity given the movement probably exaggerate its current significance and power to affect social change.

A second question to consider is just how radical a departure from the traditional culture the commune movement represents. There are some elements, such as the rejection of modern technology and creature comforts, the anti-intellectualism, and the rejection of the nuclear family, that have historical antecedents but nevertheless represent important departures from the dominant ethos. What is most striking, however, are the points of congruence with dominant American values, especially the strong emphasis on individualism, local autonomy, self-sufficiency, open space, and nature. After all, what is the young family that moves to suburbia seeking? Moreover, it is not clear that the communitarians have been any more successful than suburbanites in striking a balance between freedom and community.

Finally, there is the question of survivability. The evidence is not all in yet but it appears that the new communal groups are very unstable. There is considerable turnover of personnel and two years is about as long as the communities last. This seems to be due to several factors, including the extreme individualism of the adherents, the absence of an economic base, and the failure to provide for the future. It appears at this early date that Sonya Rudikoff might be closer to the truth in suggesting that the communes may be an inexpensive functional equivalent of summer camp for the growing population of postadolescent unemployed rather than a forerunner of a radical shift in consciousness and life style.[23]

The problem of the future will not be that of comprehensive planning for metropolitan areas but that of developing community among diverse and transient elements of the metropolitan population. As we have seen, American society has experienced considerable change in the pattern of settlement, creating even more diver-

21; David French, "After the Fall: What This Country Needs Is a Good Counter Counterculture Culture," *New York Times Magazine,* October 3, 1971, pp. 20 ff.
[23] Rudikoff, *op. cit.*, p. 69.

sity than had already existed. The combination of rapid change and growing diversity results in rather formidable barriers to creating and maintaining a sense of community. As James Q. Wilson has suggested, for most of our citizens the "urban problem" is *a sense of the failure of community*.[24] Around one's home and the places where one shops and the corridors through which one travels there is for each of us a public sphere wherein our sense of security, self-esteem, and propriety is either reassured or jeopardized by the people and events we encounter. At the very time people are drawing physically closer together and becoming increasingly dependent upon one another, we are drifting toward an extreme form of individualism and privatization of social behavior which undermines the foundations of communal life. The challenge before American society is not so much one of coping with the physical aspects of community change but of striking the right balance between freedom and community that will do justice to individual and subgroup differences yet remain compatible with the requirements of a technologically advanced society.

---

[24] James Q. Wilson, "The Urban Unease: Community vs. City," *The Public Interest*, 12 (Summer, 1968), 369-70.

TABLE I
POPULATION BY SIZE OF PLACE FOR THE UNITED STATES:
1970 AND 1960

Urban and Rural		1970		
	Places	Population	Per cent of total population	Per cent distribution
United States	20,768	203,211,926	100.0	....
URBAN				
Total	7,062	149,324,930	73.5	100.0
Inside urbanized areas	3,222	118,446,566	58.3	79.3
Central cities	308	63,921,684	31.5	42.8
Cities of—				
1,000,000 or more	6	18,769,365	9.2	12.6
500,000 to 1,000,000	20	12,966,746	6.4	8.7
250,000 to 500,000	30	10,441,689	5.1	7.0
100,000 to 250,000	78	11,484,410	5.7	7.7
50,000 to 100,000	125	8,630,741	4.2	5.8
Less than 50,000	49	1,628,733	0.8	1.1
Urban fringe	2,914	54,524,882	26.8	36.5
Places of 2,500 or more	2,287	38,612,499	19.0	25.9
100,000 or more	22	2,801,623	1.4	1.9
50,000 to 100,000	115	8,093,137	4.0	5.4
25,000 to 50,000	278	9,511,106	4.7	6.4
10,000 to 25,000	727	11,504,407	5.7	7.7
5,000 to 10,000	724	5,184,988	2.6	3.5
2,500 to 5,000	421	1,517,238	0.7	1.0
Places less than 2,500	627	726,683	0.4	0.5
2,000 to 2,500	107	238,472	0.1	0.2
1,500 to 2,000	100	172,022	0.1	0.1
1,000 to 1,500	132	164,272	0.1	0.1
Less than 1,000	288	151,917	0.1	0.1
Other urban	......	15,185,700	7.5	10.2
Outside urbanized areas	3,840	30,878,364	15.2	20.7
Places of—				
25,000 or more	205	6,932,070	3.4	4.6
10,000 to 25,000	646	9,686,526	4.8	6.5
5,000 to 10,000	1,115	7,738,587	3.8	5.2
2,500 to 5,000	1,874	6,521,181	3.2	4.4
RURAL				
Total	13,706	53,886,996	26.5	100.0
Places of 1,000 to 2,500	4,191	6,656,007	3.3	12.4
2,000 to 2,500	880	1,960,524	1.0	3.6
1,500 to 2,000	1,261	2,181,353	1.1	4.0
1,000 to 1,500	2,050	2,514,130	1.2	4.7
Places less than 1,000	9,515	3,851,873	1.9	7.1
Other rural	......	43,379,116	21.3	80.5
URBANIZED AREAS				
Total	248	118,446,566	58.3	100.0
Areas of—				
1,000,000 or more	25	70,828,671	34.9	59.8
500,000 to 1,000,000	21	14,419,672	7.1	12.2
250,000 to 500,000	35	12,478,948	6.1	10.5
100,000 to 250,000	91	14,962,419	7.4	12.6
Less than 100,000	76	5,756,856	2.8	4.9

Source: *U.S. Census of Population, 1970. PC (1)-A1, U.S. Summary,* p. 1-43.

TABLE I (continued)

Urban and Rural	Places	1960 Population	Per cent of total population	Per cent distribution
United States	19,790	179,323,175	100.0	....
URBAN				
Total	6,041	125,268,750	69.9	100.0
Inside urbanized areas	2,430	95,848,487	53.5	76.5
Central cities	254	57,975,132	32.3	46.3
Cities of—				
1,000,000 or more	5	17,484,059	9.8	14.0
500,000 to 1,000,000	16	11,110,991	6.2	8.9
250,000 to 500,000	30	10,765,881	6.0	8.6
100,000 to 250,000	66	9,872,604	5.5	7.9
50,000 to 100,000	111	7,858,514	4.4	6.3
Less than 50,000	26	883,083	0.5	0.7
Urban fringe	2,176	37,873,355	21.1	30.2
Places of 2,500 or more	1,580	27,332,504	15.2	21.8
100,000 or more	15	1,779,822	1.0	1.4
50,000 to 100,000	90	5,977,388	3.3	4.8
25,000 to 50,000	212	7,253,877	4.0	5.8
10,000 to 25,000	518	8,209.099	4.6	6.6
5,000 to 10,000	399	2,862,099	1.6	2.3
2,500 to 5,000	346	1,250,219	0.7	1.0
Places less than 2,500	596	689,746	0.4	0.6
2,000 to 2,500	112	249,559	0.1	0.2
1,500 to 2,000	86	149,220	0.1	0.1
1,000 to 1,500	122	152,177	0.1	0.1
Less than 1,000	276	138,790	0.1	0.1
Other urban	....	9,851,105	5.5	7.9
Outside urbanized areas	3,611	29,420,263	16.4	23.5
Places of—				
25,000 or more	200	6,935,191	3.9	5.5
10,000 to 25,000	610	9,237,648	5.2	7.4
5,000 to 10,000	995	6,917,615	3.9	5.5
2,500 to 5,000	1,806	6,329,809	3.5	5.1
RURAL				
Total	13,749	54,054,425	30.1	100.0
Places of 1,000 to 2,500	4,151	6,496,788	3.6	12.0
2,000 to 2,500	784	1,748,316	1.0	3.2
1,500 to 2,000	1,248	2,157,904	1.2	4.0
1,000 to 1,500	2,119	2,590,568	1.4	4.8
Places less than 1,000	9,598	3,893,640	2.2	7.2
Other rural	....	43,663,997	24.3	80.3
URBANIZED AREAS				
Total	213	95,848,487	53.5	100.0
Areas of—				
1,000,000 or more	16	51,785,410	28.9	54.0
500,000 to 1,000,000	22	15,365,801	8.6	16.0
250,000 to 500,000	30	10,624,125	5.9	11.1
100,000 to 250,000	85	13,480,252	7.5	14.1
Less than 100,000	60	4,592,899	2.6	4.8

TABLE II
VARIATION AMONG THE 224 SMSA's ON 35 SELECTED VARIABLES

Variable	N	Median	Low	High	Range
Basic Dimensions					
Population Size (1,000)	224	233	52	10,695	10,643
Land Area (square miles)	224	1,076.5	24	27,295	27,271
Density (pop. per sq. mile) ..	224	270.5	13	12,912	12,899
% Urban	224	79.2	47.3	100.0	52.7
% Change 1950-60	224	24.8	−11.5	297.9	309.4
Net Migration 1950-60 (%)	201	6.2	−21	264	285
Ethnic Composition					
% Negro	224	5.5	0	43.5	43.5
% Foreign Stock	224	15.0	0.8	51.6	50.8
% Minority	224	25.7	5.1	57.3	52.2
Educational Status					
Median School Years Completed	224	10.9	6.4	12.4	6.0
% compl. less than 5 years school	224	6.5	2.0	38.5	36.5
Economic Status					
% employed in Manufacturing	224	26.8	4.5	53.2	48.7
% White Collar	224	42.5	30.0	58.8	28.8
Per Capita Value Added by Manuf. ($)	224	1,109	0	3,615	3,615
Income Distribution					
Median Family Income	224	5,890	2,952	8,745	5,793
% Under $3,000	224	15.8	7.5	50.7	43.2
% $10,000 and over	224	14.2	5.3	42.1	36.8
Housing					
% One Unit Structures	224	82.4	16	93.7	77.7
% Sound with all plumb.	224	78.0	43.6	93.2	49.6
% Owner Occupied	224	64.1	29.4	80.8	51.4
Index of Home Equip.	224	361	275	406	131
Taxes and Expenditures					
% Gen. Revenue Intergov't ..	224	29.9	7.7	55.1	47.4
% Gen. Revenue Taxes	224	54.0	22.7	84.8	62.1
Per Capita Property Taxes ($)	224	96	17	207	190
Per Capita Total Gen. Expend. ($)	224	154	77	313	236
Allocation of Resources					
% Exp. on Education	224	47.7	21.5	69.4	47.9
% Exp. on Public Welfare	224	3.2	0	26.5	26.5
% Exp. on Health and Hosp.	224	3.0	0.1	22.9	22.8
% Exp. on Police Protection	224	4.3	2.2	8.7	6.5
Government Efficiency - Adequacy					
No. of persons per local Gov't Employee	224	42.7	29.1	102.0	72.9
Welfare					
% of Pop. on Public Asistance	201	3.2	0.7	9.9	9.2
Average Exp. per Pub. Assis. Recipient	201	$211	0	$1,625	$1,625
Crime					
Crime Rate per 100,000 persons	196	2,394	458	5,441	4,983
Violent Crime Rate	196	238	19	1,023	1,004
Property Crime Rate	196	2,062	338	4,775	4,437

Source: *County and City Data Book, 1967.*

FARM, CITY, AND SUBURBAN POPULATIONS, 1940-1970

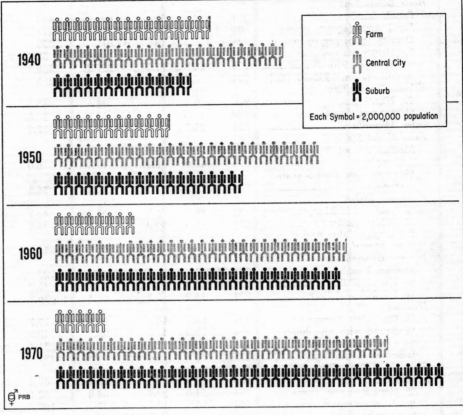

Note: Rural nonfarm dwellers, and urban residents outside of metropolitan areas, are not included in this chart. Some farm dwellers are also included in the suburban category. Definition of central city and suburb for the years 1940-1960 are according to the 1960 Census. The 1970 figures reflect some slight changes in the definitions that were used in the 1970 Census.

Sources: U.S. Department of Commerce, Bureau of the Census, *Census Population and Housing: 1970. General Demographic Trends for Metropolitan Areas 1960-1970, Final Report PHC (2)-1 United States* (Washington, D. C.: Government Printing Office, 1971).

——————. *Pocket Data Book, USA, 1971* (Washington, D. C.: Government Printing Office, 1971).

——————. *U.S. Census of Population: 1960. Selected Area Reports. Standard Metropolitan Statistical Areas. Final Report PC (3)-D* (Washington, D. C.: Government Printing Office, 1963).

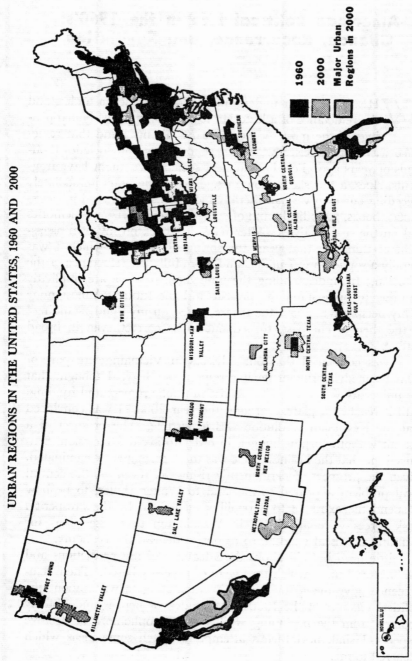

URBAN REGIONS IN THE UNITED STATES, 1960 AND 2000

1960
2000
Major Urban
Regions in 2000

Source: Map redrawn by PRB from Jerome P. Pickard, *Dimensions of Metropolitanism* (Washington, D. C.: Urban Land Institute, 1967).

American Political Life in the 1960's: Change, Recurrence, and Revolution

John Roos

WHEN I was an undergraduate I could never understand the reluctance of a historian to analyze in print the happenings of the most recent 20 years. To my mind that reluctance was best exercised with respect to events and societies thousands of years ago. For those ancient societies we might have fragments, clues, a few sketchy outlines. But for the years immediately preceding our own we had literally mountains of material in newspapers, books, periodicals, and of course our own personal memories and on the spot analyses. After reflecting back on my own assessment of things in that year, the spring of 1963, in which I was literally a sophomore, I understand more fully the reluctance of the historian. In understanding the immediate past we are implicitly claiming to understand the present and the future. Almost none of my perspectives about the future, based on my "understanding" of the then recent past, turned out to be correct even in broad outline.

I was convinced that our advisors in Vietnam were part of John Kennedy's brilliant flexible response strategy. I thought that the university would continue to rise in public respect and funding, until it reached a plateau around the year 2000. I was convinced that the Keynesian revolution was irresistible. The prospect of a tax cut without surplus budget, in order to avoid a recession, convinced me that the business cycle was to be permanently eliminated. Given the prospect of permanently rising tax revenues, the central fiscal problem appeared to me, and to Walter Heller, to be how to spend the extra $8 to $10 billion generated by the prosperity. Task forces were appointed in Washington to devise plans for spending the fiscal windfall so as not to depress the economy.

Little need be said about the adequacy of my predictions and the "history" upon which they were of necessity based. These reminiscences give me serious pause in attempting to write about the political changes of the 1960's. My endeavor here is undoubtedly doomed from the beginning. Still being a sophomore in decisive respects, I shall nevertheless attempt to sketch some ideas which occurred to me.

One consequence of the above *caveat* will be concentration more on what did not happen in the 60's than on what did. The three alternatives in the title may not be mutually exclusive. Indeed I feel that we experienced aspects of all three during the 60's. The crucial question is which areas of our national political life are best described by which title. The following pages will attempt to raise such considerations with respect to three major areas of politics in America: the party system and its central tendencies, foreign affairs, and the Presidency and the role of central government.

In a large and diverse republic such as our own, the operation of elections and political parties will be of central importance.[1] It has long been accepted by political scientists that the two-party hegemony in America has been a crucial factor in explaining the basic stability in American politics. A commonly accepted corollary is that basic shifts in attitudes and events are usually accommodated by "critical elections" in which one party redraws the basic lines of division in the electorate and dominates with its new majority for the next 30 to 40 years.[2] The best examples of such "critical elections" and subsequent dominance are Jackson and the Democrats in 1828, Lincoln and the Republicans in 1860, McKinley and the Republicans in 1896, and Roosevelt and the Democrats in 1932 and 1936.

Interpretations of where the 60's fit with respect to such cycles are many, but only four current ones will be examined. Kevin Phillips, top aide to John Mitchell in President Nixon's campaign in 1968, contends that 1968 was just such a critical election.[3] Phillips' thesis is that the 60's witnessed the dissolution of the Roosevelt coalition of the South, labor unions, intellectuals, blacks, and ethnic minorities. Phillips contends that the 1968 election was a decisive rejection of the centralized government and social planning of the Democratic party and its New Deal. The key assumption in Phillips' argument is that the Wallace vote should in substantial part be added to Nixon's to accurately calculate the new conservative majority. Phillips views the 1968 election as a watershed, moving from a 60-plus Democratic percentage in 1964

[1] V. O. Key, Jr., *Politics, Parties, and Pressure Groups* (3rd ed., New York: Crowell, 1964), p. 10.

[2] *Ibid.*

[3] Kevin Phillips, *The Emerging Republican Majority* (New Rochelle, N.Y.: Arlington House, 1969), pp. 25-42.

to a 60-plus percentage for the Republican-conservatives in 1968.

Another thesis, quite contrary, is that the 60's witnessed the beginnings of the disintegration of the traditional two-party system and the beginnings of a period of multiparty factionality and instability in American political life. This view contends that, if not in 1972, then in 1976 or 1980 a four-party system will emerge, with concomitant instability.

A related thesis was formulated at the beginning of the decade by Walter Dean Burnham. In an article entitled "The Changing Shape of the American Political Universe" Burnham uncovers a long-term decline in basic identification with participation in the two-party electoral system.[4] Looking at turnout in Presidential and off-year elections Burnham finds less than 50 per cent of the electorate engaged fully in the minimal act of voting consistently. His analysis is that such lack of basic identification and participation on the part of such a large percentage of the electorate indicates a deep alienation from the existing political alternatives. One possible consequence of such alienation would be recurrent waves of protest and a high degree of susceptibility to demagogic and extremist appeals from both left and right.

Daniel Boorstin in *The Decline of Radicalism* makes a strikingly similar prognosis, but for somewhat different reasons. Writing some 10 years after Burnham, Boorstin points to voter technology, raised minority consciousness, nationalization of the electorate, and the multiplication of opinion through TV as strains on the two-party system. The consequences he sees are similar to those envisioned by Burnham:

> If our political life is to stay indoors—if more and more of our political life is not to move from the ballet box and the legislative hall into the street or into the barricades—we must find new political voices for these new minorities, legitimate political voices, numerically registered and nationally audible.[5]

These four represent somewhat disparate analyses, yet all focus on the central question of whether the basic pattern of challenge and response by the two-party system has been broken. In one respect the 60's illustrate the recurrence of a familiar theme in

---

[4] Walter Dean Burnham, "The Changing Shape of the American Political Universe," *American Political Science Review*, LIX (December, 1965), 7.

[5] Daniel J. Boorstin, *The Decline of Radicalism* (New York: Vintage, 1970), p. 120.

American life: a shift in partisan alignments manifesting a challenge to the prevailing policy orientation. The question is whether the response will be revolutionary. In time past the challenge has, either by co-optation or isolation, eliminated the radical challenge from the political stage. A new party or new party leadership has usually created a new majority. McKinley's victory removed the Populists from the field in 1896. Roosevelt answered the challenge of discontent over the Depression. The question is whether we can now expect the discontent of the 60's, from both right and left, to be accommodated into a new majority solid enough to govern.

This much seems clear. What appeared in 1964 to be an overwhelming reassertion of the New Deal coalition was an illusion. The Democratic party faces defections on three major fronts: the South, the blue-collar working class, and the left, including some militant blacks. Nixon benefitted from the actual defection of these groups in 1968. The South and the blue-collar vote went in substantial part to Wallace, and the far left stayed at home, cutting into Humphrey's strength. The inability of the Democratic party to reconcile these factions is evident in the fratricide being currently conducted in the primaries.

Of the four interpretations above, Phillips' is the most traditional. He contends that once again an accommodation has been found by the two parties. The moderate conservatism of the new Republican party is, in his mind, the vehicle for continued majoritarian consensus. But two factors leave open the possibility that something revolutionary may have happened, or might happen. The first is the militancy of the demands of the left and the blacks, and the second is the militancy and strange diffuseness of the Wallace and McGovern vote. The Wallace and McGovern vote appears to be a protest vote of deep intensity. Racial attitudes comprise a large part of it, in Wallace's case, but this does not exhaust it. The voter is discontented in a wide and diffuse manner. Taxes, big government, privilege, bureaucracy, frustration over a war neither understood nor explained—all these and more appear to motivate many supporters of both men. The discontent appears to be wider and deeper than any accommodations presently being offered by any of the candidates of the two major parties. McGovern's showings are impressive, but he has not yet shown that he can command the support to govern rather than protest. Similarly the militant black and leftist components of the electorate, though apparently quiet on the surface, appear to this author to be also deeply alienated from the two parties. The basic conflict of the Black Political Caucus in Gary in the spring of 1972 appeared to be whether the two-party system had already failed or was living out its last chance (the conflict between Richard Hatcher and Jesse Jackson). If this analysis is correct, then there is the possibility that a new coalition formed by either of the two parties will be, like 1964, transient. This analysis sees the basic identification of major groups with the two major parties as being markedly lower. What may be deceptive is that either of the two parties could weld together a seemingly solid majoritarian coalition in 1972, and yet the underlying malaise might remain the same. A Democratic victory based on populist economic interest or a Republican victory based on a conglomeration of antistands (busing, radicals, etc.) could both be patchwork solutions easily sundered under the pressure of new events.

The cries for reform within the Democratic party after the police riots in 1968 missed the crucial point to some extent. There can be no doubt that free access to decision-making centers is a laudable goal and a necessary condition for vitality for each party and the two parties together. But it is not a sufficient condition. The reforms in the Democratic party insured that a wide variety of opinions would be expressed at the 1972 convention. But they did not insure that any opinion expressed would be able to articulate a common ground upon which lasting political alliances could be based. (Obviously no procedural change could insure such an articulation. The mistake was to believe that any procedural change could.) The last two years have seen both the Democrats and the Republicans grasping for a thread which could bind together a wide and deep enough majority to ensure the ability to govern: Nixon's patriotic appeals in the 1970 off-year elections; Fred Harris' abortive new populism; Edmund Muskie's futile pretensions to middle-course leadership; Scoop Jackson's floundering campaign to bind together all the elements of common-sense America; Hubert Humphrey's overkill of special-group appeals culminating (hopefully) in pledges of kosher kitchens in public schools for the Jewish vote. All of the major candidates are convinced that a resounding majority exists somewhere in the heartland, but no one has found the key yet,

Allegiances to parties and electoral systems are like most allegiances; they are best understood and evaluated in trying rather than calm times. The last 18 months, compared to the five years preceding, have been relatively calm. It may well be that the two-party system will again cumulate the various and conflicting opinions in the polity into a consensus large enough to govern. But it may also be that underneath this there exists as our legacy from the 60's a nation deeply divided, with the divisions ready to reappear in abnormal politics with the inevitable emergence of more overtly troubled times. McGovern, for example, is popular when criticizing property taxes. The question is whether, if elected, he can be popular when asking the citizen to make the great-hearted sacrifices democracies inevitably require? What is at stake is not simply the question of the New Deal coalition or its replacement. The central question is whether there exists any basis of coalition sufficiently broad and deep to bind together the deeply divided groups in our society in a stable way.

A similar ambiguity is found in attempting to evaluate the 60's with respect to foreign affairs. What is striking about the present campaign is that a decade which was completely dominated by a war which is still going on is followed by a campaign in which the war and foreign affairs will probably play a secondary role. And the change of the 60's was not limited to the Vietnam war, though dominated by it. I will list some of the major aspects of the changes of the 60's:

1. A shift from a competitive bipolar situation to a three-cornered situation with the emergence of China as a fledgling nuclear partner.

2. A corresponding shift of attention from Europe as the focus of concern to Asia and Third World nations.

3. A continued blurring of available and adequate definitions of "legitimate interest" and "spheres of influence" in non-European areas. In the 50's we could act with much more certainty in opposing any "Communist" government in Asia, Africa, and Latin America. The question today is enormously more complicated.

4. Experience of failure and concomitant internal frustration with both military and economic aspects of foreign aid programs.

5. A deepening simplistic isolationism internally supported in part by both right and left. The phenomenon of liberal support for Israel has been a major element in stemming this tide.

6. Development of promising and yet vague avenues of negotiation, all of which require subtle commitments, but none of which offer many dramatic, tangible results for public consumption (that is, the Salt Treaty, China trip, Russian trip, etc.).

The cumulative effect of these changes plus the Vietnam war has been to frustrate, confuse, and agonize the average citizen of all persuasions. The 50's offered the citizen clear-cut alternatives—victory or defeat, America or Russia. The alternatives were perhaps illusory, but at least clear cut. But even at the end of the 50's the strain of an increasingly complex foreign policy was beginning to tell on the public. Eric Goldman points out the discontent in foreign affairs at the end of the Eisenhower years:

> In foreign policy, the critics insisted that mere acceptance of coexistence was not enough. The United States had to make very clear what it stood for in the world—and in doing this the repetition of snappy phrases would not be sufficient. It had to give up budget-pinching in appropriating funds for matters connected with foreign policy. Millions more had to be appropriated to make sure that the United States was keeping up with and getting ahead of the Soviet Union in the race for scientific knowledge. Millions more had to be appropriated for economic aid abroad.[6]

If we began the decade with discontent, we ended it with more discontent and with a more complex reality to rail against.

It would perhaps be better if the discontent was merely on one side. The striking thing about Vietnam is that no one was really happy about it. If the question were simply hawk *versus* dove, then perhaps the conflict might be settled for good or ill. But the events of the 60's cut more ways than that. There was and is something terribly difficult to assimilate about our involvement in Southeast Asia, and it is tolerably clear that we have failed in coming to grips with that experience. We experienced a war which by any measure involved more tragic mistakes than any in our history. We experienced the anomaly of, if not defeat, then stalemate at the hands of a relatively tiny foe. We experience a war with no definite end

---

[6] Eric F. Goldman, *The Crucial Decade and After* (New York: Vintage, 1960), pp. 344-345.

point or resolution (no "victory," no "treaty"). And yet we strangely face a national election in which at this writing no issue of foreign affairs is of central importance.

To have a foreign policy means in part to be able to respond to events by reference to firmly held principles which are consistent and applicable. A foreign policy can exist in the minds of the leaders of a country without being held either in cognition or sentiment by the populace. Without judging the leaders, I think it is fair to say that the 60's left the average American without a foreign policy. In attempting to speculate on what might be public reaction to certain conceivable developments in world affairs, I am at loss. But that perhaps is a significant fact. If that is true, then the conduct of American foreign policy faces extraordinarily difficult times in the next decade. Without a minimal stability of understanding and expectations on the part of the public, conducting foreign policy becomes at least internally a game of Russian roulette. This is not to say that the average citizen ever grasps the full complexities and consequences of diplomatic and military situations. But it is something quite different if the situation is so confused that extreme militarism and extreme isolationism are real options for the populace. No matter how brilliant our present and future foreign policy might be, the 60's leave us with the enormous task of translating that policy into a set of principles which in main part can be understood and accepted by the citizenry.

The role of the Presidency and the central government was another area of major change in the 60's. In 1960 the election of John Kennedy and his vigorous style of central leadership seemed unqualifiedly beneficent to most people of liberal persuasion. For 30 years the argument over the role of the federal government *versus* state and localities had raged, and the early 60's seemed to settle the question decisively in favor of the federal government. The successful intervention in the economy through the tax cut of 1964 and the vastly expanded governmental presence in civil rights and economic redistribution appeared to mark the beginning of wide acceptance of increased central governmental activity. But by 1970 a strange coalition of right and left groups agreed on one fundamental principle: the power of the Presidency and the federal bureaucracy had grown dangerously large and powerful. Congress, the whipping boy of the late 50's and early 60's because of its obstructionist role *vis-à-vis* the Presidency, became the hope of concerned statesmen from both sides of the ideological spectrum. Calls for Congressional checks of the Presidency, revenue-sharing, dismantling of federal investigatory agencies, demands for decentralization and participatory democracy, all pointed to a deep dissatisfaction with the central exercise of power. Some of this can be attributed, especially on the liberal side, to political bending with the wind. Many Democratic intellectuals who plumped for greater power in the White House because they liked John Kennedy became rabid advocates of Congress the day Richard Nixon was inaugurated. But in addition to such factors there was again a revulsion at the failure of the 60's. After the long sleep of the 50's many citizens felt that now things were going to be not only better, but solved. When in many cases, such as the racial bifurcation in our metropolitan regions, the problems were not only not solved but worsened, the support for central authority became broadly antiauthoritarian.

The three trends identified clearly overlap. If the analysis is correct, we find as a legacy of the politics of the 60's a quiet but dangerously brooding nation. During the 60's America experienced the inadequacy of its assumed communal basis of political action. Louis Hartz in his *Liberal Tradition in America* cites the absence of any clearly articulated substantive basis of political life as the crucial facet of American politics. The liberal democratic dream of solving all conflict by procedure and compromise has, in his mind, left us incapable of withstanding the onslaught of events which raise fundamental questions about the identity of the community. Hartz contends that the failure to come to grips with the substantive questions, and the continued reliance upon procedural democracy, leaves extremism as the alternative rather than reasoned response on the basis of deeply accepted principles. The 60's proved him, in this author's opinion, at least partially right. But it is misleading to think that the problem is unique to the 60's and the time surrounding the Vietnam war. Hartz would contend that the lack of an underlying consensus was present before, and that the explosions in time of strain were simply the occasion of manifestation. The calm of the early 70's in this analysis is just as illusory as the calm of the 50's. Even before the Vietnam war discontent was rising in the nation. John Kennedy faced an electorate remarkably similar to our own in 1960. Theodore White said this about the 1960 election:

It was the atmospherics of 1960, more than anything else, that made it possible for John F. Kennedy's political exertions to triumph over the many divided pasts of the American people. And these atmospherics, as much as anything else, define the unique nature of his problem.

For 1960 was a year of national concern—but vague, shapeless, unsettling, undefinable national concern. It was a year in which the Congress of the United States saw fit for the first time to hold hearings on the National Purpose. . . . It was a political year ushered in, symbolically, by the greatest newspaper in the country, *The New York Times*, finding fit to print on its front page a dispatch from Moscow that reported that the Russians had now taken to referring to themselves as "the greatest power on earth"—a proud vulgarity hitherto reserved for Americans alone. It was a year in which Americans sensed the world about them changing as the politics of entire continents overseas changed; and they knew their own world to be changing too.

It was a year, above all, in which Americans were concerned with their identity. For Britons and Frenchmen, Russians and Germans, Arabs and Chinese, can pass through the uncadenced measure of time and history, swinging from greatness to nothingness and back again—and yet still remain Britons, Frenchmen, Russians, Germans, Arabs or Chinese. But America is a nation created by all the hopeful wanderers of Europe, not out of geography and genetics, but out of purpose—by what men sought in fair government and equal opportunity. If other nations falter in greatness, their people remain still what they were. But if America falters in greatness and purpose, then Americans are nothing but the offscourings and hungry of other lands.

This was the central problem of the campaign of 1960—and yet it was a problem that could show itself in no visible, tangible crisis.[7]

The crisis came, and soon enough it was discovered that we in fact did not know what or who we were. White's prose might, in the author's opinion, be applied to 1972. Kennedy responded with the New Frontier, and an exciting rhetoric which claimed to give us new and glorious goals. Sadly, it tasted deeply of that hubris which afflicts almost all of our attempts to resolve our fundamental questions. The one heartening aspect of our present time is that some few men appear to realize that the question of who and what we are cannot be answered in the ringing challenge of being everything and everybody. Some men seem to realize that the discontent

---

[7] Theodore H. White, *The Making of the President 1960* (New York: Atheneum, 1961), pp. 377-378.

and frustration pointed out here cannot be answered with the lie that all things are ours for the taking and doing. Some men seem to realize that perhaps the only response to our present dilemma is truly revolutionary with respect to our past. For it would be truly revolutionary to admit that we as men and as a nation have erred grievously, that we will err in the future, and that to define our common bonds is necessary but does not relieve us of the lot of most men and most nations.

Ethnic Nationalisms and the Cultural Dialectics: A Key to the Future

Joseph W. Scott

The Nature of Culture

CULTURE, in the simplest language, refers to the thoughtways, feelingways, and actionways of a people, be they a nation or a subsociety. As a concept, it refers to the established orientations which a people has for managing its relationships in the collectivity and its relationships to the forces and conditions of the physical environment. The key elements of culture are beliefs, sentiments, norms, and values. Almost all behavioral scientists would include in the realm of culture all the cognitive, affective, behavioral, and value orientations shared by a people. With these basic elements of culture, a people constructs complexes which we call ideologies, social structures, institutions, organizations, laws, and policies.

Everywhere and among each people culture will be found and it is constantly being elaborated and renewed. It is being renewed because it is always inadequate in the face of the constantly changing social and physical imperatives of survival.

Culture functions as a people's "survival kit," as a people's social solution. It is in sum a conglomeration of invented, borrowed, and evolved instrumentalities for dealing with the social and physical environment. The functions of culture are many. Culture orientates, regulates, engenders, and generates; it polarizes, socializes, conceptualizes, and disguises. In other terms it can be simultaneously liberating, enslaving, illuminating, and blinding.

Even the theories, models, and equations which record the conditions of survival and the coping actions of a people also belong to the realm of culture. Thus a people's concepts about the world and its actions toward the physical and the social conditions of the world are written large in its culture. It is at once a record and an inspiration; it is a map of past history and a map to the future.

At another level of abstraction, we must admit that one function of culture is political. It is generated through political processes, managed by political agents for the interests of specific political groups, and thus it is a political force. To the extent that culture takes the form of political policies which guide, manage, and control the lives and life chances of the citizens of a society, it is a political force. To the extent that culture is taught in schools as American history, sociology, and psychology and is used to indoctrinate or incapacitate certain peoples of the society, it is a political force. Because political institutions are mechanisms for making culture, and political policies and ideologies are some of the aspects of culture made by such institutions, politics is both a product and a progenitor of culture. Culture can be therefore both liberating and enslaving.

The Culture of Colonialization

Of all the European descendants, the Anglo-Americans have had the most influential role in shaping the culture of the United States, the so-called American culture. Ironically, even in the midst of espousing the high ideals of freedom, liberty, equality, and justice for all peoples, the Anglo-Americans set upon a course in history which negated these very ideals. They developed sets of cultural practices which were opposites to these ideals. The political, economic, educational, and biological ideologies which they developed have been negations of these ideals. When the American ideologies and institutions are examined closely, they constitute a cultural complex which we might in a shorthand way refer to as *the culture of colonialization*. The culture of colonialization refers to the cognitive, affective, and behavioral orientations conceived and used systematically to support and rationalize the political subjugation and economic exploitation of ethnic minorities. We are all too familiar with thoughtways, feelingways, and actionways of racial and ethnic discrimination. We also know that learning racial discrimination in the United States is like learning the alphabet, and that prejudice of the ethnic and racial variety is normative in the United States.

Anglo-Americans came to this continent with a colonial mentality and they have elaborated this cultural mind-set over the past three centuries in the New World. This society has a shining record of racial and ethnic subjugation. No society ever before perfected slavery like this society did, and no society ever expended so much of its financial resources to kidnap, transport, and hold in slavery so many people.

The cultural heritage of Europe caused the Anglo-Americans to institute a society which was in large part antithetical to the ideals the newcomers espoused. American culture thus abounds with ideas and techniques for subjugating, exploiting, and misleading the minorities in this country. Far from having a preponderance of policies, ideologies, and institutions which constitute accurate representations of the original ideals of equality, etc., we find that American culture abounds with their contradictions. The history of immigration and emigration, ideologies, laws, policies, and institutions on the whole does not constitute a record of people being liberated. The history constitutes a record of various peoples being oppressed and excluded.

In truth, American culture is really a continuation of European expansionism, and thus it is very much a continuation of the European culture of colonialization. Since this country began, the Anglo-Americans have been about the business of procuring and retaining cheap labor and natural resources, and thus the country has been oriented towards out-and-out colonialization. American colonialization began in the early 1660's with the enslavement of the Indians and Africans in this country, and it continued with the conquering of the Mexicans in the Southwest and the Puerto Ricans on the island of Puerto Rico. Thus there are minority groups within this country who were conquered and forcibly made citizens of this nation: the Africans, the Mexicans, and the Puerto Ricans. For the most part they have not been immigrants to the United States. They were not voluntary American subjects. They did not ask to be taken over by a foreign power. They did not volunteer to give up their cultural traits and be transformed. They did not agree tacitly as others did by coming to the United States to assimilate Anglo-American culture. Africans, Mexicans, and Puerto Ricans were forced to acquiesce to American culture and institutions against their wills by force of arms.

The Africans, the Mexicans, and the Puerto Ricans under the political jurisdiction of the United States government are in effect colonized subjects and they have been treated differently from European immigrants: they have not just been deprived, they have been exploited; they have not just been segregated, they have been subjugated; they have not just been displaced, most have been dispossessed of their political rights and many of their cultural traits as well as their lands.

The culture of colonialization was first worked out on the Indians and the Africans, and it was subsequently applied to the Mexicans of the Southwest after 1846 and to the Puerto Ricans on the island of Puerto Rico after 1898. Since procuring cheap labor and natural resources are very much a part of the survival of the system in the United States, the constant need of colonized peoples has caused the Anglo-Americans to continue to elaborate cultural complexes which negate and repudiate the ideals of equality, justice, freedom, and liberty for all. The constant need of these colonized peoples also helps keep alive the culture of colonialization and keeps up the pressure for renewing the colonial aspects of the culture. Cognitive, affective, and behavioral orientations conducive to successful control over such peoples are being worked out in the area of school desegregation even as I write.

The European Immigrant Experience

The process of acculturation which I am about to describe was fairly typical for most immigrants from Europe but was not typical of the Africans, Mexicans, and Puerto Ricans. After the English came and started this society, the immigrants arrived and met collectively with political, economic, religious, and social discrimination perpetrated by the English. Specifically, the Anglo-Americans denied them entry into the institutions and social groups by means of attitudinal and behavioral barriers. The immigrants' initial reactions were to gravitate together in order to deal with their common foe and common plight.[1] Since they were restricted to specific geographical areas of the city, they tended to form ghettos and to organize around the traditional values, norms, sentiments, and beliefs of their old countries. The first generations had to be contented with making little economic or no social progress. They were confined largely to advancement within their ghetto communities.

Their children who came into more contact with Anglo-American institutions outside the ghettos underwent a cultural indoctrination apart from that which took place within the ghettos. The

---

[1] See a discussion of this experience by The Puerto Rican Forum, *A Study of Poverty Conditions in the New York Puerto Rican Community* (New York, 1970).

children found themselves more able to associate with Anglo-Americans as they learned Anglo-American culture. They found that they could not advance themselves outside the ghetto unless they took on the cultural characteristics of the dominant group. They found that they could gain entry into some institutions of Anglo-American society when they learned the thoughtways, feelingways, and actionways of the Anglo-Americans. Thus the second generations became bicultural peoples—caught between two cultures, neither completely in one nor the other. Since access to the advancement they sought in America was controlled by the Anglo-Americans, they danced to the Anglo-American tunes as called.

This Anglo-conformity acculturation process produced conflicts between the first and second generations of immigrants but these conflicts became secondary to the overall quest for advancement in American society. The second generations in seeking to achieve positions like Anglo-Americans sought to associate with Anglo-Americans and sought to participate in the institutions of the Anglo-Americans more than those of the ghettos. Most of the second generations gave up their languages, their customs, and their distinctive cultural traits and adopted Anglo-American cultural patterns. A larger number even intermarried into Anglo-American communities.

The immigrant experience was not without conflict. The Anglo-Americans by virtue of their superior power positions were able to control the rewards and punishments for conformity and nonconformity. They controlled access to occupations, educational attainments, residential areas, social clubs, and marriage partners of the dominant group. Thus as the immigrants came and settled within these borders, many found themselves in an alienating environment. They found themselves blocked from attaining many of the just goods and statuses of this society. They found that the Anglo-Americans had erected barriers to entry and participation in the established institutions of the society, and the price they had to pay to advance socially, politically, and economically in American society was Anglo-American conformity. This opened up culture conflicts. As the immigrants challenged the Anglo-Americans, various cultural dialectics began. Anglo-American culture was confronted and opposed by what were described as "alien" cultures. Hot and cold warfare followed and out of the conflict came a resolution heavily weighted on the side of Anglo-American cultural conformity, allowing for behavioral and organizational pluralism.

Anglo-American cultural conformity was inevitable because the immigrants had come voluntarily for one reason or another to seek a better life and with the aim and desire to become American citizens and to accept to some extent the culture within these borders. To be sure, they came at the urgings and with the encouragements of the Anglo-American leaders who had held privileged positions as traders, merchants, landowners, and politicians. But they came voluntarily with the expectation of having to acquiesce to some extent to the dominant group of Anglo-Americans.

Today, however, the cultural dialectics are different.[2] They are different because the major minorities today are *not* immigrants. The major minorities are peoples who have been colonized: the Africans, the Mexicans, and the Puerto Ricans are not citizens by virtue of being naturalized immigrants. They are victims of conquest. This perhaps is the most important reason why they have not been fully assimilated into the mainstream of American society.

Because these conquered groups have not been able to follow the "natural" assimilation processes of other groups, different cultural dialectics are going on. In each of these groups highly organized and virulent nationalist movements have emerged. Among each of these minorities, large vanguard groups are about the business of indoctrinating the masses with ideas, sentiments, and values designed to bring about national liberation. These cultures pose antitheses to the culture of colonialization.

Anglo-American conformity,[3] which is really Anglo-American nationalism, is presently being opposed by African-American nationalism, Mexican-American nationalism, and Puerto Rican-American nationalism. Vanguard groups within each of these ethnic enclaves are resurrecting and developing ideas, behaviors, and materials with the aim of achieving territorial, political, and economic liberation. In sum, the cultures of liberation constitute complexes of cognitive, affective, behavioral, and value orientations to enable the colonized subjects within the boundaries of the United States to deal with

---

[2] For a discussion of cultural dialectics see Sékou Touré, "A Dialectical Approach to Culture," *The Black Scholar*, I (November, 1969), 11-26.

[3] See Milton M. Gordon, *Assimilation in American Life* (New York: Oxford University Press, 1964).

the sociopolitical and socioeconomic conditions of survival. Specifically, the cultures of liberation now in the making include both material and nonmaterial instrumentalities for overcoming the economic exploitation, political domination, and cultural genocide perpetrated by the dominant elements in the society. The political ideologies of these nationalist groups begin with the conceptualization that they are first and foremost a colonized people who have had Anglo-American culture forced upon them. Secondly, they have concluded that assimilation is untenable and unwanted because acceptance of Anglo-American conformity includes political domination which is a price too large to pay in exchange for full access to the "good life" of this society. Assimilation is also unwanted because the minority problem is not a lack of assimilation but a lack of remuneration. Africans, Mexicans, and Puerto Ricans believe that they should receive more adequate remuneration from the economy rather than more marginal remuneration from the economy. Thus all three groups call for more reparations, not more participation, and most of them even go as far as to say that what they want is national separation, not integration.

What is happening is that the Anglo-American ideas and ideologies of colonialism are being opposed. The falsehoods which the dominant group has foisted on minorities by misrepresenting their histories are finally being discovered for what they are and for what they were intended to do. These various historical misrepresentations are being raised in sharp relief for all to see. Through the emergence of their cultural nationalisms, the lost, stolen, and hidden cultural traits of the Africans, the Mexicans, and the Puerto Ricans are being resurrected and corrected. This process of resurrecting the indigenous cultures and inculcating the young with them is the process which is setting the stage for the development of a revolutionary ethnic movement which will reach effective proportions within a decade.

African-American Nationalism[4]

The recent African-American nationalism movement started in 1965 when the civil rights movement proved irrelevant to the great problems of young blacks. Marching, picketing, demonstrating, and

---

[4] See E. U. Essien-Udom, *Black Nationalism* (New York: Dell, 1969).

petitioning had reached a point of diminished returns, and the masses of young blacks wanted new approaches to the problems they were facing. This new mood became evident with the Watts riot of 1965 and the Detroit riot of 1967. After the Detroit riot more than 100 cities experienced some type of rioting, and the movement for integration, civil-rights style, had come to a halt. Several young black men and women emerged from the ranks of the old civil rights force and began to espouse doctrines of "Black Power." Some of the doctrines added up to collective integration rather than individual integration, others to collective separation. Some doctrines advocated communal separation and others national separation. I will deal from this point on with groups and individuals espousing national separation.

The most famous of these groups was the Black Muslims. Malcolm X, speaking for the Nation of Islam, had been calling for national separation. He had been calling for revolution to achieve this separation. He had been calling for a black nation for black people by means of a land revolution if necessary.

The Honorable Elijah Muhammad, the head of the Nation of Islam, had called for a black-controlled territory and state on this continent. He actually demanded the five southeastern states of the United States because the great majority of the blacks have labored and lived in these states since they were kidnapped from Africa. An African-American heritage which they have worked out over the past 300 and some odd years is a heritage growing up largely in this geographic area. Millions of black people have been buried there. Much black sweat has been mingled with the soil there. Black blood, sweat, tears, and labor have paid for this land.

The Black Muslims continue to preach and practice racial separation. They have spent their time and energy in apolitical activities since the death of Malcolm X. They are a religious-economic group with exclusively religious and economic programs and enterprises. The Honorable Elijah Muhammad shuns political activities like voting and political campaigning. He also shuns running members of the Nation for public office. He also shuns any revolutionary activities of the paramilitary variety. Social and economic developments are the chief mechanisms for building a black man's nation, and these are the only activities the Nation engages in.

On the other hand, there is the Republic of New Africa.[5] It was founded in 1967 by many former members of the civil rights rank and file. It is a secularized version of the Nation of Islam, the Black Muslims. It advocates national separation on this continent too. It wants the same southern states, and gives the same reasons for claiming rights to this land. It differs, however, from the Nation in that it is a political-paramilitary group. It has no discernible economic or social program. Presently, the representatives of the RNA are setting up a territorially free nation on a small plot of land in Mississippi. They are preparing to expand from here their sovereignty over more and more land as circumstances permit. The African-Americans, they maintain, are a captive people and these southern states are captive lands. Thus the RNA has declared itself the government of all African-Americans and is working to set them free territorially and politically. From such independence will come the solutions to economic deprivation and political and social oppression facing blacks in the United States.

Described as an African Nation in the Western Hemisphere, the RNA is the symbol for the black chanters of "nation-time" who can be heard in every city wherein there are at least 10,000 African-Americans.

Chicano Nationalism[6]

In 1969 the first national Chicano Youth Liberation Conference was held. An organization called the Crusade for Justice hosted the conference. They adopted a plan which has come to be known as *The Spiritual Plan of Aztlan*. It is a document calling for Chicano nationhood—that is, national separation—and Chicano sovereignty over what were the northern parts of Mexico before 1846: California, Texas, Colorado, Arizona, and New Mexico. The Plan of Aztlan calls for Chicano control and ownership of the territories which were seized during the Mexican-American War. It is a call for nationalism and revolutionary action to achieve territorial, political, and cultural liberation.

The plan also outlines an action program for mobilizing all

---

[5] See Abubakari Obadele Imari, *Revolution and Nation Building* (Detroit: Songhay, 1970).

[6] See Antonio Camejo, *Documents of the Chicano Struggle* (New York: Pathfinder, 1971), and Mario Compean and Jose Angel Gutierrez, *La Raza Unida Party in Texas* (New York: Pathfinder, 1970).

Chicanos in the United States in a collective struggle for Chicano independence from Anglo domination. It suggests that Chicanos everywhere wage revolution if they want freedom and prosperity.

The political analysis begins with the fact that Mexican-Americans are a people who were subjugated through conquest. The analysis reports that the Anglo-Americans invaded their lands and took them by force of arms. Thus reclamation of these lands is at the base of the Chicano uprising. Through land, freedom and sovereignty can result. Through land and political independence, prosperity by the sweat of their brows is possible. The Chicanos reject the fact that conquest gives a country legitimate rights over another country. They reject the rights over the Southwest claimed by the United States government.

The conference concluded that social, economic, and political independence are the only sure ways to escape economic exploitation, political domination, and cultural genocide. A struggle therefore must be waged against the Anglo-Americans who control everything in the lives of Chicanos.

Youth organizations like the Mexican-American Youth Organization and others have begun political education and political organization. They have helped organize the Chicano third-party movement in some of the southwestern states, and they have led school boycotts and other protest activities in the field of education.

One of the most important vanguard groups is the Alliance of the Free City-States from Northern New Mexico. It is spreading Chicano nationalism. Through such political organizations the Chicano masses are moving to reclaim their lands. One motto is: *Tierra o Muerte* (land or death). Territorial and cultural integrity has become the rallying point politicizing Chicano youth. This new ideological perspective and these new value orientations heighten the contradictions between Anglo-American words and deeds, killing what remaining faith the Chicano masses may have in the present institutions and assimilation. The Chicano movement today is about nation-building and national consciousness.

Borinquen Nationalism[7]

Puerto Rico is probably the oldest remaining colony in the

---

[7] For a discussion of Borinquen Nationalism see Young Lords Party, *Palante* (New York: McGraw-Hill, 1971).

world. For 500 years it has been controlled by one nation or another. Puerto Rico was discovered on Columbus' second trip to the New World in 1493. It was thereafter controlled by Spain for 400 years. The Spanish first tried to enslave the indigenous Indian populations, and being unsuccessful with the Indians they imported and enslaved Africans.

Today the Puerto Rican people are a racially mixed ethnic group of African, Indian, and Spanish bloods. In short, they are a multiracial, multicultured people.

The United States took control of Puerto Rico in 1898 after the Spanish-American War. In 1898 United States troops invaded the island shortly after Spain granted political "autonomy" to Puerto Rican revolutionaries. They took control of the government and the people, and Puerto Rico came under the domination of the United States. Shortly after that, in 1900, Congress passed the Foraker Act which established civilian American rule rather than American military rule in the island. The American government, once in control of the island, began to revamp the social institutions, the educational institutions, and the economy. It also began to divide up the land and permitted large sugar companies to take over most of the cultivatable land. From this time on American businessmen invested more and more money in Puerto Rico, to the point that now most major corporations are American owned and most Puerto Ricans are dependent upon American enterprises for economic survival.

In 1917 the Puerto Ricans in masses were made citizens by legislative decree. From this time on, the language and culture of Puerto Rico came under attack, and the English language and other aspects of Anglo-American culture were imposed forcibly. The Puerto Ricans became political subjects of the United States government, controlled but not enfranchised.

The Young Lords Party, a Puerto Rican group, is an outgrowth of the Young Lords Organization which had been a street gang in Chicago. The Party really started as an amalgamation of "corner youth" and "college youth." The college youth were of the Society of Albizu Campos—a nationalist group. The corner youth were members of a street gang which was organized to fight other street gangs in the process of protecting its "turf" or neighborhood.

The Party began in midyear 1969 and at that time it began to organize in earnest. It planned social campaigns to help the

Puerto Rican community of which it was a part. At the present time it is conducting political education and health campaigns in Puerto Rican neighborhoods across the big cities of this country.

Since October, 1969, the Party has been active in the field of health, organizing hospital workers, mobilizing TB and lead poisoning detection services, and urging better city sanitation services. On the surface its campaigns appear as social betterment activities, but these betterment activities are only means to gain the attention, the respect, the confidence, and the loyalty of the masses. Through these services it has been able to politically educate and behaviorally demonstrate what immediate control over community institutions can do for a people.

The Party's political program calls for raising a national liberation struggle to free Puerto Rico from Anglo-American domination. Its methods call for the politicalization and the radicalization of all Puerto Ricans both on the mainland and the island. Puerto Rican nationalism is the key unifying force.

One Party motto is: "Where a Puerto Rican is, the duty of the Puerto Rican is to make revolution." Thus the Party is about the task of uniting all segments of the Puerto Rican people in order to press the United States government for political and economic independence. The Party is a revolutionary group trying to radicalize the Puerto Rican masses in order to move them to act in their own political interest and strike a blow for national separation and thus national independence.

Politics and Culture

If we consider political processes, we can see that some new cultures are in the making. There are several vanguard ethnic groups actively unearthing old cultural patterns and generating new ones. These groups are not only about the business of resurrecting and making culture; they are also about the business of indoctrinating the youth with new cultural ideas.

What is quite apparent is that the most influential political youth movements in the United States today are the ethnic power movements: the Black Power Movement, the Bronze Power Movement, the Yellow Power Movement, the Puerto Rican Power Movement, and the American Indian Power Movement. Politically, these movements represent nearly all of the major minority groups in America today, about 40 million people. Their influence goes beyond this number, for they have inspired the Student Power Movement and the Women's Liberation Movement in both secular and sacred sectors of the society. Some say the reactionary white ethnic power movements now in embryo have been inspired by these movements.

Key goals in all the movements are self-determination, self-legitimation, and self-valuation. The cultures of liberation are opposition cultures. They are countercultures. They are contracultures. Like all cultures they are purposive and utilitarian. Their utility lies in that they function so as to neutralize the social, economic, political, and psychological ideas which presently control the minorities in this country. The means and ends of the new cultures are political. The inculcation process raises into relief the invalidity of many Anglo-American ideas, sentiments, and values which the dominant group used to distort the images of the minorities in this society and to produce inferiority complexes in the minorities. The new cultures are purgative. They are opening vistas to future actions by resurrecting formerly blunted and repressed collective strategies. This collective process of self-legitimation is becoming the basis for the revolutionary movements now under way in the United States.

Revolutionary movements, however, are doomed to splinter and die without a unifying ideology. The unifying ideology within each ethnic enclave is nationalism. Ethnic nationalism forces recognition of cultural patterns which heretofore had been lost, stolen, or hidden from the mainstream of the society by the educational systems and the mass media of communication. Cultural traits which were formerly kept out of the inculcating apparatus of the society are now being taught both inside and outside the ethnic enclaves. The ethnic studies programs and ethnic studies institutes are the most indicative evidence of this new institutional process of acculturation.

Ethnic nationalism has produced new ideologies, new standards of beauty, new personal styles, new speech patterns, and new patterns of self-legitimation in America in recent years. Ethnic nationalism has produced new political and social arrangements in some communities in the United States too. Ethnic political parties and ethnic-dominated school boards are still other developments which ethnic nationalism has produced.

Although the African-American, Mexican-American, and Puerto Rican-American power movements are young and their accomplishments are not many, and the changes they have produced are not revolutionary, the movements cannot be dismissed. The possibly 40 million politicized and radicalized people which they may represent are not going to permit themselves to be dismissed. Ethnic cultures of liberation are afoot and are being carefully cultivated. A day of reckoning may not be more than a decade away, and the small trickle of the movements today may turn into a mighty river of people who will desire and seek the partitioning of the United States—the key to the survival of the United States.

Religion and Philosophy

Theology and the New American Culture: A Problematic Relationship

Stanley Hauerwas

MY title calls the relationship of theology and the new American culture "problematic." That relationship is a problem, I think, on many sides and various levels. The issue involves questions I do not even know how to ask meaningfully, let alone resolve.

First of all, I have all sorts of problems with a term so amorphous as "American culture." I know there is something distinctive about being American, that is, being heir of and participant in this nation's history and culture. Yet if forced to characterize that distinctiveness, I find myself either mouthing meaningless abstractions about democracy, freedom, and equality — or simply lost in the sheer diversity of people and experience which make up the country. So it is definitely problematic for me to attempt relating theology to something as hard to pin down as concepts like "American culture" or "the American character."

Moreover, the turbulence of the 1960's makes me suspect that America well may have undergone some fundamental changes which indicate the beginnings of a new culture. Yet I am even more puzzled about how to identify and properly characterize this "new American culture" than I am the old. Is the new culture that which is the development of our technological society, or is it rather the "counterculture" of American youth? Are the seemingly momentous changes in the American scene really "new," or only different ways of construing the familiar American pragmatic and individualistic spirit? In other words, is the so-called "new American culture" something different in kind or but one or several variations on traditional American values and institutions?

Finally, the relationship of these kinds of questions and theology is highly problematic. Today there are numerous "theologies of culture" — not least because it is so unclear as to what such an enterprise entails. Without broaching that thorny matter, I can at least insist that the question of theology's relation to the "new American culture" be separated from that of religion's relationship to a culture. Theology is a normative discipline. In the context of the questions we are raising here, theology is concerned with how

71

religious people *should be* related to culture, regardless of how in fact they are so related. Historically, of course, religion has played a decisive role in the formation of the American spirit. But such a descriptive account has no normative weight for the theologian. At best, awareness of religion's role will inform his enterprise since the theologian must have some idea as to what has been in order to know what should be.[1]

At least such has been the traditional view of theology as normative. One of the most striking aspects of contemporary American theology, however, has been its willingness, even avidity, to enter into dialogue with its culture. Today's theologians appear eager to rush in where historians and sociologists fear to tread. Or to change the image, American theologians no longer sit around the hearth of philosophy, but warm themselves with the cultural themes of the day. It is the leaping flames of cultural issues they contemplate, seeking to discern implicit or explicit "religious" significance in that fire.[2] And no longer is the theologian's handbook Aristotle's *Metaphysics,* but rather Reich's *The Greening of America.*

The difficulty with the resulting theology is, however, deciding why Reich's (or X's or Y's) account of modern American society should be accepted rather than Parsons' (or X's or Y's). With such theology, the theologian's claims seem to be only as good as the cultural commentator he happens to prefer. Nor is it clear how such theology is to be distinguished from journalism.

I do not wish to deny many healthy aspects of the theologian's concern with contemporary culture; but in actual practice the

---

[1] For example, my own analysis below presupposes the kind of work done by Perry Miller in *Errand into the Wilderness* (Cambridge, Mass.: Harvard University Press, 1956) and H. R. Niebuhr in *The Kingdom of God in America* (New York: Harper, 1937).

[2] Harvey Cox's *The Secular City* (New York: Macmillan, 1965) is the classic example of this kind of theology. Many lesser lights continue the attempt over different aspects of culture they find more significant. For example, see Myron Bloy, "The Counter-Culture: It Just Won't Go Away," *Commonweal,* October 17, 1971, pp. 29-34, and Robert Johnson, *Counter Culture and the Vision of God* (Minneapolis: Augsburg, 1971). A summary of Michael Novak's work would make a fascinating account in this respect as he originally gave a theological blessing to the "youth movement" but then has begun to be more and more disenchanted with it. For a well-balanced assessment see his "American Youth and the Problem of God: A Theological Reflection," *Proceedings of the Catholic Theological Society* (New York, 1972), pp. 138-155. Many of the essays in this volume are of interest for the subject of this essay.

development has tended to trivialize the theological task. An indication of this danger is the highly faddish and arbitrary nature of such theology. For example, in 1965 Harvey Cox in *The Secular City* gave an almost unqualified baptism to the new "secularity" with its pragmatic and technological style.[3] This was necessary, according to Cox, because theology is called upon to make religion relevant and responsive to the new forces of our society. (Thus reversing the ancient Christian assumption that the Christian's task is to make the world relevant to the Gospel.) Yet only four years later we find Cox praising the emphasis on fantasy, play, and celebration in the antitechnology counterculture.[4] Perhaps Cox has begun to suspect that there is nothing more boring or pathetic than the irrelevancy of the "relevant theology" of the generation just past. Nonetheless, he has created a hard theological world to live in: the theologian must somehow keep up with every new movement the media decide to create.

Such criticism of the recent theology of culture, however, does not reach the basic difficulty. Often the implicit assumption in this kind of theologizing is that the prime duty of theology is to help create or reconstitute Christendom. Such a suggestion may appear odd, since the theology I am criticizing tends to be itself critical of past failures of the church to stand over against the pretensions of American righteousness. It vigorously opposes the willing domestication of the Gospel to believing in belief. Such theology dissociates itself from the church's rather crude baptism of the "American way of life." And this theology insists that its perspective is not determined by the church's good faith, but rather by the bad faith of the church expressed in the acceptance of racists, capitalists, and a dehumanizing society. Thus for the theologians

---

[3] The issue of the relation of religion and "secularity" is of course an important and significant problem for the theologian. The problem with *The Secular City* was the assumption that the meaning of "secularity" and its relation to our contemporary culture was clear. For an excellent collection of essays concerned with this issue see Childress and Harned, eds., *Secularization and the Protestant Prospect* (Philadelphia: Westminster Press, 1970).

[4] Harvey Cox, *The Feast of Fools* (New York: Harper, 1969). Cox explicitly denies that there is any conflict between his earlier and later books and calls the latter only a "companion piece" to *The Secular City*. However, it is extremely hard to see how he can have both worlds; the "festive radical" he calls for surely seems bent on tearing down a good deal that the pragmatic-technological culture wishes to preserve. He is right, however, that there is a continuity between the books as he continues to have a rather touching faith in the goodness of his fellow creatures.

of the "new American culture" the current counterculture movement seems to offer the church a way out of its all-too-willing service to the old culture which has now revealed its true warmaking,
racist, and technologically repressive character. Such a way out,
however, leads through the same error of the past: confusing the
demands of the Gospel with the reigning idealities of culture. The
New Left and the counterculture are, in fact, no less aspects of
the American phenomenon than are its pragmatic-technological
forms.

Thus theologians continue to foster the idea that the church's
mission is to translate the Gospel into the pieties of contemporary
culture — that her mission is to spiritualize our civilization and our
lives by identifying the current moralisms with the meaningfulness
of salvation. The church's very success in the past now weds her
to the continued bad faith that she is shepherd of the goodness
of our culture.[5] But such a view of the church's mission, I would
argue, is theologically askew. The church is not called to build
culture or to supply the moral tone of civilization, old or new. The
church is called to preach that the Kingdom of God has come close
in the person and work of Jesus Christ.[6] It is only as the church

[5] James Sellers says, for example, "Christian theology plays its role by
seeking to identify those elements in the [American] tradition that express
the Gospel, while it is at the same time open to those new elements in our
contemporary situation that express new challenges and call for new expressions of the Gospel." *Public Ethics: American Morals and Manners* (New
York: Harper and Row, 1970), p. 226. Herbert Richardson attempts to
identify theology with what he calls the sociotechnic age. Thus, he says, "A
sociotechnic theology must develop new ethical principles which will enable
men to live in harmony with the new impersonal mechanism of mass society.
This ethic will affirm the values of a technical social organization of life in
the same way that earlier Protestantism affirmed the values of radical individualism and capitalism." *Toward an American Theology* (New York: Harper
and Row, 1967) p. 25. Sellers and Richardson have the virtue of not being
mesmerized by the "righteousness" of the counterculture but their theological
difference with the counterculture theologians is only over which part of the
culture they wish to make the engines of theology serve. To provide one final
example, Leroy Moore suggests that the great unfinished theological task of
the American church is to construct a theology to support the pluralism and
freedom of the American culture. "From Profane to Sacred America: Religion and the Cultural Revolution in the United States," *Journal of the
American Academy of Religion*, 39 (September, 1971), 322-324.

[6] Since I am primarily concerned in this context to criticize what I interpret to be a new form of the "Christ of culture" position, my understanding
of the relation of "Christ and culture" may appear more negative than it is.
A culture may offer many positive forms of life congruent with the demands
of the Gospel. My concern in this essay, however, is to deny that this con-

becomes a community separate from the predominant culture that she has the space and rest from which to speak the truth to that culture.[7]

The church's task, then, is not to choose sides among the competing vitalities of the current culture, but to speak the word of truth amid warring spirits. For the truth she speaks is not any truth; it is the truth of the Kingdom which the bounds of this earth do not contain. That is the reason why the first word the church always speaks to its culture is a word of incompleteness and finitude. However, this is not a word men gladly hear. It is characteristic of our personal and national existence to claim that we have a hold on truth which gives security in this life. We indulge the illusion that we can and do imbue our life and culture with meaning that is not subject to the ravages of time and human perversity. This is the reason a society only confesses its past sins within a framework of later rectitude. To do otherwise would necessitate admitting that the society's call for loyalty and devotion can only be accepted with qualification, or perhaps not at all.

The theologically interesting aspect of the current cultural "crisis" is, therefore, the tension it reveals in the idealism of the American spirit. For, as Reinhold Niebuhr demonstrated in *The Irony of American History,* the great strength and great weakness, the great wisdom and great folly of America have been the assumption that her beginning and history somehow captured the ideal possibilities of man.[8] To be sure, America often betrayed her ideals

---

gruence can be *a priori* asserted in the name of relevance or social reform, but occurs only because Christians first take a critical and discriminating stance toward the society in which they happen to find themselves.

[7] I suspect that this is also true for the university. However, it remains to be seen if the university's commitment to truth in the abstract is sufficient to withstand the temptation to become mistress to the reigning culture. For a position close to my own in this respect see James Schall, "The University, the Monastery, and the City," *Commonweal,* April 7, 1972, pp. 105-110.

[8] Reinhold Niebuhr, *The Irony of American History* (New York: Scribner's, 1962). Some may interpret this essay as a reassertion of Niebuhrian realism against the idealism and romanticism of the new politics. However, this would be a serious misunderstanding for even though I continue to have deep sympathies with Niebuhr's insights I think much of the recent criticism of "Christian realism" as a position has been just. It would take me too far afield to go into this matter but generally I think Niebuhr failed to appreciate the positive nature of society, or, in more theological terms, he tended to continue to assume, admittedly in a more dynamic fashion, the Lutheran dichotomy between the orders of creation and redemption. However, even if that is the case many of Niebuhr's contemporary critics ignore his positive apprecia-

for lesser goods; but her very hypocrisy proved but another aspect of her spiritual pride. For America's ability to see critically her shortcomings has been interpreted by Americans as another sign of her essential righteousness and distinctiveness among the nations. The theologians of the "new American culture" question no more than those before them that a righteous America is possible. The debate between the representatives of the old and the new cultures concerns only whether we have fallen, or to what degree the fall has occurred, so that the necessary nostrums may be applied.

The interesting "problematic relationship" for me in this essay is therefore the tension created by a necessary theological stance. As a theologian I must be a critic who somehow stands apart from his culture, while remaining at the same time part of it. In attempting such a task I am sure I will make some horrendous errors concerning my perception of the nature of the American culture, both old and new. However, such a risk must be taken, since the Word to which the theologian is first responsible does not go out to the world to come back empty. The theologian shares in the church's desire not to keep a place above the battle, but a place within it, so as to speak the truth about the human condition in its localized cultural dress. Relevancy is not the criterion of truth. It is, however, an obligation of the church and the theologian if they are to avoid narcissistic infatuation which breeds the self-righteousness of men who have forgotten that Christ belongs not to themselves but to the world.

In this essay I am attempting to suggest what I take to be pertinent theological aspects of the current crisis of American culture. For purposes of analysis, I will distinguish between the crisis associated with our institutions and the crisis of persons. I hesitate to employ such a distinction, for it separates the inseparable and tends to suggest a cleavage between the social and personal factors of our life. As a way of sorting out issues, however, I think the distinction will prove functionally useful.

The account of the crises of American institutions is a familiar litany. Our cities are decaying. They are filled with black refugees from the South, who must try to survive strangled by white insen-

---

tion of community for the flourishing of the self. Moreover, the critics are wrong in their claim that Niebuhrian realism is essentially conservative. This appears to be the case due to Niebuhr's refusal to develop any principles of justice on which discriminating social judgments could be based. In the absence of a substantive view of justice, Niebuhr's realism was and is open to conservative distortion.

sitivity and stupidity. Integration of the blacks has proved more difficult than was originally envisaged; the blacks resist it for reasons of manhood and identity, while whites fight integration in order to preserve the "quality education of the neighborhood school." Then there is the continuing problem of poverty. We have discovered a poor in the midst of society's plenty whom the growth of a mixed-capitalist economy does not seem capable of reaching. On top of it all, we are becoming aware that we are callously destroying our environment, so that we can neither drink our water nor breathe our air without endangering health. And all these problems seem to be occurring at a time when our political institutions are not able to provide even the most basic services for society to keep running at a minimal level.

Brooding over these immense problems is of course the war in Vietnam. The war seems to stand as sign and symbol that America has indeed fallen from the ranks of the righteous. In Vietnam we have engaged in and helped perpetrate an evil so terrible that no possible rationalization can be offered to explain or excuse what we have done.[9] America seems to have sided with the forces of death and destruction against the forces of life. The only question left is which ones will prevail.

These are extremely serious problems; taken together they pose a real threat to our society's current form of existence. What I am concerned about here, however, is how this common litany of our problems serves to substantiate the claim that we are living in an "apocalyptic" or "crisis" time. Such a proclamation is not a new phenomenon in American life. But framing the current revision of the claim reveals some of the basic illusions associated with the American dream. For this apocalypticism is based on our prior claims to greatness and innocence. That is to say, our apocalypticism is a sign of a disease deeper than the actual problems which we Americans face. It is noteworthy that the radical critiques of American society as corrupt continue to presuppose, as their model of the good society, a purer and more perfect America which supposedly existed in the past. The American radical is not the born cynic but

---

[9] I do not mean this to be taken as my own ethical judgment about the Vietnam war. Rather, I am discussing the war insofar as it has become a cultural symbol. It is one of the marks of our ethos that it is so difficult to discuss the war as an issue of ethical ambiguity, for either one must think it a complete evil or a complete good.

the lover who has discovered his beloved works part time in a
brothel.

In a decisive way, then, our times render problematic the notion
that America represents a new start and opportunity for mankind.
We are not, were not, a nation conceived in innocence. The new
Eden or the new Israel we have never been and will never be.[10]
Yet many continue to presuppose the myth of innocence by suggesting that America's way out of her current crisis is to make a
completely new beginning. We have betrayed the original covenant;
our hope now lies in making a new contract which allows us to
begin again, leaving behind our sin of the past.

This illusory quest for our lost innocence, however, only deepens
our problem. It perverts the accuracy of how we describe our current situation. For example, Americans seem unable to believe that
our present troubles may possibly be due to the very hardness of the
issues, inadvertence, or sheer stupidity.[11] If we are in a mess, we
prefer to explain it in terms of evil men conspiring to put us there.
The war in Vietnam is brutally painful to us. Even if one allows
for the incredible deviousness associated with American involvement
in Vietnam, the truth is that honorable men with good intentions
tragically committed us to the present course. But to admit such a
truth means that as a nation Americans must face the fact that we
exist in a world of ambiguity. And within that world innocence is
bought only at the price of illusion. Put differently, accepting the
hard truth means that we must somehow learn that life is often

---

[10] For a fascinating account of the idea of innocence in early American
literature see R. W. B. Lewis, *The American Adam* (Chicago: Phoenix Books,
1955). John Barth's *The Sot Weed Factor* is a marvelous satire concerned with
the myth of America's birth in innocence (New York: Grossett and Dunlap,
1966). See also Thomas Merton's *Conjectures of a Guilty Bystander* (Garden
City: Doubleday, 1968), pp. 32-40.

[11] It never seems to occur to the current radicals that part of our problems
is the result of the incompatibility of positive moral values. For example, the
early S.D.S. manifesto, the *Port Huron Statement*, seems to assume that we
can reduce poverty, provide better housing, destroy racism, and at the same
time decentralize the governmental process and decrease our dependence on
technology. Zbigniew Brzezinski is closer to the truth when he says, "Today's
America has set higher standards for itself than any other society: it aims at
creating racial harmony on the basis of equality, at achieving social welfare while
preserving personal liberty, at eliminating poverty without shackling individual
freedom. Tensions in the United States might be less were it to seek less—but
in its ambitious goals America retains its innovative character." *Between Two
Ages: America's Role in the Technetronic Era* (New York: Viking, 1970),
p. 257.

neither good nor bad, but simply tragic. Even more difficult, we must learn how to embody that fact in our experience. Thus Americans might come to see, for example, that we cannot remove the stain of sin by immediate withdrawal from Vietnam, nor even by fighting the war for heightened moral purposes. There is, perhaps, no choice except between evils.

In this matter of overcoming the myth of innocence, the crucial issue before Americans is whether we can include within the account of our history the reality of the black man's existence and struggle. I am not talking about whether we finally are able to integrate the blacks into the larger society, important and necessary as that is. (Integration, in fact, might well be a way of avoiding the hard problem which the black American raises for his white compatriots.) Nor do I mean that our white histories should be written to include the contributions blacks have made to our nation, though that also is necessary. Rather, I want to point up the fact that the black population stands in our midst as a people who have suffered the injustice and humiliation of being systematically oppressed and exploited. As such, black people are a constant check on the American presumption of innocence with its corollary of omnipotence.

As Vincent Harding has put it so well:

> The black experience in America allows for no illusions, not even that last ancient hope of the chosen American people whom God will somehow rescue by a special act of his grace. America began with such hopes, but they were tied to the idea of a Convenant, that men would have to do God's will for them to remain as his chosen ones. Somehow, just as America forced black men to do so much of its other dirty but productive work, the nation evidently came to believe that whites could be chosen while blacks did that suffering which has always been identified with the chosen ones. Now that is over. The black past has begun to explode and to reveal to a hidden chosen people that to be the anointed one is to be crushed and humiliated by the forces of the world. So, for all who would see it, the Afro-American past illuminates the meaning of being chosen. Perhaps this is what white Americans must see: that they will either join the ranks of suffering and humiliation or there will be no chosen people on these shores. Either they will submit their children to some of the same educational terrors they have allowed black children to endure or there is no future for any. Either they will give up their affluence to provide necessities for others or there will be neither affluence nor necessities for anyone. Perhaps we were chosen together, and we cannot move towards a new beginning until we have faced all the horror and agony of

the past with absolute honesty. Perhaps integration is indeed irrelevant until the assessment of a long, unpaid debt has been made
and significant payments begun. Perhaps atonement, not integration, is the issue at hand.[12]

To speak of institutional crises as finally a matter for atonement
may sound odd, since such crises are only solved by action and new
programs. It is my contention, however, that while new programs
and new institutional forms are certainly necessary in our society,
they do not reach to the heart of our current problems. I suspect
that as Americans we will find some way to "muddle through." The
great tragedy will be if we do so in a way which keeps us trapped
in the illusion that further action will free us from the past. A
viable moral future for America is possible only if we embrace our
sinful past not as an accidental side show, but part and parcel of
what it means to be American. That may be asking far too much
of any nation; but we can do nothing less if the moral substance of
our society is ever to be based on truth rather than illusion.

Severe as it is, the crisis of institutions in America in some ways
pales in comparison with the crisis of persons. For in the midst of
the most affluent economy in the world and the freest political
system, we find a quarrelsome and dissatisfied people. This dis-
quietude appears in its most dramatic form among the youth
identified with the New Left and the counterculture.[13] Common
to these is a kind of conventional wisdom about contemporary
society. These young people see themselves trapped in an increasingly and seemingly irreversible technological society which leaves
nothing to chance. We each become cogs in a completely planned
system. The bureaucrat and the expert are the new power brokers
in this society. And their power is all the more secure because, with

---

[12] Vincent Harding, "The Afro-American Past," in *New Theology* No. 6
(New York: Macmillan, 1969), 175-176.

[13] I do not mean to imply that there are not often profound differences
between those associated with the New Left and members of the counterculture. However, for my purposes there is no reason to try to carefully distinguish between them. The standard works describing this phenomenon are
of course Theodore Roszak, *The Making of a Counter Culture* (Garden City:
Anchor, 1969); Charles Reich, *The Greening of America* (New York: Bantam,
1970); Jacobs and Landau, *The New Radicals* (New York: Vintage,
1966); and for a good collection of Movement literature see *The Movement
Toward a New America: The Beginnings of a Long Revolution,* edited by
Mitchell Goodman (New York: Alfred Knopf, 1970).

ideology now relegated to the irrational past, they no longer have to justify their position.[14]

In such a technological society democracy becomes but a sham, since government manipulates the masses through the media. Freedom thus becomes but a word for submitting to the choices of those who run the technological machinery. Work becomes pointless and empty. Reich describes work in this society as "mindless, exhausting, boring, servile, and hateful, something to be endured while 'life' is confined to 'time off.' At the same time our culture has been reduced to the grossly commercial; all cultural values are for sale, and those that fail to make a profit are not preserved. Our life activities have become plastic, vicarious, and false to our genuine needs, activities fabricated by others and forced upon us."[15]

The greatest loss we feel in such a society is the loss of self. The system strips us of all personal uniqueness in order to make us productive members of the technological mass society. We tend to become our roles, and thus are alienated from our true selves. Moreover, in such a society all attempts at community are killed, for "modern living has obliterated place, locality, and neighborhood, and given us the anonymous separation of our existence."[16] Thus we are left as machines without souls; we are condemned to a life of meaningless consumption so that our technological society can continue to function.

Against such a system, American youth see the only hope in forming a counterculture based on love and friendship. It becomes a political act to "do your own thing," for "the system" cannot stand any form of deviation. Style thus becomes a matter of political substance as it embodies the "idea that an individual need not accept the pattern that society has formed for him, but may make his own choice."[17] Genuine participatory democracy must be made

---

[14] It is interesting that Roszak relies so heavily on Jacques Ellul's book, *The Technological Society* (New York: Vintage, 1964), for the implications of Ellul's analysis is that there is no way of opting out or fighting a technological society without becoming part of it. This is but one example of the failure of the New Left to find adequate intellectual positions that would make intelligible the profound dissatisfaction they feel.

[15] Reich, *op. cit.*, pp. 6-7. One wonders why Reich thinks work was otherwise in the past.

[16] *Ibid.*, p. 7.

[17] *Ibid.*, p. 395. The New Left makes no attempt to distinguish between a political and a cultural revolution. That is why it often appears totalitarian. It wishes to transform the political form of society to get at the general culture. In some ways Reich's naive view of the necessity of changing "consciousness"

a reality, even if it means the violent overthrow of the current rule.

What is impressive about this position is not the analysis of our society associated with it, but rather the profound dissatisfaction to which it witnesses. The dissatisfaction, however, is all the more tragic because of its failure to perceive accurately and face the reality of our contemporary experience. The New Left and the counterculture are thus more interesting as a symptom of our times than as a herald of our future.[18] But these movements are indeed a significant symptom. The language of their protest reveals their profound commitment to traditional American values—the very values that are often the source of their dissatisfaction. What is so striking about Reich's description of Consciousness III, for example, is not how new it is, but how very American it is with its optimistic and individualistic assumptions about man.[19]

first is nearer to the truth, but that implies a far longer, harder, and more ambiguous process than many associated with the New Left want to contemplate. For that reason Reich is considered by many of the New Left to be dangerous, since he assumes social change can occur without a transfer of power.

[18] Brzezinski, op. cit., p. 232. He goes on to claim that the New Left "is an escapist phenomenon rather than a determined revolutionary movement; it proclaims its desire to change society but by and large offers only a refuge from society. More concerned with self-gratification than with social consequences of its acts, the New Left can afford to engage in the wildest verbal abuse, without any regard for the fact that it alienates even those who are potential supporters. Its concern is to create a sense of personal involvement for its adherents and to release their passions; it provides a psychological safety valve for its youthful militants and a sense of vicarious fulfillment for its more passive, affluent, and older admirers." Though I am sure there is much truth in this kind of ad hominem, we must be careful not to let the excesses of the youth culture blind us to its importance. For without such protest, I suspect we would feel a good deal less the oddness of our everyday life than in fact we do.

[19] Reich, op. cit., p. 338. The romantic element in Reich's account of our modern situation is unmistakable. He assumes that if we could just strip from our existence the old forms of consciousness and structures, we would find the naked-beautiful-creative-loving self. The Port Huron Statement also argues that men have "unfulfilled capacities for reason, freedom, and love," and "unrealized potential for self-cultivation, self-direction, self-understanding and creativity." The current attempt of theologians to identify with this understanding of man makes one wonder how deeply Reinhold Niebuhr's work is capable of penetrating the American spirit.

The contradictions in Reich are obvious but perhaps the most important is the tension between his stress on community and individuality. Though he insists that the self can only be realized in community (p. 417), it is a community only of autonomous, self-realizing individuals who must refuse to accept any group responsibility, for "the individual self is the only true reality" (p. 242). Thus the individual of Consciousness III rejects all general standards and classifications since each person is intrinsically different, and values are but the subjectivistic choice of our sovereign will. While we can use no person as a means,

Undoubtedly many Americans do feel profoundly alienated. But this alienation is not necessarily due to an oppressive technological culture.[20] Nor is the estrangement due to a fundamental denial of the original promise of America. Rather the alienation is rooted precisely in the fulfillment of that promise—ironic as it seems. The current malaise of our people stems not from the failure of the American dream, but from the fact that we are now closer than ever to realizing it. And we are beginning to suspect that dream may be a nightmare. In America we have sought to create a society of individuals—autonomous, self-sufficient, and stable—and the criterion of our success was taken to be the progressive emancipation of the individual from the "irrational" social constraints of the past.[21] Such freedom, it was assumed, would allow for a breakthrough of creativity and universal brotherhood, for the particularistic ties of kinship and tribe were taken to be the barrier to human fellowship. But to our dismay, we now discover that this "freedom is accompanied not by the sense of creative release but by the sense of disenchantment and alienation. The alienation of man from historic moral certitudes has been followed by the sense of man's alienation from fellow man."[22]

The freedom America gives the individual has occasioned the furious quest for community in our society. The attraction of many to the New Left lies in being given a sense of participating in a reality larger than the confines of one's own ego. But the amorphous and self-destructive nature of "The Movement" cannot be sufficient to supply the community required, without that community itself

---

it is equally wrong to alter oneself for someone else's sake (p. 244). What makes Reich's position so ironical is he entirely fails to see that he has restated the bourgeois individualism of pluralist democracy in a new style. He has reaffirmed the ethic of the middle class in a form that its children will accept.

[20] Of course, I do not mean to deny that technology poses many different and complex problems for our society. But as it is often used in radical literature, technology is but a symbol for all that is wrong with our society. That makes the term descriptively about as interesting as saying, "We are all sinful."

[21] Robert Nisbet, *The Quest for Community* (New York: Oxford University Press, 1953), p. 4. My general debt to Nisbet's thought should be apparent in this essay.

[22] *Ibid.*, p. 10. In this paper I am concerned with the more general cultural aspects of this phenomenon. However in my "Politics, Vision, and the Common Good" I have tried to relate these individualistic and utilitarian assumptions to the nature of pluralist democracy and the resulting political problems. *Cross Currents,* XX (Fall, 1970), 399-414.

becoming totalitarian.[23] Groups and societies are not sustained
simply because men desire to be together, but because they share
common purposes and loyalties. The high failure rate of the
communes currently being formed is due largely to the fact that
no society, even very small ones, can sustain itself for the sole purpose of letting everyone "do his own thing."

The other side of the American quest for community is our
search for the self or identity. Contrary to the New Left assertion
that technological society robs us of our identity, the problem is
that it leaves us free, or even forces us to choose what we shall be.
It would take us too far afield to engage here in an extensive comparison of our modern legal-rational social order as compared to
traditional societies; suffice it to say that all modern sociological
analysis confirms that we live in a highly differentiated society.[24]
Such a society is individualistic and voluntaristic, for it separates
men from their communal or ascribed societal structures. Men no
longer belong to groups that give them a place within the whole,
but join associations built around specific goals and purposes. Such

---

[23] One of the striking things about the development of the New Left is
how dependent it is on the paradigm of community and solidarity which many
of its leaders shared while working in the early civil rights movement in the
South. In effect, these people have moved from one cause to another in an
attempt to preserve their original experience of community. Moreover, their
political ideal derives from this experience as they wish somehow to apply this
experience of community to wider society. In a sense, the New Left is a
sectarian community trying to make a church of society. For as the *Port
Huron Statement* says, participatory democracy must provide the necessary
"means of finding meaning in personal life"—that is, it must at least provide
the opportunity for salvation. For an interesting but unsuccessful attempt to
relate the New Left to traditional forms of Christian sectarianism see Arthur
Gish, *The New Left and Christian Radicalism* (Grand Rapids: Eerdmans,
1969). In this context the New Left differs significantly from the adherents
of the counterculture as the former continues to exemplify and embody the
American faith in man's dominance over his environment, both political and
natural, through work and activity. It may be that some form of the more
passive counterculture is a significant alternative to the American spirit.

[24] For a good summary of this contrast see James Nelson, *Moral Nexus*
(Philadelphia: Westminster Press, 1971), pp. 131-144. This sociological point
is important for it makes clear why America was able to give actual institutional form to its basic value commitments. Every society emphasizes some
values as peculiarly its own, but seldom have societies had the institutional
means to make their "preferred" values dominate all other forms of values
embodied in other social relations as has America. By characterizing America's
stress on individualism I do not mean that other societies do not share this
value nor that Americans do not share some values that tend to qualify their
individualism. However, I have isolated the idea of "individualism" here
because I think it illuminates the current American malaise.

voluntary associations make no claim to supply a unified world view. Paradoxically, in such a society the more independence we achieve the more interdependent we become; but our interdependence is highly formal since we meet one another only in specific roles and functions.

Philip Slater characterizes our quest for independence by describing the kind of vicious circularity that results:

> Technological change, mobility, and the individualistic ethos combine to rupture the bonds that tie each individual to a family, a community, a kinship network, a geographical location—bonds that give him a comfortable sense of himself. As this sense of himself erodes, he seeks ways of affirming it. But his efforts at self enhancement automatically accelerate the very erosion he seeks to halt. It is easy to produce examples of the many ways in which Americans attempt to minimize, circumvent, or deny the interdependence upon which all societies are based. We seek a private house, a private means of transportation, a private garden, a private laundry, self-service stores, and do-it-yourself skills of every kind. An enormous technology seems to have set itself the task of making it unnecessary for one human being ever to ask anything of another in the course of going about his daily business. Even within the family Americans are unique in their feeling that each member should have a separate room, and even a separate telephone, television and car, when economically possible. We seek more and more privacy, and feel more and more alienated and lonely when we get it. What accidental contacts we do have, furthermore, seem more intrusive, not only because they are unsought but because they are unconnected with any familiar pattern of interdependence.[25]

---

[25] Philip E. Slater, *The Pursuit of Loneliness* (Boston: Beacon Press, 1970), p. 7. Slater's book is easily the most suggestive of the popular critiques of contemporary American society. For Slater, technology is not an evil in itself; the power of technology becomes perverse only when we attempt to regulate it with the assumptions of an individualistic society. It is extremely interesting to compare Slater's book with Reich's. On the surface they seem to be in agreement, since both find our society overcompetitive, impersonal, garish, and boring. Yet Slater's analysis is fundamentally antithetical to the naive individualism characteristic of Reich's book.

For an analysis that I find in many ways similar to Slater's, yet more profound, see Simone Weil, *The Need For Roots* (New York: Harper, 1952). For example, she says, "When the possibilities of choice are so wide as to injure the commonweal, men cease to enjoy liberty. For they must either seek refuge in irresponsibility, puerility, and indifference—a refuge where the most they can find is boredom—or feel themselves weighted down by responsibilities at all times for fear of causing harm to others" (p. 13). Even though this was written with France in mind, there is no better analysis of the difference between

Thus living in a highly pluralistic society means that we are called upon to make more choices every day, "with fewer 'givens,' more ambiguous criteria, less environmental stability, and less social structural support, than any people in history."[26] In contrast to traditional social orders, our public institutions no longer contribute to the formation of the individual personality. "Personal identity becomes, essentially, a private phenomenon."[27] Men are now free to construct their personal identity as we are left to ourselves to choose our friends, marriage partners, neighbors and even "ultimate" meanings. Our culture is "no longer an obligatory structure of interpretive and evaluative schemes with a distinct hierarchy of significance. It is, rather, a rich, heterogeneous assortment of possibilities which, in principle, are accessible to any individual consumer."[28]

But as we are thrown back upon ourselves, when we lose the sense of moral and social involvement, we become prey to sensations of anxiety and guilt. For we perceive the pain our aloneness causes others and our consequent guilt eats on our soul; but our only choice

---

the American middle class and the young as the former retreats into the suburbs of uncare to avoid the moral agony of being alive in such times, and the latter rush to claim total responsibility to assure their moral righteousness. We no longer seem to have any way to appreciate the man that faithfully fulfills his limited duties in this time and this place. To quote Weil again, "Uprootedness is by far the most dangerous malady to which human societies are exposed, for it is a self-propagating one. For people who are really uprooted there remain only two possible sorts of behavior: either to fall into a spiritual lethargy resembling death, like the majority of the slaves in the days of the Roman Empire, or to hurl themselves into some form of activity necessarily designed to uproot, often by the most violent methods, those who are not yet uprooted, or only partly so" (p. 47).

[26] Slater, op. cit., p. 21. Contrary to the radicals' charge, Americans are not forced to conform by an oppressive system, but their very individualism produces uniformity. In a highly cooperative and traditional society variety and eccentricity can be tolerated. It is assumed the social order is a going concern. In a highly individualistic society, however, eccentricity represents to the individual the threat of societal chaos and anarchy that he cannot bear to contemplate. In other words, the conformist aspects of American society are a correlate of our inability to handle the freedom that society forces upon us. In America there is seldom a battle between individualism and conformity, but a conflict between antithetical styles of conforming. For a still provocative treatment of this theme, see Winston White, Beyond Conformity (Glencoe: Free Press, 1961).

[27] Thomas Luckmann, The Invisible Religion (London: Macmillan Co., 1967), p. 97. For similar analyses that have influenced my presentation see Peter Berger, The Sacred Canopy (New York: Anchor Books, 1969), and Berger and Luckmann, The Social Construction of Reality (New York: Doubleday, 1966).

[28] Luckmann, op. cit., p. 98.

seems to be to call our self-hatred the pursuit of happiness. There appears to be no external reality strong enough to call us from the monad-like form of our existence, for value has become privatized. Morally, it is assumed that our ethical positions are but subjective preferences. The only way of establishing the best preference is by observing which are held by the largest number of individuals, or those that can be forced by power. Religion becomes a matter of voluntary choice and thus must be marketed in forms palatable to the pagan pieties of those who still feel they should be "religious." Thus by relegating all values to subjective choice, we cut ourselves off from any resources that might call us out of infatuation with our aloneness. Even if religious institutions wished to speak critically to the American culture, they would find their resources spent by having already accepted the option of that privatized religiosity so amenable to the American spirit.

The new upsurge in religiosity among the young is but a variation on the individualistic piety of their parents. The rise of "Jesus groups" and the interest in Eastern mysticism are to be expected, for when "the institutional framework of religion begins to break up, the search for a direct experience which people can feel to be religious facilitates the rise of cults."[29] The religious search is one aspect of the kind of political immersion and/or drug experience shared by many today. Each in its own way is an attempt to fly from the self, to dissolve the self in "mystical" experience or political involvement.

Yet this flight from the self is not just the province of the young. Their experience in this respect is not more intense than that of their elders. For none of us has yet discovered how to live morally in our consumer society without becoming a collector of the seemingly endless array of goods constantly produced for our pleasure. In our aloneness we are tempted to think that surely our lives have more significance than increasing our wealth to buy more and different goods, or bequeathing to our children the ability to consume more than we ourselves were able to do. Even if we turn our attention to helping those in our society who have less, we are struck by absurdities. For example, the idea that helping the poor is to

---

[29] Daniel Bell, "Religion in the Sixties," *Social Research*, XXXVIII (Autumn, 1971), 474. In no way should what I am saying be taken as a denial of the religious integrity of many who share this kind of religious experience. The mystic has an honored position among the religions of the world.

provide them with the opportunity to share the kind of life that the
affluent now find so unsatisfactory. We are thus tempted to roman-
ticize what it means to be poor. Some have even begun to play at
being poor, in order to escape the self-hatred occasioned by the
meaningless existence brought on by our wealth.

Put another way, the attempt to find our identity in this society
inevitably seems to create a tension between becoming a useful
member of society and a real person. For to be "useful" means we
must be able to play well a repertory of roles; but to be a real person
implies we possess a core of personal reality which controls the roles
so that we are not swallowed up by our societal existence. But we
live in a world that rewards those most adroit at completely
identifying with their roles.[30] Yet the more adaptive we become to
our roles the more we wish to deny ourselves; we can no longer
distinguish who we are from our public appearance which, by the
way, we cannot stand.

The wish we spoke of earlier—to return to a purer, more simple,
innocent America—can thus be seen as the social form of our personal crisis. As Daniel Bell characterizes it, the desire is "to step outside one's social skin, to divest oneself of all the multiple roles which
contain behavior, and to find a lost innocence which has been over-
laid by rules and norms. The search for feeling is a search for
fantasy and its unrestricted play."[31] Such a longing assumes that if
we could just divest ourselves of our degenerate culture, underneath
the decay we would find a self morally worthy and uncomplicated.
But secretly we know that all we would find is the emptiness of a
life that has no moral form, and that suspicion paralyzes our souls
and we abandon ourselves to complete activity. What we flee in
our alienation is not external structures but the internal guilt of our
existence occasioned by living in a suffering world as rich men who
have lacked for nothing except the meaning that makes life worth
living. We have failed to understand that the only way to gain

---

[30] For example, Alvin Toffler says, "What is involved in increasing the
through-put of people in one's life are the abilities not only to make ties but
to break them, not only to affiliate but to disaffiliate. Those who seem most
capable of this adaptive skill are also among the most richly rewarded in
society." *Future Shock* (New York: Random House, 1970), p. 105.

[31] Bell, *op. cit.*, p. 488. A topic I have not treated associated with the new
culture is the rediscovery of the body and sensuality. I suppose one of the
reasons for this is my uncertainty whether the body has ever been lost. However, for an interesting analysis of religion and the "new American culture"
written from this point of view, see Leroy Moore's article cited above.

wholeness in such a world is to grasp and understand the suffering and the world's needs with a patience that refuses to create more suffering in the name of some who suffer.

Theologically it is tempting to grasp this search for the self as true religion. But such an interpretation is no more viable than the attempt to develop a new "civil religion," "story," or "myth" for the American ethos.[32] No doubt a renewed sense of national purpose would provide many a solution for the personal crisis of our times.[33] But such a purpose, I suspect, would only create new myths which would create more persistent illusions about our capacities. For the flight from the self which I have been describing is not simply a flight from the peculiar difficulties of living in American society. Like the American dream itself, I fear it is an attempt to flee the human condition of finitude, limitation, and guilt. The radical and the nonradical have much to criticize about the American culture, but the very extent of their criticism is a clue that they seek an escape from the limitation of personal and social existence. In such a context the primary task for adherents of the Gospel is to remind ourselves and others that such an escape is not possible or desirable. The Gospel's primary thrust is not to provide the details

---

[32] Robert Bellah's famous article, "Civil Religion in America," made respectable again the idea of a theology of support for American ideals. It is indeed a temptation hard to resist as so many of the values of the American ethos seem to have such a natural relation to the Gospel. Bellah's article can be found in *Secularization and the Protestant Prospect,* pp. 93-116. To see the influence of Bellah, see Novak's suggestion of the need for a new American "story" and Richard Neuhaus' idea of the new American "myth." Novak, *Ascent of the Mountain, Flight of the Dove* (New York: Harper, 1971), and Neuhaus, *In Defense of People* (New York: Macmillan, 1971). Neither Novak nor Neuhaus makes clear the relation of theology to the development of such a "story" or "myth," or how such a "story" can embody the sense of the tragic I have tried to articulate above.

[33] Theologically, the attempt to alleviate our personal aloneness by constituting the American people, as such, as the primary group of our society must be resisted. Such an attempt inevitably runs the risk of imbuing the political order with more significance than it deserves. The greatness of realism, for all of its weaknesses, was its appreciation of the ambiguity of the political. A national purpose we need, but not at the cost of the development of the individual through groups less quantitatively extensive than the nation but qualitatively more substantive. Nisbet, I think, is quite right that the great danger of the current quest for community is the totalitarian potential of constituting the state as the one source of ultimate meaning for society. Politically the hard problem confronting America is how to embody at once a substantive sense of the common good as an alternative to interest group or pluralist democracy as an end in itself without destroying the authentic diversity that a healthy society must have.

for the development of a just society, but rather to give men the strength to see their problems and condition honestly and without illusion. Only on such a basis is it possible to establish social justice, for lasting justice can only be built and sustained by a people who have no fear of the truth. A justice not so grounded becomes but the injustice of the next generation for it has no defense against those that would claim it in the name of their peculiar version of the truth.

The hard struggle that the American people now confront is not a struggle to overcome external adversities, though there is still much to be done. Rather, it is a crisis of spirit. It requires we face honestly what we have been and what we must do in a world where death is the one sure reality. The problem of living in America is that there literally seems to be nothing worth dying for. We manufacture "moral-political" causes to hide this from ourselves but the emptiness of our lives cannot long be filled with such goods. For to be willing to die means our lives have significance yet without significance our self-hatred is so intense it must seek to destroy any significance we see in the lives of others. We fail to see that significance is only possible when we are able to accept ourselves, our nation, and our "crises times" as having less than an eternal form, or, in more traditional language, as standing under the judgment of God's eternal kingdom.

Catholicism and Cultural Change in the 1960's*

Philip Gleason

A REAL cultural shift doesn't happen very often. Skepticism about whether one took place in the 1960's is quite natural, especially in view of the rapidity with which cultural fashions have come and gone in the past 15 years. The New Conservatism had hardly crested before it was succeeded by the End of Ideology, which was displaced with equal speed by the New Left. In the religious sphere, the revival of the early 50's gave way to the Death of God 10 years later. This proved even more ephemeral. With its companion, the Secular City, it was left behind in a welter of new movements—occultism, mysticism, and various forms of millenarian religious revolutionism. Paradoxically, the dizzying pace of change itself seemed to argue that nothing very profound was going on.

Yet American Catholics should be more open-minded than others on this question of a radical cultural shift. They know such things can happen, for their Church went through a seismic upheaval in the 1960's. The most traumatic shocks seem to be over, but there are lingering tremors and the whole Catholic landscape has been transformed. This religious earthquake coincided with the social and political storms of the recent past. Although it had its own distinctive sources and character, the Catholic revolution both influenced the general American cultural crisis and was influenced by it.

The spectacle of the Catholic Church in eruption probably had the most pervasive impact on the general cultural picture. What permanence was left if the Catholic Church could blow up? It was surprising, as Garry Wills points out, how many people outside the Church were disconcerted and angered by the crack-up of Catholicism. The importance of the Roman Church as a symbol of permanence and stability was not appreciated until it began to crumble. In doing so it aggravated what Walter Laqueur calls "the feeling of

---

* This paper was presented in modified form as an address at Brigham Young University, March 28, 1972.

confusion, decadence, and disintegration which manifested itself in culture and politics alike" in the 1960's.[1]

The revolution in the Church did more than occupy a segment of the chaotic background of the 60's. It also released the energies of individuals and groups who attached themselves to other movements.[2] Priests and nuns became familiar figures in the civil rights movement. Father James Groppi's open-housing marches in Milwaukee made him, for a time, the most publicized white leader in the black revolution. Catholic radicals, led by the redoubtable Fathers Berrigan, stole the whole show in the peace movement. Three men who gave a new shape to American politics were Catholics—John F. Kennedy, Robert Kennedy, and Eugene McCarthy. Their relation to the Catholic revolution defies easy summation, but one can hardly doubt that the relation existed. All were in some sense men of the "new politics"; they were also representatives of a novel kind of American Catholicism.

The high visibility of Catholics in public life accounts in part for the unprecedented attention Catholicism has won from the media in the past decade. But it was what was happening to the Church internally that really intrigued Americans. They watched in fascination as the Barque of Peter, now increased to ponderous tonnage, swung around to take new bearings, bustled into the work of trimming ship and dropping ballast, and then was swept by mutiny, fire, and explosion. Well might the *National Review* ask, "What, in the name of God, is going on in the Catholic Church?"[3]

It was a good question in 1965, and is not an easy one to answer even now, seven years later. This essay offers one interpretation of what happened to the Church. It stresses the interaction of Catholicism with the American environment; but we must begin with a review of the European background.

---

[1] Garry Wills, "Catholic Faith and Fiction," *New York Times Book Review*, January 16, 1972, p. 1; Walter Laqueur, "America and the Weimar Analogy," *Encounter*, May, 1972, p. 25; Daniel Bell, "Religion in the Sixties," *Social Research*, XXXVII (Autumn, 1971), 447-497, discusses the Catholic situation in the context of a broader cultural analysis.

[2] In an elegant variation of this point, Francine du Plessix Gray writes: "The Catholic Church can be compared to a zoo of wild beasts, held in captivity for over a millennium, whose bars Pope John removed. There are as many new pacifists among the rampaging animals as there are liturgical innovators and structural reformists." *Divine Disobedience: Profiles in Catholic Radicalism* (New York: Vintage, 1971), p. 94.

[3] This question appeared on the cover of the *National Review*, May 4, 1965.

Influences from Abroad

As part of what used to be called the Church universal, American Catholicism has closer ties with Europe than any other religious tradition in the United States. The lines of jurisdictional authority lead directly to Rome. American Catholics were famous for their devotion to the Pope, and thousands of priests were trained in Rome. Missionary priests and sisters from Europe were essential to the growth of American Catholicism, and in some parts of the country are still numerous and important. The mass of the faithful are of immigrant stock; many of them cherish familial or emotional ties with various European homelands.

American Catholics have always leaned heavily on Europe for ideas. Philosophy and theology were imported from France in the 1940's and 50's and from German-speaking areas in the 1960's. The tone has changed notably from the days of G. K. Chesterton to the era of Hans Küng, but European intellectual luminaries have always filled the house on lecture tours in the United States. And back in the days of the post-World War II religious revival, bright Catholic undergraduates read the works of English converts like Evelyn Waugh and Graham Greene, or of French Catholics like Leon Bloy, Francois Mauriac, and Georges Bernanos.

Practically all the self-consciously reformist movements that grew up among American Catholics in the 1930's and 40's drew upon European models for inspiration. Catechetical reform, the liturgical renewal, the ecumenical movement, Catholic Action groups like the Young Christian Workers and the Young Christian Students, all had links with Europe. The French Worker Priests of the 40's and 50's were widely admired by Catholic intellectuals in this country. Contact with them strongly affected Daniel Berrigan, even to the point of inspiring his costume of turtleneck sweater, ski jacket, and beret.[4]

Against this background, it is quite understandable that American Catholics were predisposed to respond actively to the *aggiornamento* set in motion by Pope John XXIII. The personality of Pope John, his simplicity and transparent goodness, touched the great mass of American Catholics who had no direct contact with any of the new currents of thought among European Catholic thinkers. While the American Catholic intelligentsia, who did know some-

---

[4] Gray, *op. cit.,* pp. 52, 67 ff.

thing about the ferment of ideas in Europe, were even more enthusiastic about the prospect of updating the Church, bringing it into closer touch with the modern world, opening the windows and letting in some fresh air, as Pope John had said.

No one could have foreseen the forces that Pope John's Council was to unleash. The Second Vatican Council went on a long time. Preliminary work lasted more than two years, and the sessions of the Council spanned three more years. People's ideas and expectations changed. It was a great educational experience for the bishops and their advisers who were present and for the multitudes who followed events from afar, saw the great spectacles on television, and heard or read innumerable explanations—or sometimes exposés —of what was happening.

The Council undertook an immense task—to bring the Church to a new understanding of itself, of its forms of worship and discipline, and of its relation to, and responsibilities toward, other Christian Churches, non-Christian believers, and the whole modern secular world. The various solemn statements of the Council embodying the position of the Catholic Church on these issues are documents of fundamental importance. They mark a historic new departure for Catholicism, the long-range effects of which cannot yet be measured.

But even more important, for the contemporary scene at least, was the postconciliar spirit. The Council shook everything loose. The splits that developed in the ranks of the Council fathers revealed deep disagreements about what the Catholic faith was, and what its implications were, among those who were thought of as authoritative teachers on such matters. The journalistic treatment of progressive *versus* conservative battling demystified the whole proceeding and hastened the polarization of Catholic attitudes. By the middle 1960's some American Catholics felt that the Council had changed everything and looked forward to a rapid actualization of all the new departures it implied. Other Catholics were already visibly uneasy about just how much "everything" included, and fearful lest the deposit of faith be departed from. The great mass of Catholics distributed itself between these extremes, most not knowing what was afoot but prepared to move with the Church.

The impact of the Council was felt throughout the Church, but quite unevenly. In a work published in 1969, for example, a French writer could say that the Church in his country was "calm," while in nearby Holland all was in ferment.[5] By then the American Church was in a state approaching uproar. We must look to the American context to understand why the conciliar spark set off such a detonation.

The American Context

Both internal and external factors were at work in the American context. Developments indigenous to the Catholic group itself constitute the internal factors. The external factors impinged upon Catholicism from the larger arena of national life in the 1960's.

In the quarter century since the end of World War II Catholics have definitely "made it" as members of the American middle class. That sums up the most important internal factors. In 1945 Catholics were distinctly below Protestants and Jews on all the main indicators of socioeconomic status. Two decades later, they had overtaken Protestants, but not Jews, in terms of wealth and occupational status, although still slightly behind in percentages that attended college.[6] Among younger Catholics the differences in educational attainment tend to disappear as well. Special efforts had been made for a long time to upgrade Catholic schools and encourage promising students to go as far as they could. By 1961, Catholics were represented proportionately in the ranks of graduate students.[7]

As Catholics came up in the world so rapidly, they lost their sense of being outsiders. They saw the world in much the same light as other Americans. In short, they became thoroughly assimilated and Americanized.[8] The better-educated progressives were uncomfortable about the vestiges of ethnic loyalty still felt by laggard elements in the Catholic population and for a time the Irish

---

[5] Robert Rouquette, S. J., "France," in M. A. Fitzsimons, ed., *The Catholic Church Today: Western Europe* (Notre Dame, Ind.: University of Notre Dame Press, 1969), p. 232. For the Church in Holland, see *ibid.*, pp. 1-28.

[6] Norval D. Glenn and Ruth Hyland, "Religious Preference and Worldly Success: Some Evidence from National Surveys," *American Sociological Review*, XXXII (February, 1967), 73-85. Cf. also, Andrew M. Greeley, *Come Blow Your Mind With Me* (Garden City, N. Y.: Doubleday, 1971), pp. 166-168.

[7] Cf. Andrew M. Greeley, *Religion and Career: A Study of College Graduates* (New York: Sheed and Ward, 1963).

[8] For a fuller elaboration of the argument made here see my essay, "The Crisis of Americanization," in Philip Gleason, ed., *Contemporary Catholicism in the United States* (Notre Dame, Ind.: University of Notre Dame Press, 1968), pp. 3-31.

Catholic tradition was made a kind of public whipping boy. At the same time, intellectuals and the liberal Catholic press mounted a sustained critique of "the ghetto mentality" and "separatist tendencies." Acceptance of prevailing American norms was also reflected in embarrassment over the deficiencies of Catholic intellectual life and in the pursuit of "excellence" on the part of Catholic colleges and universities. By the middle 1960's, Catholic professors were asking for full academic freedom, and the institutions in which they taught resembled more and more the standard secular model of the American university.

Assimilation to the norms of modern secular society led naturally to a series of identity crises among various groups of Catholics and the institutions they had founded in an earlier day when their faith had seemed to set them definitively apart from others. What was the point of having an organization of Catholic sociologists, for example, if Catholic sociologists did not differ from other sociologists in the way they studied their subject, taught it, or did research in it? The Catholic Sociological Society had been founded in the 1930's on the explicit premise that there was such a thing as "Catholic Sociology." By the early 1960's, Catholic scholars repudiated that belief.

Such identity crises become commonplace in the 60's. By now virtually every Catholic organization has agonized over whether it has any business existing. Catholic intellectual positions that once seemed permanently established dissolved, leaving even Catholic philosophers, theologians, and moralists feeling that they have nothing distinctive to say as Catholics. What can be observed clearly in these specialized disciplines is also happening in a more diffuse way among educated Catholics generally as they ask themselves: "Just what do I as a Catholic believe that others equally well-informed and well-intentioned do not also believe, and what grounds have I for believing it?"

It should be emphasized that this development was under way as a result of indigenous processes internal to American Catholicism even before the Council. But the Council accelerated the movement tremendously. It called into question old attitudes and beliefs and reformulated doctrines hitherto thought of as fixed. Above all, it dramatized the startling fact that the unchangeable Church could change, and was indeed calling upon its faithful to change. This naturally had the effect of reinforcing the disposition, brought on by assimilation, for Catholics to question their habitual assumptions and ask themselves why they were acting as they did.

But beyond that, the kind of changes the Council mandated seemed to be of the same general sort as those brought on by the indigenous processes of assimilation. The effect of assimilation, after all, was to bring Catholics into more intense interaction with the non-Catholic world, and into closer conformity with its spirit and outlook. And one of the main thrusts of the Council—especially in the *Pastoral Constitution on the Church in the Modern World*—was precisely that Catholics should break away from their old exclusiveness and self-absorption, and go out to meet the modern world in a spirit of openness, ministering to its needs, and cooperating with all the movements for good at work within it.[9] They were not to lose their identity as Catholics in doing so, of course; but just what that Catholic identity consisted in became increasingly problematic.

This brings us to the second general category of domestic influences on the contemporary Catholic scene—the pressures exerted by the ferment in American society at large. This aspect of the situation has been neglected by commentators on the Catholic upheaval, and it deserves much fuller analysis than I can give it here. In a nutshell, this was the situation: Catholics whose old beliefs were severely jolted by the Council were told to involve themselves actively in the world; but the world they were encouraged to plunge into was being torn apart by radical denials of its basic assumptions and passionate efforts to bring about fundamental change. The religious doubts and uncertainties of Catholics, and the confusion that marked the release of pent-up energies, were more than matched by the social and political tumults raging across the land.

Experiences of this sort interpenetrate one another. We are all involved in each other's spiritual crises, and the 60's were rife with spiritual crises. On the one hand, Catholics heard it said that their Church was corrupt and its leaders bankrupt. On the other, they heard that their country was a racist, imperialist monster, its leaders war criminals. From other quarters sounded the cry: Let us be done with all this! We can build a new earth and a new heaven! The rhetoric of revolutionary politics merged with that of religious prophecy. The tactics of militant confrontation were carried into

---

[9] Thomas F. O'Dea, *The Catholic Crisis* (Boston: Beacon Press, 1968), lays particular stress on the importance of this conciliar document and its teaching.

solemn ecclesiatical assemblies. Gestures of ritual sacrifice accompanied political dissent.

Everything became intermingled, confounded together, chaotic. What could one catch hold of? Some were gripped by a vision, or seized by a passion, and committed themselves to a clear-cut cause. Others stood by in bewilderment, pulled now in this direction, now in that. Some wearied of the hubbub and turned away to cultivate their own gardens. Still others continued to watch in fascination, trying to hang onto something solid amid the clashing winds of doctrine. New theologies came and went like flashes of summer lightning as churchmen strove to read the signs of the times and speak to modern man's condition. When the storm abated, a kind of spiritual exhaustion overspread the scene.

This picture may seem too lurid, overdone. Admittedly, it is partial and impressionistic. Yet the 60's were a decade of frenzied agitation, whose intensity was heightened for Catholics by the merging together of the religious crisis and the society-wide political and cultural crises. Not all Catholics were equally affected, however. The conjunction of forces struck with greatest impact on young people and religious professionals.

Groups in the Eye of the Storm

Almost everything happening in American society in recent years hit hardest among young people, even unemployment. The modern civil rights-black revolution began with a Supreme Court decision affecting school-age children, and young people furnished the vanguard of freedom riders and other militant activists. Young men were most directly affected by the war; they had the draft cards it meant something to burn. Turmoil on the campuses, the drug scene, the sexual revolution, experiments in aquarian age life-styles —all of these are phenomena primarily centered in the more youthful segments of the population. Accompanying these developments, our traditional national preoccupation with youth blossomed into a full-blown cult of youth. Young people were proclaimed the best educated, most sensitive, most idealistic, most committed generation America had ever produced. The message seemed to be that salvation lay with the young—all power to the kids!

Young people of Catholic background could not help but be caught up in all this. Indeed, given the high Catholic birthrate in the previous generation, there is probably a larger proportion of

Catholics among young people than in any other age segment of the population. More of them than ever before were in college, right in the eye of the storm. They were at the point in their personal life-cycles where they had to grapple with the tasks of self-discovery and ideological identity formation. Like all young people, they were ripe for experimentation, idealistic, impatient with the past, in-tolerant of half measures, and a trifle smug about their own sin-cerity and general virtuousness. Most of them came from politically conservative backgrounds, and were perhaps slower than those from other traditions to move into the forefront of political radicalism. But they moved with the radical tide.

As far as religion was concerned, young Catholics were caught in a real maelstrom. The seas of faith are always troubled for adolescents and young adults, but those who matured in the 1960's encountered a veritable hurricane. They were peculiarly susceptible to all the influences discussed earlier. They were the most assim-ilated of any generation of American Catholics; the Vatican Council and its aftermath left them without established religious guidelines; and the society around them was seething with rejections of the past and new affirmations for the future. No one should be surprised if many of them fail to practice their religion as traditionally under-stood, prefer to think of themselves as Christians or humanists rather than Catholics, and seek new ways to meet their spiritual needs, new goals around which to orient a life of service to the good, the true, and the beautiful.

Many in the younger ranks of Catholic religious professionals—that is, priests, nuns, and brothers—were subject to the same pres-sures that affected all young people. Both casual observation and the available sociological research suggest that it is the younger priests and members of religious communities who are most dis-contented and likely to resign from the priesthood or leave the religious life.[10] But leaving aside the factor of age, there are two

---

[10] The factor of youthfulness is related in a complex way to many other factors. See Andrew M. Greeley, *Priests in the United States. Reflections on a Survey* (Garden City, N. Y.: Doubleday, 1972), especially pp. 160-161, and chapter 11. Greeley speaks of a generation "slope" rather than a generation "gap" among priests, with each 10-year age category "being more 'modern' in its religious attitudes and more 'liberal' in its sexual morality than its immediate elders." *Documentation for General Meeting of National Conference of Cath-olic Bishops, April 27-29, 1971. Detroit, Michigan* (Xerox), p. 47.

other reasons why clerics were particularly affected by the turmoil of the 60's.

The first is quite obvious: these people are religious professionals; their whole lives are bound up in the Church. Religious concerns are much more a full-time preoccupation with them than with any other group, except perhaps a small minority of Catholic lay activists, journalists, or professional observers of the religious scene. Hence they were the first to be moved by the surges of change in the Church. They were also particularly apt to respond to the moral appeal of idealistic movements at work outside the Church—the civil rights movement, for example, the grape-workers strike, or the peace movement. Indeed, the failure of the official Church to take sufficiently strong action against the evils of our society is one of the most common complaints made by her discontented clerical professionals.

Secondly, because these people are professionals, they are subject to the direct administrative authority of ecclesiastical officials to a far greater degree than is the case with laymen. Rigid and oppressive authoritarianism in the Church exists largely by reputation for laymen; but not for priests and religious! A layman, let us say, reads in the newspaper about an arbitrary or stupid action on the part of a bishop or superior of a religious order. He may groan inwardly. He may say to himself, how absurd. He may become indignant. He may write letters or join protests. Yet 99 times out of 100, he can continue his activities absolutely as though that act of ecclesiastical authoritarianism had never occurred. This was not the case for the curate who was told to be within doors at the rectory at 10 p.m.; the pastor who was summarily reassigned; the sisters who were denied permission to engage in some activity they wished to carry on; or (as it used to be) the theologian who was ordered to stop publishing on a sensitive topic.

When priests and religious complained of authoritarianism and oppressive structures, they knew whereof they spoke. Hence they welcomed with particular warmth the prospect raised by the Council that greater flexibility, openness, and collegial exercise of authority was to be introduced into the Church. These changes were not just theoretically desirable: they meant that the bosses would have to work within new rules. And when the bosses showed little disposition to create the new, flexible, democratic structures, when they tried to go right back to business as usual, there was bound to be enormous disappointment, resentment, and frustration.

These feelings no doubt played a significant role in the decisions of many of the professionals who resigned their priestly office or left their convents. But the effect goes beyond that, for many of those who stayed simply quit paying attention to the voices of official leadership in the Church and followed their own rules whenever they could. Not everyone did this, of course; yet respect for authority was undermined.

In setting aside the authority of those above them, however, the professionals weakened their own. Why should they be taken seriously as moral and religious guides? By what authority did they pronounce judgment on the Pope, the bishops, the American government, or the attitudes of their parishioners? Why shouldn't the layman in the pew set up his own authority against theirs? It wouldn't be such a novelty for laymen either, since they were well experienced in enduring clerical scoldings without changing their minds about anything.

A good many laymen, indeed a sizable majority in all likelihood, have not really been so severely shaken by all this upheaval as the foregoing discussion would suggest. Most of them go to Mass regularly as they always did, depend on their faith to give meaning to their lives, and seek salvation through it. Yet even in this great mass of traditional Catholics, unsophisticated Catholics, mediocre Catholics, if one wishes to call them that, a sense of malaise is widely diffused. It is perhaps most closely linked with the crisis of authority, which means, at the level of ordinary experience, a weakening of confidence and an uneasiness about the direction in which things are going, or a vague fear that no one knows which way they ought to go.

Andrew M. Greeley, the most consistently knowledgeable and penetrating commentator on American Catholicism, describes the present moment as "a period of emotional exhaustion." "Powerful currents of excitement, hope, disappointment, anger, frustration and bitterness have swept the Church," he continues. "Now our energies are spent. We are weary of controversy, of stridency, of the cycle of elation and discouragement which has been typical of the last several years."[11] This description applies to the relatively small

---

[11] Greeley, "The New Agenda," *The Critic,* May-June, 1972, p. 36. Greeley's essay, "American Catholicism 1950 to 1980," is a splendid review and analysis. See *Come Blow Your Mind,* pp. 109-165.

Catholic elite who have been actively involved in the developments of the 60's, rather than to the Catholic masses referred to above. Yet the apathy of the elite is not so different in its enervating consequences from the vague uneasiness of the masses. Thus, while the worst of the crisis may be over, the prospects for creative response are not hopeful while the mood of numbed indifference continues.

It seems likely, however, that this time of pause will be brief. The energies awakened in the 60's will reassert themselves. Indeed, the phenomenal growth of Pentecostalism, or charismatic renewal, in the Church reveals unsuspected springs of vitality. It is also interesting in its combination of novel forms of religious expression with strong commitment to the institutional Church. The fact that Father Greeley followed up his diagnosis of the present doldrums with a sketch of "the new agenda" for future action shows that, although he may suffer from battle fatigue, he is not retiring from the struggle. The same is true of other Catholic leaders and intellectuals. This, then, may prove to be a time of regrouping.

Romanticism and Crisis

One of the tasks appropriate to this moment is taking stock of the situation—seeking to analyze what has happened, what may be anticipated in the future, and what is to be done. As a historian I am more than willing to leave the anticipating and the prescribing to others. Indeed, I cannot conclude without trying to get a little further back from the present than my review of the very recent past has so far permitted. What I wish to suggest is a historical parallel which has application to the overall cultural scene in the nation as well as in the Church. In both spheres, I would argue, we have witnessed a profound irruption of the romantic spirit. The 1960's were a new age of romanticism.[12]

The terms romantic and romanticism are vague and uncertain in meaning. Indeed, romanticism has beeen defined so variously that one of the greatest students of the early 19th-century movement, A. O. Lovejoy, once argued that the term had lost its usefulness as a verbal sign—it had come to mean so many things that it no longer meant anything at all.[13] Without getting into a discus-

---

[12] Philip Gleason, "Our New Age of Romanticism," *America*, October 7, 1967, pp. 372-375, develops this thesis, citing literature not referred to here.

[13] A. O. Lovejoy, *Essays in the History of Ideas* (New York: Capricorn, 1960), p. 232.

sion of the essential nature of romanticism, I would argue that there are enough parallels between the temper of our own times and that of the historical romantic period to justify calling this a new age of romanticism.

Consider first certain broad similarities. Historical romanticism was born in a revolutionary epoch.[14] Its beginnings were closely tied to the French Revolution and the millennial hopes it aroused. We always think of Lord Byron, the archetype of the romantic hero, in connection with the struggle for Greek independence, a fighter for national liberation. Revolution became the watchword of the 60's, and had its Byronesque heroes in men like the younger Fidel Castro and, above all, Che Guevara. Although quite a swimmer, Chairman Mao is no longer Byronesque; but he is a poet-revolutionary and the symbol of a new kind of exotic *Chinoiserie*.

Historical romanticism exalted poetic vision, the power of imagination, and quasi-mystical intuition over the discursive processes of reason. Feeling and instinct took priority over rational analysis. Romanticism was strongly tinged with an antiscientific spirit, at least insofar as science was thought of in 18th-century mechanistic terms. It was antiurban and abhorred the dark Satanic mills of nascent industrialism. All these attitudes are widely prevalent today, and are given quite explicit statement in works like Theodore Roszak's *Making of a Counter Culture* and Charles Reich's *Greening of America*. So also the contemporary vogue of the American Indian corresponds to the vogue of the noble savage that marked early romanticism.

The original romantics were enemies of routine, discipline, and restraints on the individual. They rejected the forms of classicism and the institutionalized patterns of the past. They championed

---

[14] ". . . the Romantic period was eminently an age obsessed with the fact of violent and inclusive change, and Romantic poetry cannot be understood, historically, without awareness of the degree to which this preoccupation affected its substance and form." M. H. Abrams, "English Romanticism: The Spirit of the Age," in Northrop Frye, ed., *Romanticism Reconsidered* (New York: Columbia University Press, 1963), pp. 28-29. On this same point see Jacques Barzun, *Classic, Romantic, and Modern* (2nd rev. ed., Boston: Little, Brown, 1961); Ronald W. Harris, *Romanticism and the Social Order, 1780-1830* (New York: Barnes and Noble, 1969); and Eugene N. Anderson, "Response to Contemporary Crisis," in John B. Halsted, ed., *Romanticism. Problems of Definition, Explanation, and Evaluation* (Lexington, Mass.: Heath, 1965), pp. 96-103. Anderson's essay originally appeared in the June, 1941, issue of the *Journal of the History of Ideas*, along with several other articles on romanticism.

individual freedom and personal authenticity. But this did not mean
they slighted the need for mutual concern and fellowship. On the
contrary, they were commited to fraternity, and deeply concerned
with communal solidarity. It was simply that they depended upon
love and brotherhood, rather than external authority or forms of
law, to maintain order and coherence in society. Like so many
today, they believed that true community was a natural outgrowth
of man's capacity for goodness and love; that it had no need for a
structure of authority and officers to enforce it; and that it was
perfectly compatible with the utmost freedom for the individual.[15]

Especially in Germany, the romantic longing for community was
linked with a consciousness of a people's historic group identity.
The German writers spoke of the *Volksgeist*—the spirit of the nation. Historians have emphasized the importance of these ideas in
the rise of German nationalism.[16] For our purposes, however, it is
more relevant to note the kinship between these ideas and the contemporary upsurge of ethnic consciousness. Indeed, the new ethni-
city is a kind of incipient nationalism. It too speaks of distinctive
historical experiences shaping a people's soul—in fact, "soul" is the
very term blacks use to designate their spiritual uniqueness. It
dwells on the importance of language: most obviously in the case of
the Chicanos; but some writers argue that blacks too have a distinctive utterance and that white American speech is inadequate to
express the genius of their people. Even the contemporary emphasis
on recovering the history of American ethnic groups has a parallel

---

15 Cf. Chapter IV, "Romanticism: Community," in Ludwig Kahn,
Social Ideals in German Literature (New York: Columbia University Press,
1938); Werner J. Cahnman, "Max Weber and the Methodological Controversy
in the Social Sciences," in W. J. Cahnman and A. Boskoff, eds., *Sociology and
History: Theory and Research* (New York: Free Press, 1964), pp. 104 ff.
Speaking of contemporary hippie communal thinking, Bell writes: "In this
Elysium, each person does his own 'thing,' and there is little compulsion to
obey any rules. All men are good if they only follow their own natures, in
contrast to the pressures of the social structure. In their formal ideology there
is no leader; like Adam Smith's invisible hand, natural grace leads to natural
harmonies. As one description of 'Drop City,' a rural commune in Colorado,
puts it: 'Drop City is a tribal unit. It has no formal structure, no written laws,
yet the intuitive structure is amazingly complex and functional . . . . everything
works itself out with the help of the cosmic forces.'" Bell, *op. cit.*, pp. 493-
494.

16 Hans Kohn, "Romanticism and the Rise of German Nationalism," *The
Review of Politics*, XII (October, 1950), 443-472; Kohn, *Prelude to Nation-
States; the French and German Experience, 1789-1815* (Princeton, N.J.: Van
Nostrand, 1967), chap. XXIV.

in the romantic period when national self-consciousness spurred the collection of documents and the exploration of a nation's heritage.

There are also a number of more specific parallels between the 1960's and America's antebellum age of romanticism. Today's ecologists, for example, share the reverence for nature immortally associated with the names of Emerson and Thoreau. Scholars have recently been stressing the romantic temper of the reform movements of the 1830's and 40's,[17] and it is striking how many of them have counterparts today. Abolitionism is paralleled by the civil rights-black liberation movement. Nonresistance by nonviolence. Opposition to the Mexican War by opposition to Vietnam. Women's rights by women's liberation.

Horace Mann led a crusade to reform American schools in those years, and humanitarians like Dorothea Dix fought for improvement in the treatment of the insane and prisoners. Those movements have analogs today. The resurgence of interest in communes in the last few years is surely the greatest outburst of the utopian spirit since the days of Brook Farm. Changes in styles of dress and personal adornment are similar. Beards came back in style in the 1830's and 40's; sideburns followed soon after. The apostles of what was then called "The Newness" also favored Byron collars, loose, flowing outfits, and gay, flowery blouses.[18] Even phrenology has made a mild comeback recently. And the various occult and mystical tendencies of our own times are reminiscent of the more bizarre phenomena of the antebellum years, such as spiritualism, which swept the country after the rappings of the Fox sisters in 1848. Nor in these days of sexual liberation should we overlook the departures from conventional norms embodied in Mormon polygamy and the "complex marriage" system of the Oneida Community.

---

[17] Cf. John L. Thomas, "Romantic Reform in America, 1815-1865," *American Quarterly*, XVII (Winter, 1965), 656-681; David Brion Davis, "The Emergence of Immediatism in British and American Antislavery Thought, *Mississippi Valley Historical Review*, XLIX (September, 1962), 209-230.

[18] Cf. Robert Carter, " 'The Newness,' " *Century Magazine*, XXXIX (1889), 129, and Thomas W. Higginson, *Cheerful Yesterdays* (Boston: Houghton, Mifflin, 1898), Chap. III, "The Period of the Newness." Josiah Quincy, president of Harvard from 1829 to 1845, ran into trouble with the students because he was tactless enough to criticize their dress "or the whiskers which (greatly to his disgust) began to sprout toward the end of his administration." Samuel E. Morison, *Three Centuries of Harvard* (Cambridge, Mass.: Harvard University Press, 1937), p. 251. Cf. also Richard King, *The Party of Eros* (Chapel Hill, N.C.: University of North Carolina Press, 1972), chap. 6, "The New Transcendentalism."

We are specifically concerned here with religion, and in this sphere likewise we find broad similarities. The antebellum era was also a time of religious upheaval. Its most obvious signs then were the great waves of revivalism associated with the name of Charles G. Finney. Revivals do not loom very large today—although Catholic Pentecostalism resembles the intense Evangelicalism of the Finney revivals. But evangelical enthusiasm spread far beyond the revivals themselves in the 1830's and 40's. Indeed, many of the movements mentioned earlier should be understood as offshoots of the religious fervor inspired by Evangelicalism. For the sense of man's sinfulness, his need for conversion, the conviction that with God's grace he could be made holy, all had important social implications. The world itself might be made over by the outpouring of God's spirit![19]

Apocalyptic visions and expectations of the millennium permeated the religious and social scene in the 1830's, firing the efforts of multitudes of reformers. In our own day, kindred visions of a world made new generally assume the form of secular social radicalism or revolutionary politics. But there is an underlying similarity of outlook and spirit. And, as I suggested before, the religious ferment of the 1960's was profoundly affected by, and intertangled with, the prevailing social upheaval. Thus it does not seem to me to be straining things unduly to see analogies to the millennialism of the 1830's in the recent theologies of hope, of revolution, and in what is called broadly political theology. Nor would it be wholly fanciful to regard Daniel Berrigan and Philip Berrigan as latter-day counterparts to that prince of religio-social radicals, William Lloyd Garrison.

Obviously, there are vast differences between the romantic past

---

[19] William G. McLoughlin, *Modern Revivalism* (New York: Ronald Press, 1959); Timothy L. Smith, *Revivalism and Social Reform in Mid-Nineteenth Century America* (New York: Abingdon Press, 1957); Bertram Wyatt-Brown, *Lewis Tappan and the Evangelical War Against Slavery* (Cleveland: Case Western Reserve Press, 1969). Intense religiosity permeated the correspondence of leading abolitionists. See G. H. Barnes and D. L. Dumond, eds., *Letters of Theodore Dwight Weld, Angelina Grimké Weld and Sarah Grimké, 1822-1844*, 2 vols. (New York: D. Appleton-Century, 1934). Even temperance reformers linked their cause with millennial hopes. The American Temperance Society in 1831 wrote that, with the success of their movement, "The word of the Lord, unobstructed, will run very swiftly; and, pouring with double energy its mighty, all-pervading influence upon the whole mass of minds, will be like the rain and the snow that come down from heaven, and water the earth, and cause it to bring forth and bud. The frost and the snows of six thousand winters will be forever dissolved; and the spring-time of millennial beauty, and the autumnal fruit of millennial glory will open upon the world." *Permanent Temperance Documents of the American Temperance Society* (Boston: S. Bliss, 1835), p. 53.

and the neo-romantic present. The argument is not that history is "repeating itself" in any literal sense, or that we can draw precise conclusions or detailed guidelines for action from study of the past. This is expecting too much. It is bound to lead to the sort of disenchantment with history expressed not long ago by Martin Duberman, who had earlier hoped to find answers in the antebellum years to America's racial problems in the 1960's.[20] But the similarities between past and present are as real as the differences. Consideration of both serves not only to put the present in perspective, but also to suggest lines of reflection that we might otherwise have overlooked.

In the case at hand, the romantic parallel suggests a number of relevant inquiries. Take the question, Did America go through a cultural shift in the 1960's? Might we not pose the counterquestion: Did romanticism represent a cultural shift? If it did, and if one grants a kinship between romanticism and the present, then one must posit an intervening cultural shift in the opposite direction— otherwise there would have been nothing to shift away from in the 1960's. But if cultural shifts occur as frequently as this, do they really amount to more than changes in taste and intellectual fashion?

Cultural shift or not, romanticism was not final. It was one moment succeeded by others in the flow of human history. The same is true of our own day, our own cultural crisis. This reflection drawn from the comparison of past and present is not without practical significance. It means, on the one hand, that partisans of the counterculture would be well advised to hedge their emotional investment in its permanent realization, and, on the other hand, that champions of tradition might abate their anxieties over the threatened dissolution of precious values and institutions. The task of weaving old and new together requires the collective work and wisdom of us all.

---

[20] Martin Duberman, *The Uncompleted Past* (New York: Random House, 1969), pp. 336-356. In 1968 Duberman endeavored to shed some light on the contemporary racial scene by a historical parallel between abolitionism and the Black Power movement. See his article, "Black Power in America," *Partisan Review*, XXXV (Winter, 1968), 40-43.

An Apocalyptic Voyage: God, Satan, and the American Tradition in Norman Mailer's Of a Fire on the Moon

Thomas Werge

The human will is, as it were, a beast between God and Satan. If God sits thereon, it wills and goes where God wills. . . . If Satan sits thereon, it wills and goes as Satan will. Nor is it in the power of its own will to choose, to which rider it will run, nor which it will seek; but the riders themselves contend, which shall have or hold it.

—Luther, *The Bondage of the Will*

Man is not . . . ignominious baggage; but a stupendous antagonism, a dragging together of the poles of the Universe . . . . here they are, side by side, god and devil, mind and matter, king and conspirator, belt and spasm, riding . . . together in the eye and brain of every man.

—Emerson, "Fate"

From the keen steel barb there now came a levelled flame of pale, forked fire. As the silent harpoon burned there like a serpent's tongue, Starbuck grasped Ahab by the arm—"God, God is against thee, old, man; forbear! t'is an ill voyage! ill begun, ill continued . . . . In Jesus' name no more of this, that's worse than devil's madness. . . . Shall we be dragged by him to the bottom of the sea? Shall we be towed by him to the infernal world?"

—*Moby-Dick*

God . . . was an embattled vision: God had created man in order that man might fulfill God's vision, but His vision of the future was at war with other visions of existence in the universe. Some of those other visions were not only out in the stars, and in the galaxies, but were right here, intimate, on earth. God was, for instance, at war with the Devil. Certainly the Devil had a most detailed vision of existence very much opposed to His own. In any case the war had gone on for so long that nearly everything human was inextricably tangled. Heroism cohabited with technology. Was the Space Program admirable or abominable? Did God voyage out for NASA, or was the Devil our line of sight to the stars?

—*Of a Fire on the Moon*

I

NORMAN MAILER observed several years ago that American Protestantism, with the exception of Tillich and other Protestant existentialists, had become "oriented to the machine, and lukewarm in its enthusiasm for such notions as heaven, hell and the soul."[1] The religious tradition of the West had been preoccupied with the soul and had delineated its progress from earth to heaven and its struggling movement between darkness and light, Satan and God, as part of a cosmic and apocalyptic drama. Although Roman Catholicism had remained somewhat more concerned than Protestantism with such conceptions, argued Mailer, Christianity in general had left them behind and become tepid in the process.

Mailer's indictment of religion in America necessarily implies an indictment of America's vision of itself. From the Puritans to Emerson, Melville, and Twain, America is seen as a central, indeed, as the central place and idea in the divine drama and struggle. If the individual soul is suspended between heaven and hell, grace and sin, America's suspension was even more precarious. As the "city upon a hill," America lived and moved with the eyes of God and the world upon its covenanted saints. The drama of its experience was an elevated and magnified version of the drama of the individual soul. Emerson's definition of man as a "stupendous antagonism" in which "god and devil" clash for supremacy defined America as well, and Melville's Ahab, Twain's Connecticut Yankee, and every significant character of the major American authors of the 19th century articulated in his symbolic dimension some aspect of the American mind and soul.

Seen in this light, Mailer's indictment of the lukewarm faith of America comes to echo Emerson's castigation of the "pale negations" of the Unitarianism of his own time. A "decaying church and a wasting unbelief," states Emerson, are *national* calamities in whose wake literature itself becomes "frivolous." A bland and abstract religious faith necessitates an equally tepid language, and words eventually "lose all power to stimulate the understanding or the affections." The absence of religious and moral conviction makes impossible an efficacious language, and "meaning" and "purpose," in literature as in experience, disappear. Such a pros-

---

[1] "Catholic and Protestant" in "The Hip and the Square," in *Advertisements for Myself* (New York: G. P. Putnam's Sons, 1959), p. 426.

pect is as hideous for Mailer as it is for Emerson. For in the same discussion in which he indicts the efficient blandness of contemporary religion, Mailer insists that "the final purpose of art is to intensify, even, if necessary, to exacerbate, the moral consciousness of people . . . . [when] one is using words, [he is invoking] a sense of moral commandments, moral strictures."[2]

Throughout the American tradition, those authors who have been able to reawaken the moral efficacy of the word—to "pierce the rotten diction" of lukewarmness, as Emerson says, and "fasten words again to visible things" through image and symbol—have been preoccupied with two conceptions that have special relevance to Mailer's *Of a Fire on the Moon.* First, they dramatize the movement of the individual soul and the movement of America as a purposeful symbolic journey or voyage of exploration in which self-knowledge, knowledge of nature, and knowledge of God are reciprocal and dominating concerns. On the journey, events are charged with dramatic meaning and significance. Although *Moby-Dick,* to which Mailer explicitly refers in *Fire on the Moon,* is the most striking example of such a journey, it is a pervasive metaphor in Puritan literature, Emerson, Hawthorne, Thoreau, Whitman, and Twain. Rooted in the Biblical and Augustinian tradition, the metaphor defines man as pilgrim and his experience as teleological. Second, the dramatic significance of the voyage is made more profound—and more apocalyptic — by man's continual awareness of Satan as well as God, sin as well as romantic possibility, evil as well as good. The voyage consistently embodies an apocalyptic, indeed, often a Manichaean conflict between light and darkness, God and Devil.

Each of these conceptions has a profound importance for the American experience. America's "election," like that of the regenerate soul, necessitates an awareness of its divine mission and purpose. Exhorts Emerson: "We must accept in the highest mind [our] transcendent destiny . . . [as] guides, redeemers and benefactors, obeying the Almighty effort and advancing on Chaos and the Dark." There is nothing lukewarm in Emerson's affirmation, and its exultant tone marks a dominant strain in America's awareness of its own divine and transcendent meaning.

Yet even the elect—indeed, especially the elect—must journey

---

2 Richard G. Stern, "Hip, Hell, and the Navigator: An Interview with Norman Mailer," in *Advertisements for Myself,* p. 384.

in the consciousness not only of election but of the damnation that is its stark alternative. There is no middle ground except lukewarmness between election and damnation, and the Book of Revelation, from which Mailer quotes a long passage in the near-center of *Fire on the Moon,* emphasizes that the lukewarm, the neutral, are anathema in the sight of God. The Puritan preoccupation with the soul of America confronting the either/or of its existence is reflected in its use of the logic of exclusive disjunction. If America is not celestial, it is satanic. If it is not light, it is darkness. If the saints are not to comprise a city of God upon a hill, says John Winthrop, "we shall be made a story and a by-word throughout the world: we shall open the mouths of enemies to speak evil of the ways of God . . . we shall shame . . . God's worthy servants, and cause their prayers to be turned into curses upon us, till we be consumed out of the good land whither we are going."

Throughout the 19th century, America continues to be seen as Saviour or Satan, and its voyage as salvific or destructive. In Twain's early writings, America's mission is benevolent; but Twain's Yankee "saves" the past only by destroying the society he sets out to redeem, and *The Great Dark* describes a journey of nightmare and nihilism. Melville's Ahab becomes the destroyer. In "Prayer of Columbus," Whitman's Columbus is a prophet, but one profoundly aware that the impulses that led him on his journey may have originated in his own madness. And the corrosive irony of the final epigraph in Twain's *Pudd'nhead Wilson*—"*October 12, the Discovery.* It was wonderful to find America, but it would have been more wonderful to miss it"—reflects the despair resulting from the discovery that America's apparent innocence belies its real corruption. In this particular work, slavery is the serpent in the garden. But in a more inclusive sense, America had betrayed its promise, and its election, of necessity, could now only become its damnation. The dream was transformed into nightmare, and paradise into hell. America's prayers, in Winthrop's words, had turned to curses, and its saints had become devils.

Finally, the technological revolution in America during the 19th century intensified rather than diminished these same concerns about the nature of the American soul. 'Steam was till the other day," writes Emerson, "the devil which we dreaded." But Fulton and others thought that "where was power was not devil, but was God . . ." Henry Adams had entered a "supersensual world" of unintelligible and random energy in which the dynamo had displaced the Virgin. But "as he grew accustomed to the great gallery of machines, he began to feel the forty-foot dynamo as a moral force, much as the early Christians felt the Cross." There were new forces, to be sure, but man's nature inevitably would respond to them morally, and in doing so man would recognize that "the idea that new force must be in itself a good is only an animal or vegetable instinct . . . . hidden energies . . . tended to become destructive." For one part of the American soul, the dynamo could remain a Cross; for another, as for Twain in the apocalyptic ending of *A Connecticut Yankee,* in which the thousands of electrocuted bodies of the knights of Arthurian England testify to the Yankee's destructive efficiency, the dynamo could intensify the malevolence, but not the goodness, of America's divided soul. Yet in each case, the quantitative changes brought about by the machine, traumatic and overwhelming as they were, served to reinforce the traditional qualitative vision of the nature and meaning of the American journey.

II

In the contemporary literary world of pap and Portnoy, *Of a Fire on the Moon* stands as a significant and profound expression of the American tradition. Fifteen years ago, Mailer defined the malaise of our time as the resigned feeling that "everything has been getting smaller and smaller and less and less important, that the romantic spirit has dried up, that there is almost no shame today like the terror before the romantic. We're all getting so mean and small and petty and ridiculous."[3] In light of the banal preoccupations of a great deal of what passes for American literature today, Mailer's judgment would seem accurate. Indeed, the nature of Mailer's questioning on first contemplating the possibility of writing about Apollo 11—"he hardly knew whether the Space Program was the noblest expression of the Twentieth Century or the quintessential statement of our fundamental insanity"[4]—would itself be incongruous to any mind steeped in moral relativism and naturalism. "Noblest expressions" and "quintessential statements"

---

[3] *Ibid.,* p. 382.

[4] *Of a Fire on the Moon* (Boston: Little, Brown, 1970), p. 15. All references are to this edition and are included in the text.

of anything, even in relation to the voyage to the moon, are hardly
in vogue. And the moral absolutism of Mailer's polarities would
have little meaning for those trained to seek after, indeed, at times
to lust after, ambiguity. Yet Mailer never softens the starkness of
those polarities:

> Nothing in the future might ever be the same—that was cause
> for unrest—nor could the future even be seen until one could an-
> swer the obsessive question: was our venture into space noble or
> insane, was it part of a search for the good, or the agent of diab-
> olisms yet unglimpsed? (p. 140)

In replying to critics who accused him of using extravagant language, Thoreau stated in *Walden* that he feared only that his expression might not be extravagant *enough* to be adequate to the
truth of which he had been convinced.

> *Extra vagance!* it depends on how you are yarded. . . . I desire
> to speak somewhere *without* bounds; like a man in a waking mo-
> ment, to men in their waking moments; for I am convinced that I
> cannot exaggerate enough even to lay the foundation of a true
> expression.

The consciously heightened and exaggerated quality of Mailer's
language throughout *Fire on the Moon*—a language thought admirable by several critics and abominable by others[5]—has for its
most obvious justification the sheer and inconceivable exaggeration
of the event itself. One could not write about the voyage to the
moon in the terse and simple sentences of Hemingway. To those
who see the voyage as possessing the symbolic significance with
which Mailer invests it, his style and ideas are harmonious.

---

[5] The reviews of Mailer's style and ideas in *Of a Fire on the Moon* are often
as diametrically opposed in their judgments as the polarities of Mailer's vision.
Concludes one sardonic critic: "The reader must await another momentous
event for any further personal information by Mailer about Mailer." Another
states that *Fire on the Moon* is a superb, beautiful, and profound book that
"might well remain unequaled." Benjamin DeMott, in a thoughtful consideration of the work in *Saturday Review*, January 16, 1971, pp. 25-27, 57-58,
argues that *Fire on the Moon* "does matter; this much lies beyond question."
There is nothing trivial or marginal, he states, in Mailer's accomplishment.
Despite its flaws, the work is "a stunning image of human energy and purposefulness," and "at those moments when [it] rises to the level of its highest
aspirations, it is itself an act of revelation—the only verbal deed to this moment
that begins to be worthy of the dream and the reality it celebrates."

Beyond this justification, however, lies one of equal importance.
Mailer's attempt to "fasten words again to visible things," in Emerson's phrase, is made especially difficult because of the "rotten diction" pervading the mission of Apollo 11: the statistical and programmed data of the computers and the similarly bloodless language of the astronauts. Words and things, language and the
senses, have become as divorced in the technological world Mailer
attempts to describe as they had in the supersensual world of Henry
Adams. Those at NASA, "like real Americans . . . always talked
in technological code," a code generated in part by an American
desire to minimize the senses and to remain antiseptic because of
our fear of them: "If we honor or fear the presence of odors,"
for example, "because they are a root to the past . . . are indeed
our very marriage to time and mortality, why then it is no accident
that the Wasps were . . . the most Faustian, barbaric, draconian,
progress-oriented, and root-destroying people on earth. They had
divorced themselves from odor in order to dominate time, and
thereby see if they were able to deliver themselves from death! No
less! It is fiendish to get into exaggeration so early [in the work],
but . . ." (p. 10)

Mailer's use of exaggeration, then, is highly self-conscious. It
is demanded by the enormity of the event and by the technological
code that encases the event in a computerized data that robs it
of meaning. When the astronauts are asked if they worry over the
Lem's ability to ignite and ascend—"would the motor ignite, or
did the moon have a curse?" wonders Mailer—their answers are
of "various contingencies" and "a wider variety of trajectory conditions."

> [they were] talking about not being able to join up, wandering
> through space, lost forever to life in that short eternity before they
> expired of hunger and thirst. Small hint of that in these verbal
> formulations. . . . The heart of astronaut talk, like the heart of
> all bureaucratic talk, was a jargon which could be easily converted
> to computer programming, a language like Fortran or Cobol or
> Algol. Anti-dread formulations were the center of it, as if words
> like pills were there to suppress emotional symptoms. (p. 25)

One astronaut could have completed any given sentence for another, states Mailer, for their impersonal and interlocking phrases
were part of a language meant to reduce and control all phenom-

ena. Indeed, *initial*-controls were central to their dominance of nature and of any potential irrationality:

> EVA . . . referred to their walk on the moon; but the sound of the letters E, V, A might inspire less perturbation than the frank admission that men would now dare to walk on an ancient and alien terrain where no life breathed and beneath the ground no bodies were dead. (p. 32)

Despite the language of the astronauts, and despite the difficulty of consistently conceiving them as individually heroic—given their mechanized and technological existence—[6]Mailer does conceive their voyage as dramatically purposeful and even apocalyptic. Nowhere does Mailer depart most strikingly from the naturalists of our own time—and become continuous with the most profound part of the American tradition—than in his conviction that God and the Devil are locked in combat: 'What if God wrestled for the soul of man in some greased arena with the Devil? . . . the time of apocalypse was certainly near" (pp. 469-470). The drama is a divine and eschatological one, and the voyage to the moon cannot be understood apart from it.

Mailer's conviction of man's purposefulness has played a constant part in his writing. In 1958, he stated that God to him existed as "a warring element in a divided universe" and that "we

---

[6] Mailer's difficulty in defining the astronauts as "heroic" stems in part from their apparently technological and machine-like natures. As individuals, they insist that they are representatives of a "collective will." Indeed, Armstrong, on being asked to admit that his endeavor was equal in magnitude to Columbus' adventure, seems to Mailer virtually to reply, "If not me, another," and to assert that "there had been only one Columbus—there were ten astronauts at least who could do the job, and hundreds of men to back them up" (p. 38). Finally, however, the astronauts are not machines; of their courage as individuals Mailer has no doubts and for it he has only admiration. His more profound difficulty with their heroism has its origin in their necessarily persistent faith that the universe is benign and that the emptiness of space will conceal no malevolence. Given this inevitable conviction, their "resolute avoidance of a heroic posture" follows logically; the astronauts seem set on demonstrating that "heroism's previous relation to romance had been highly improper—it was technology and the absence of emotion which were the only fit mates for the brave" (p. 108). For "the astronauts, brave men, proceeded on the paradoxical principle that fear once deposed by knowledge would make bravery redundant. It was . . . the complacent assumption that the universe was no majestic mansion of architectonics out there between evil and nobility, or strife on a darkling plain, but rather an ultimately benign field of investigation" (p. 109) that leaves Mailer most outraged.

are a part of—perhaps the most important part—of His great
expression, His enormous destiny; perhaps He is trying to impose
upon the universe His conception of being against other conceptions
of being very much opposed to His. Maybe we are in a sense the
seed, the seed-carriers, the voyagers, the explorers, the embodiment
of that embattled vision; maybe we are engaged in a heroic activity,
and not a mean one."[7] Such a vision, he argued, was not only
"arduous" in its conception but "the only thing that makes any
sense to me. It's the only thing that explains to me the problem
of evil."[8] Although Mailer anticipates in *Fire on the Moon* the
naturalistic objection that it is more "comforting" to see meaning
rather than absurdity in the voyage to the moon by remarking that
"it was somehow superior to see the astronauts and the flight of
Apollo 11 as the instrument of . . . celestial or satanic endeavors,
than as a . . . meaningless journey to a dead arena" (p. 152), it
is clear that he believes thoroughly in the vision.[9]

It is precisely Mailer's willingness to take seriously the problem
of evil, the palpable reality of Satan, that deepens his sense of the
journey as *either* celestial *or* satanic. He is as scandalized by scientific attempts to combine and synthesize opposing theories about
the origin of the moon or the nature of light[10] as he is by political

---

[7] Stern, *op. cit.*, pp. 380-381.

[8] *Ibid.*, p. 381.

[9] *Ibid.*, esp. p. 376 and pp. 380-384. To say that Mailer "believes thoroughly
in the vision" is not to say that *Fire on the Moon* is without its doubts and
ironies—indeed, Mailer argues that he "preferred" this vision to a vision of
absurdity or to no vision at all. Nonetheless, when he states that "his sense of
irony once aroused, his sense of apocalypse could never be far behind" and that
he is "quick to hunt for reason in absurdity" (p. 150), he suggests that irony is
an inevitable part, but never even nearly the whole, of his vision and work.
Like Ishmael, his awareness of his—and man's—limitations in trying to find
meaning in an overwhelming phenomenon often leads to ironies of self-depreca-
tion. But, again like *Moby-Dick*, *Fire on the Moon* is an extremely serious work
whose heightened language and meaning are not ultimately ironic. The use of
irony in each work never dominates the genuine seriousness and conviction of
its tone or its view of man's experience.

[10] Writes Mailer: "Nobody could be certain whether light was composed
of little pellets, or traveled like sound in a wave, or was both. Both!" (pp.
165-166). His impatience with such a synthesis, whether scientific, political, or
moral, stems from the glibness with which it often may be advanced and the
ease with which it disposes of mystery ("When it came to ultimate scientific
knowledge we were no further along than the primitive who thought light came
from God. Perhaps it did. No physicist could begin to prove it didn't. So we
didn't even know what a flame was" [p. 166]). Given his own view of man as
ultimately "twin-souled"—a creature of good and evil rather than of one exclusively—his quarrel is not with the recognition of complexity but with the

attempts to argue that the voyage can be justified because of "spin-offs" that will benefit America in practical ways (the notion that the journey can be made to answer the "any nation that can send men to the moon . . ." syndrome). All this, says Mailer, is "cement." Finally, he states, "God or Devil at the helm—that was the question behind the trip . . ." (p. 456). His use of exclusive disjunction is as continual and rigorous as any Puritan's. He cannot call the ground after lift-off "hallowed":

> For all he knew, Apollo-Saturn was still a child of the Devil. Yet if it was, then . . . the Devil was beautiful indeed. Or rather, was the Devil so beautiful because all of [us] were nothing but devils [ourselves]. For the notion that man voyaged out to fulfill the desire of God was either the heart of the vision, or anathema to that true angel in Heaven they would violate by the fires of their ascent. A ship of flames was on its way to the moon. (p. 103)

Mailer's description of the "ship of flames" at its launching emphasizes this same disjunctive conception of the either/or. The mystery of fire, "impenetrable" and awesome, may be the mysterious fire of salvation and purification. Or the fire may be the quintessence of Satan and damnation. And "the flames," writes Mailer, "were enormous":

> Two mighty torches of flame like the wings of a yellow bird of fire flew over a field, covered a field with brilliant yellow bloomings of flame, and in the midst of it, white as a ghost, white as the white of Melville's Moby Dick, white as the shrine of the Madonna in half the churches of the world, this slim angelic mysterious ship of stages rose without sound out of its incarnation of flame and began to ascend slowly into the sky, slow as Melville's Leviathan might swim, slowly as we might swim upward in a dream looking for the air. (pp. 99-100)

The "Niagaras of flame" and the "apocalyptic fury of sound" are as overwhelming as "the thought that man now had something with which to speak to God—

> the fire was white as a torch and long as the rocket itself, a tail of fire, a face, yes now the rocket looked like a thin and pointed witch's hat, and the flames from its base were the blazing eyes of

---

overly facile way in which *x* is equated with *y* or in which *x* and *y* combine to form a bland substance in which neither is seen as really existing.

> the witch. Forked like saw teeth was the base of the flame . . .
> Now it seemed to rise like a ball of fire, like a new sun mounting
> the sky, a flame elevating itself. (pp. 100-101)

It is significant that the supernaturally awesome whiteness and
forked flames of Apollo 11 are here joined to the American literary
past through Mailer's allusions to *Moby-Dick*. For if whiteness is
the color of celestial innocence and love, states Melville, it also may
be the absence of color and the sign of transcendent horror and
dread. It is being and goodness, annihilation and demonism—"the
most meaning symbol of spiritual things, nay, the very veil of the
Christian's Deity; and yet . . . the intensifying agent in things the
most appalling to mankind." And the "levelled flame of pale,
forked fire" that marks Ahab's ritual of witchcraft, the "forking
flames" of the tryworks and the *Pequod* itself, "laden with fire,"
are echoed in Mailer's description of this ship of flames.

Finally, the flames of this "new sun" allow Mailer no respite:
"to look into a fire hot as the manifest of [God's] immanence might
be equal to staring into the fires of Apollo 11" (p. 166). In Ishmael's warning—"Look not too long in the face of the fire, O Man!
. . . believe not the artificial fire, when its redness makes all things
look ghastly"—resides the hope that the "natural sun," the "only
true lamp," will make all things bright and reveal in a gentler light
"those who glared like devils in the forking flames." Ishmael, of
course, cannot sustain without agony his faith in the "natural sun";
yet damnation and despair seem the alternative. For Mailer, then,
the flames may be satanic; Apollo may be after all not the god of
the sun but the Apollyon of the Book of Revelation; and in citing
the eighth chapter of Revelation—again, cited nearly in the exact
center of his work—Mailer's preface to the Biblical description of
the seven angels of the Apocalypse ends once more with his awareness of Satan:

> he continued to brood about the chasm between technology and
> metaphysics, the psychology of machines and the dreams of men,
> the omens of the future amid the loss of taboo, the horror of the
> ascent and his fear of the heavens—was the Devil chief engineer
> of the ship which went to the moon? (p. 208)

In the midst of the satanic fire of the tryworks, Ishmael's vision
of the flames is inseparable from his vision of Ahab. Ahab refers
to his "soul's ship" as the journey proceeds. And here, "plunging

into that blackness of darkness," the fiery ship seems to Ishmael "the material counterpart of her monomaniac commander's soul." On the voyage to the moon, Armstrong is the commander. To command Apollo 11, indeed, to become and remain an astronaut in the face of irrational machinery and sudden death, in the face of the fire that killed three astronauts in an instant, reflects Mailer, "one might need some of the monomania of Captain Ahab" (p. 331). Although he had come close to death on an earlier space voyage, "there is never a hint Armstrong ever thought of trying another profession" (p. 331).

Indeed, it is Armstrong whose startling use of the word "soul" before the journey begins shatters the code of technology and reveals his sense of man's nature. He is pressed by reporters as to why the journey is necessary. Finally, after refusing to answer in the language of economics, or "spin-offs," or practical results, he replies that it is necessary because "it's in the nature of the human being to face challenges."

> He looked a little defiant, as if probably [the reporters] might never know what he was talking about, "It's by the nature of his *deep inner soul.*" The last three words came out as if they had seared his throat by their extortion. How his privacy had been invaded this day. (p. 42)

Yet Armstrong's private vision of the single-minded nature of man's soul was also the common vision of America. The astronauts were iron men, "the core of some magnetic human force called Americanism, patriotism, or Waspitude . . . with a sense of mission so deep it was incommunicable even to themselves, as if they had signed on as the core, no, rather as the most finished product of a human ore whose purpose—despite all thoughts it had found that purpose— was yet undiscovered" (pp. 315-316).

Aldrin, an elder in the Presbyterian Church, celebrated Holy Communion on the moon. He was, states Mailer, "a traditionalist with a faith that never seemed to alter" (p. 338). If the real nature of the astronauts' purpose was "yet undiscovered," Aldrin, "not only a technologue but a high priest," finds its meaning and resolution in religious intensity, sacrament, and ritual. As a believer in predestination and an agent of God's will,

> was there a single question whose lament might suggest that if the mission were ill-conceived or even a work of art designed by the

Devil, then all the prayers of all good men were nothing but a
burden upon the Lord, who in order to reply would be forced to
work in the mills of Satan, or leave the prayers of his flock in
space[?] Not likely. Aldrin did not seem a man for thoughts like
that, but then his mind was a mystery wrapped in the winding-sheet
of a computer with billions of bits. (p. 395)

For Aldrin, man's potential or actual demonism—on the moon as
on the earth—could be absolved by form, ritual, and Host. The
voyage was designed not by the Devil but by the Lord, and its
purpose was His own.

Finally, however, it is not Aldrin but Ahab—or Armstrong—
with whom Mailer is most preoccupied and by whose presence he
is most obsessed. Although they both are religious men, Armstrong's
mysticism departs from Aldrin's more formal and traditional perception. He had lived with death and the numinous since he was a boy
through awesome and recurring dreams in which, said Armstrong,
"I could, by holding my breath, hover over the ground. Nothing
much happened; I neither flew nor fell in those dreams. I just
hovered" (p. 333).[11] Armstrong, then, is the dreaming mystic and
technologist who most perfectly symbolizes the "incredible contradictions" of America's soul. All the astronauts, to be sure, lived
with cosmic oppositions in their souls.

On the one hand to dwell in the very center of technological reality
(... that world where every question must have answers ...) yet to
inhabit—if only in one's dreams—that other world where death,
metaphysics and the unanswerable questions of eternity must reside,
was to suggest natures so divided that ... they contain[ed] in their
huge contradictions ... the profound and accelerating opposites
of the century itself. (p. 47)[12]

---

[11] In light of the preoccupation of American literature with the questions of
defining reality, of the dream, and of wedding, in Hawthorne's words, the
"actual" and the "imaginary," it is significant and appropriate that Mailer
builds his theory of the "psychology of astronauts" on the "*fact*" of Armstrong's
dream (p. 48). The "pearls of one's legends were not often founded on real
grains of sand" (p. 45). But here, Armstrong's dream, itself a fact, becomes the
foundation for the attempt to unite the incongruous elements of an unimagin-
able yet factual journey. Mailer's descriptions of technology, like Melville's
descriptions of cetology, delineate facts; and in each case, these "facts" become
incredible, staggering, and dream-like. Finally, they become not only symbolic
but inseparable from the "factual dream" of the journey, and, transformed by
the imagination, part of the union of the imaginary and the actual that
comprises each work.

[12] These "profound and accelerating opposites" characterize the century
and the voyage in such a way as to make them inseparable. In their apocalyptic

But Aldrin's faith in the marriage of God's purpose and man's voyage to the moon resolved such oppositions through tradition and sacrament.

Yet only Armstrong, the mystic and dreamer, "could be the man to [first] enter the sanctums and veils of the moon" (p. 333). His dream of hovering and his apparently calm apprehension of death were facts as certain as technology, but their implications were at once more profound and more obscure than technology. Armstrong's view of the teleological significance of the voyage—despite his conviction that it was a manifestation of the nature of man's soul—remained less clearly visible and more hidden and elusive than that of Aldrin. To Mailer, preoccupied with the warring polarities in man's nature and in the soul of America, and committed to Emerson's definition of man as a "stupendous antagonism," Armstrong's conception of the voyage as the quintessential expression of man's nature and soul could only raise once more— and with renewed intensity—the ultimate question of the voyage's real purpose and real end: good or evil, God or Devil.

Mailer's fascination with Armstrong, then, involves more than the polarities of technology and dream, reason and faith. Finally, Armstrong becomes the incarnation of the innocence or evil of America itself. He was, says Mailer on first observing him, of all the astronauts the "nearest to being saintly," yet "there was something as hard, small-town and used in his face as the look of a cashier over pennies" (pp. 29-30). If the personalities of Aldrin and Collins were fairly comfortable to grasp, Armstrong was "extraor-

---

contradictions, the times, the journey, and the astronauts are as one: "The century would seek to dominate nature as it had never been dominated, would attack the idea of war, poverty and natural catastrophe as never before. The century would create death, devastation and pollution as never before. Yet the century was now attached to the idea that man must take his conception of life out to the stars. It was the most soul-destroying and apocalyptic of centuries. So in their turn the astronauts had personalities of unequaled banality and apocalyptic dignity. So they suggested in their contradictions the power of the century to live with its own incredible contradictions and yet release some of the untold energies of the earth. A century devoted to the rationality of technique was also a century so irrational as to open in every mind the real possibility of global destruction. It was the first century in history which presented to sane and sober minds the fair chance that the century might not reach the end of its span. It was a world half convinced of the future death of our species yet half aroused by the apocalyptic notion that an exceptional future still lay before us. So it was a century which moved with the most magnificent display of power into directions it could not comprehend. The itch was to accelerate—the metaphysical direction unknown" (pp. 47-48).

dinarily remote." Their speech was easy and stolid, Armstrong's was agonized. Yet his difficulty in speaking became, paradoxically, his most impressive quality. He could, of course, rattle off the technological code; but in a deeper sense—as when he uttered "soul"—Armstrong seemed to have "such huge respect for words that they were like tangible omens and portents . . . of psychic presence, as if finally something deep, delicate and primitive would restrain him from uttering a single word of fear for fear of materializing his dread."

> So, once, men had been afraid to utter the name of the Lord, or even to write it in such a way as to suggest the sound, for that might be enough to summon some genie of God's displeasure at so disrupting the heavens. (pp. 30-31)

The nature of Armstrong's soul, like the nature of his respect before the divinity of authentic words, might be "particularly innocent or subtly sinister" (p. 23). But there can be no doubt that Armstrong, whose mysticism is not bound by the sacramental ritual of Aldrin's traditional worship, is as much at the center of Mailer's drama as Ahab is of Melville's.

Just as Mailer's reflections on Armstrong begin his consideration of the nature of the quintessential American whose voyage to the moon is apocalyptic, so his reflections on Armstrong conclude his description of the end of the voyage itself. An awareness of a casual remark made by Armstrong during the astronauts' conversation with the President—and preceding the President's comment that "this is the greatest week in the history of the world since the Creation"—[13] is necessary to our understanding of this final description.

---

[13] In the moments before the landing of the Eagle, states Mailer in retrospect, "one got ready for the climax of the greatest week since Christ was born" (p. 111). His allusion to the birth of Christ at this point needs to be seen in the light of his earlier response to a statement of Wernher Von Braun: "He had declared that reaching the moon would be the greatest event in history since aquatic life had moved up onto land, and that was a remark! for it passed without pause over the birth and death of Christ" (p. 79). Here, the President's exultant remark immediately precedes a chaplain's prayer of thanksgiving to God the Father that concludes "in the name of the Lord." If the generally religious nature of the response to the astronauts' safe return—or deliverance— is obvious, Mailer's previous juxtaposition of his own remark and Von Braun's (despite Von Braun's ostensibly Christian belief as shown in the same interview in which his "aquatic life" comment occurred) suggests the difficulty of defining its more particular religious meaning for an America at once pluralistic, proud of its "new creation," and professedly humble before its God.

> ARMSTRONG: *We're sorry you missed that* [All-Star baseball]
> *game.*
> NIXON: *Yes, well—you knew that, too.*
> ARMSTRONG: *We hear that—*
> NIXON: *The rain—*
> ARMSTRONG: *The rain. Well, we haven't been able to control
> the weather yet, but that's something we can look forward to as
> tomorrow's challenge.* (p. 452)

Although we are not told whether the remark was made in innocent
humor, we are justified in supposing that it was not. Armstrong—
like Melville's Ahab, or, better still, Twain's Yankee?—had little or
no "comic spirit," and his smile, "the smile of an enterprising small-
town boy," leads us once again at the beginning of Mailer's work to
the same recurring alternatives:

> He could be an angel, he could be the town's devil. Who knew?
> You could not penetrate the flash of the smile—all of America's
> bounty was in it. (p. 30)

It is in the light, or the darkness, of Armstrong's remark and
America's "bounty" of innocence or evil, benevolence or destruction, that Mailer's concluding description of the astronauts must be
seen.

> The anthem was played. The astronauts stood at attention. It
> had ended. It was done. Armstrong's face looked remarkable.
> Never as at this hour . . . had it had so much of the shriven and
> scourged look of that breakfast food face which smiles in innocence
> at us from every billboard. A truly American saint. Of course, the
> Devil has power to assume a pleasing shape. . . . [Just before the
> launch], his head in his helmet, he had the hard flat-eyed ego-
> centric look of a kitten, eyes hardly cracked, who will be someday a
> cat. It had been a moment to suggest that in the mysteries of Arm-
> strong's makeup, there might be a bona-fide devil in one soul if a
> saint in the other—assume he was twin-souled, yes—and if [Mailer]
> had a glimpse of him as a mystic, he could see him now again as a
> cat-technician who would tamper with the rain. "Haven't been
> able to control the weather yet, but . . . tomorrow's challenge."
> (p. 454)

Armstrong and America are twin-souled—angel and devil, innocence and evil, expressions at once of heaven and hell—and their
antagonisms are made still more complex by Satan's ability to
assume the shape of goodness.

Yet in the face of this complexity, Mailer's recurring emphasis on the either/or nature of the American journey is not swallowed up in ambiguity or the curse of lukewarmness. Indeed, the intensity of his final vision of man and the moon is itself "apocalyptic." The moon may be releasing a city of the dead, a revelation of the afterlife because of Apollo's voyage, and anomalies may be rising from hell: "he was obliged to wonder if man had finally become a cancer in the forms of the Lord" (p. 457). If Mailer were "without compass to the designs of the father," the meaning of the moon can be found only in the stark alternatives: "she could be a disguise of Heaven or as easily the Infernal Shades" (p. 457). And the consequences of the voyage are not limited to America but extend to the world. The city upon a hill remains a light to, or a darkness over, mankind. The President's reply to Armstrong's remark about controlling the weather is nothing less than "right, right." The astronauts, "the end of the old or the first of the new men" (p. 49), as "heroes or monsters"

> were out to savage or save the rest of the world, and were they God's intended? (p. 441)

The intensity of Mailer's ambivalence precludes any glib answer to his own question. If his own "culture" of crazies, dropouts, and drug users would easily define America as satanic and its voyage as damned, and if the Wasp with equal thoughtlessness would define America as God and its journey as blessed, Mailer is too convinced of the possibility of grace and election to echo the glib rebel and too aware of sin and the demonic to speak as a Wasp. Ultimately, then, "where did you put your feet so that finally you might begin?"

Mailer finds his beginning in an object—a rock from the moon —and in his favorite saying: "Trust the authority of your senses" (p. 470). There is no incongruity but rather the greatest harmony between Mailer's allusion to the author of the saying—St. Thomas Aquinas—and the tone of his allusion to the rock: "Marvelous little moon rock. What the Devil did it say?" (p. 471). The senses mark man's humanity and limitations, and even when they are deceived —as when one saw in Armstrong only saint or devil—they inhabit a world of religious and moral meaning. The question could be, indeed, is Ishmael's: "What the Devil did it say?" But that leviathan and moon rock do "say" something is clear; the universe is not mute.[14] The rock is for Mailer a sign and a symbol, and although "she"—the gender he "instinctively" gave it—may be as old as three billion years, she was young and tender as "the subtle lift of love which comes up from the cradle of the newborn" (p. 472).[15] He liked the moon rock, and thought, "his vanity finally unquenchable—that she liked him." Finally, then, "he had his sign, sentimental beyond measure . . . even if he and the moon were nothing but devils in new cahoots" (p. 472).

The moon rock, sign and symbol of an affirmation newly born of the apocalyptic voyage, even here cannot escape the specter of the devils. But, still more important, the sign and the specter embody meaning. Words are moral commandments, moral strictures, and our life is a moral, indeed, a religious drama.[16] The sign of the moon rock is the culminating omen that words and things cannot be cheated of their power or meaning by a naturalistic interpretation of man and the universe. It speaks to the nature of the voyage, the nature of the soul, and the nature of language. And it gives to Mailer "certitude enough to know he would write his book and in some part applaud the feat and honor the astronauts," for

> the expedition to the moon was finally a venture which might help to disclose the nature of the Lord and the Lucifer who warred for us; certainly, the hour of happiness would be here when men who

[14] Contrast to Mailer's interpretation of the moon rock as sign and symbol Mircea Eliade's description of the prevailing modern view of the world and experience: "The cosmos has become opaque, inert, mute; it transmits no message, it holds no cipher . . . the world is no longer felt as the work of God." *The Sacred and Profane: The Nature of Religion,* trans. Willard R. Trask (New York: Harcourt, Brace & World, 1959), p. 17.

[15] Cf. pp. 150-151: "If God finally was the embodiment of a vision which might cease to exist in the hostilities of the larger universe, a vision which indeed might be *obliged* to prevail or would certainly cease to exist, then it was legitimate to see all of human history as a cradle which had nurtured a baby which had now taken its first step." See also pp. 111-113.

[16] Mailer's insistence that "anyone [can] lose his soul" (p. 140) and his continual awareness of death—indeed, his work shares with the traditional literature of imagined moon voyages a sense of the voyage as a journey into and beyond death and a confrontation with the afterlife (see esp. p. 35 and pp. 108-109)—give his apprehension of life as a religious drama a striking immediacy and intensity. "What I would hope to do with my work," he has stated, "is intensify a consciousness that the core of life cannot be cheated. Every moment of one's existence one is growing into more or retreating into less. One is always living a little more or dying a little bit. . . . the choice is not to live a little more or to not live a little more; it is to live a little more or to die a little more." Stern, *op. cit.,* p. 385. Again, the either/or nature of the drama is apparent.

spoke like Shakespeare rode the ships: how many eons was that
away! Yes, he had come to believe by the end of this long summer
that probably we had to explore into outer space, for technology had
penetrated the modern mind to such a depth that voyages in space
might have become the last way to discover the metaphysical pits
of that world of technique which choked the pores of modern consciousness—yes, we might have to go out into space until the
mystery of new discovery would force us to regard the world once
again as poets, behold it as savages who knew that if the universe
was a lock, its key was metaphor rather than measure. (p. 471)

III

In his review of *Fire on the Moon* (see note 5), Benjamin
DeMott argues that one of the work's greatest virtues is its conviction that "something important can happen on earth, can
demand a total draft of a man's resources of intelligence, respon-
siveness, awe, and projective capacity for its representation. Fewer
and fewer men seem ready to grant this elementary truth." DeMott's
statement is valid and compelling; it echoes, of course, Mailer's
earlier insistence that "everything has been getting smaller and
smaller and less and less important." Yet the "elementary truth"
that life possesses moral significance no longer seems so elementary
or self-evident. As a truth, it would seem to presuppose and necessitate religious conviction and to demand some sense of the reality
of "Lord and Lucifer" and "metaphysical pits" as well as a conception of man as a moral creature and "stupendous antagonism."
Mailer is one of the few contemporary American authors who
possesses such a conviction of the essential religious drama of man's
experience—the movement of his soul between heaven and hell—
and he is perhaps the only one whose prose could sustain the symbolic dimension and apocalyptic significance he perceives in the
voyage to the moon.

Finally, Mailer's intense ambivalence toward America's errand
into a new wilderness reflects the polarities he sees in America and
in the journey of the soul. It echoes the ambivalence of the Puritans,
of Edwards, and of the great American authors of the 19th century.
"God or Devil at the helm," writes Mailer, "that was the question
behind the trip." His question—who is man's, and America's,
"navigator"?—echoes their own and reflects the continuity of the
American tradition.[17] And for Mailer as for the tradition, the

---

[17] Mailer uses the explicit image and idea of the "navigator" throughout

question and the attempts to answer it assume a conception of man that is not naturalistic but religious and a conception of the world that is not relativistic but purposeful and apocalyptic. "Can engines, comets, or bombs teach the nations to sing the *Dies Irae?*" asks Perry Miller.

> When the end of the world was a descent from Heaven, it was also a Judgment; if it becomes more and more a contrivance, it has less and less to do with good and evil. Humanity lusts after the conflagration, even after nature seems unlikely to provide it. But then, if humanity has to do the deed itself, can it bring about more than the explosion? Can it also produce the Judgment? Explosion, in its stark physical simplicity, although satisfying the most venerable requirements for stage effects, turns out to be . . . not what was wanted after all. Not for this was the errand run into a wilderness, and not for this will it be run. Catastrophe, by and for itself, is not enough.[18]

The astronauts' and America's continuation of the errand in their voyage to the moon is for Mailer neither a symbol of catastrophe nor a symbol of facile hope. In and for themselves, neither is enough. For Mailer, Lord and Lucifer, good and evil continue their struggle within the soul and throughout the universe. That America is again their central battleground reflects the durability of its errand and the agony of its simultaneous awareness of sin and grace, damnation and election. That Mailer's expression of this traditional awareness in a setting of yet another voyage of exploration is not resolved by despair or euphoria, nor by the conventional "ambiguity," but by a tormented ambivalence in which goodness and satanic pride are each real and compelling, reflects the depth of his vision. And that he "sanctions" the voyage without minimizing its potential for evil reflects a hope for America and for man rooted not in sentimentality but in a moral realism that remains acutely conscious of the reality of the fall and the presence of the demonic. For Mailer, the polarities and complexities of the 20th

---

Fire on the Moon. It is associated at once with man's conscious sense of purpose, with his unconscious, and with God's design in the universe. Cf. Mailer's concluding statement in "Hip, Hell, and the Navigator": "the unconscious . . . has an enormous teleological sense . . . It is with this thing that [we] move, that [we] grope forward—this navigator at the seat of [our] being" (p. 386).

[18] "The End of the World," in *Errand into the Wilderness* (Cambridge, Mass.: Harvard University Press, 1956), p. 239.

century do not diminish but rather intensify the traditionally "stupendous" antagonism that comprises the nature and voyage of man's
soul. It remains—as does America itself—a "dragging together of
the poles of the Universe" in which "god and devil, king and conspirator," in Emerson's words, contend for dominance. Its ultimate
end, like its journey, continues of necessity to signify nothing less
than apocalypse.

The Changing Temper of American Philosophy

C. F. Delaney

WHEN the question of a "new age" is put to a philosopher there are two quite different ways in which he can define the issue and accordingly respond. On the one hand, he might construe his task as that of a clarifier of some general claim about cultural revolutions. From this perspective he would set about the task of analyzing the concept of a cultural revolution in terms of some loose analogue of necessary and sufficient conditions. These criteria having been laid down, he could then make suggestions as to whether or not those conditions obtain which would justify the claim that we are in the midst of such a cultural revolution. On the other hand, he might construe his charge more specifically as that of assessing the present state of his own field to see if something like a shift in perspective is manifest in this narrower domain. In this paper I am going to take the latter tack. I will, first, briefly survey the contemporary scene in philosophy to illustrate the "changing temper" I am to talk about; secondly, locate these phenomena in a broader historical context; and, thirdly, try to get at the reasons underlying the changes on which I am focusing. The major part of the paper will be devoted to the third point.

One of the most striking facts about recent American philosophy is its renewed interest in public affairs. There is a resurgence of interest generally in political philosophy, philosophy of law, and ethics in the most concrete of senses. The normative issues of the ordinary man seem again to have captured the philosopher's attention. "War," "justice," "ecology," and "abortion" are now the subjects of serious study by some of the leading philosophers in this country. Specifically, *The Monist* (January, 1972) was on "Philosophy and Public Policy," and three of the next six issues are devoted to such themes as "Contemporary Moral Issues," "Women's Liberation," and "The Philosophy of War," not to mention "Pragmatism Reconsidered." Furthermore, some of the most successsful new journals and books to appear on the philosophic scene in recent years deal exclusively with these issues. A new professional quarterly, *Philosophy and Public Affairs,* describes itself as "filling the need for a periodical in which philosophers with different viewpoints can bring their distinctive methods to bear on problems that con-

cern everyone." Richard Bernstein's popular *Praxis and Action*
provides an excellent historical introduction to an understanding of
human action, and, in a more specific way, John Rawl's recent *A
Theory of Justice* promises to be one of the most important philosophical contributions of the decade. Finally, and most difficult to
document, there seems to be a new tone of concrete urgency even
at the professional meetings.

Now all of this on the contemporary scene is striking and suggests some radical shift only because it was noticeably lacking in the
American philosophical community for the previous 30 years. The
period from the 1930's through the 1950's was one of "professionalism" and "tough-mindedness" and also one of speculative aloofness.
Philosophers were talking only to one another, and at that, only
about rather esoteric speculative issues. Professional philosophy was
quite removed from the "problems of men."

If one takes a wider historical view, however, it will be obvious
that this concern for public affairs was not at all lacking in earlier
American philosophy; in fact, it was characteristic of it. The philosophical community of the 1920's under the leadership of Dewey
(with Mead in the background) and through intermediaries like
Holmes, Frankfurter, and Brandeis was intensely interested in and
exercised a profound influence on the life of the American community. When pragmatism held center stage professional philosophy
was firmly embedded in ordinary human concerns.

When this historical perspective is taken, then, a certain pattern
emerges with regard to American philosophy's involvement in and
concern with what I am calling public affairs. First, we have
classical pragmatism with its activist conception of philosophy;
secondly, the positivistically inspired speculative years; and finally,
our present reorientation to activist concerns. It is in and through
this historical contextualization that I think we can begin to comprehend the manifest change in contemporary American philosophy.

Acknowledging that such a delineation of trends itself provides
a species of understanding, my intent in this paper is to move beyond
this. I would like to suggest that there is a rationale of a philosophical nature behind these manifest shifts in attitude, that is, that
theoretical reasons lie behind these public phenomena. Accordingly,
what I will try to do in this paper is to sketch the outlines of an
account in terms of which we can *understand* the changing temper
of contemporary American philosophy.

My thesis is that the key to understanding these changes is in each instance a certain shift in perspective on the fact-value distinction, a shift which does have practical bearing. My account has three stages. First, I will sketch in broad strokes what I will call the classical pragmatic perspective whose activist orientation is based on a certain theoretical and practical interrelation of facts and values. Secondly, I will characterize the positivist period in American philosophy as a speculative period grounded in a sharp separation of facts and values. And finally, there is what I see as a tendency toward a return to pragmatic themes with a new reintegration of facts and values.

a) *Classical Pragmatism: John Dewey.* For Dewey, as for all pragmatists, the abstract issues of epistemology and ethics are concretely embedded in a theory of inquiry, and inquiry is defined as that rational process of transforming problematic situations by bringing about the conditions which contribute to their satisfaction. Inquiry provides the matrix within which knowing and evaluation are concretely interrelated. There is a normative component in even what we call "factual" inquiry because it terminates in a judgment as to what ought to be the case *vis-à-vis* a certain problematic situation. Ought-to-be's give rise to ought-to-do's in terms of which an existential reconstruction of the situation is effected, a reconstruction which is the ultimate ground of warranted assertability. Conversely, given the normative component in factual inquiry, it is not implausible that there could be a factual basis for what we call "normative" claims. Claims with regard to what we ought to do are grounded in an empirical assessment of a morally problematic situation and predictions as to how alternative courses of action might remedy it. But at this point I would like to back up a little and sketch in more detail the pragmatic theory of knowing and evaluation before focusing on its practical import.

Reflective understanding, for Dewey, does not occur in a vacuum. It is called forth by a felt indeterminacy, a tension within our experience. This tension must be articulated and specified to the point of being recognizable as a specific problem if inquiry is to get off the ground. So formulated, the concrete problem will be the regulative principle of the inquiry inasmuch as its demands will furnish the guidelines for possible resolutions. Secondly, there is the suggestion of possible solutions. In a hypothesis we move beyond what is immediately present to something which would, if present, resolve the initial difficulty. Thirdly, there is need for a logical elaboration of the hypothesis which will exhibit its relation to other information available and enable us to devise a means for its testing. Finally, there is the experimental testing which leads to the hypothesis' acceptance or rejection. It is rare that simple observation will suffice at this stage, but the logic of the procedure demands that our theories return to the empirical level at which the problem arose for their ultimate vindication. The successful conclusion is one which effects a transformation of the problematic situation into one which is clear, untroubled, and settled. It is a judgment with regard to what we ought to do (if only conceptually) if we are truly to resolve the problem.

Dewey intends this account to be a historically grounded description of the methods which have been effective in gaining reliable knowledge. From this description we can derive rules which will be normative with regard to future inquiries. In our concrete dealings with the world we gradually learn the best means for gaining and warranting knowledge. Rules are eventually learned and explicated, and these serve as leading principles for directing further inquiries and may in turn be modified by the consequences of these inquiries. The process is self-corrective, and it is this that grounds our confidence in it.

The process of evaluation proper, Dewey maintains, is quite similar in structure. Again we have a situation in which there is conflict and need, and certain conditions which, if brought into existence, would provide a satisfactory resolution of the difficulty. The context in which valuation occurs, then, is a situation in which there are practical conflicts pertaining to what course of action one ought to pursue. There is a conflict among our immediate wants and desires, not all of which can be satisfied. Action is blocked, so reflection is called forth. Based on the nature of the conflict and the consequences of various alternative courses of action a certain hierarchy of values is established for the specific situation. In the establishment of the hierarchy "natures" and "consequences" are necessary but not sufficient conditions for a specific value judgment. Socially inherited rules must be employed as leading principles in determining what we ought to value and do in practical circumstances. The desirable, then, although not unrelated to actual desires, goes beyond them in suggesting what will effect the integration the situation calls for. There is even an analogue to confirmation here, for the actual consequences which follow from initiating a course of activity can serve to test the correctness of the value judgment.

Moreover, valuation thus understood is also a self-corrective reflective process. From past evaluations we can derive standards which are guides for the future, while acknowledging that these guides themselves can be modified by or in the light of experience.

This theory of evaluation has important practical consequences. On this account values are amenable to rational analysis on two counts: first, the process of evaluation is structurally isomorphic with the general process of rational understanding; and, secondly, specific evaluations are grounded in facts in the sense of the "natures" of the beings involved and the "consequences" of the various courses of action. Even more importantly, however, given this rational account of value, metaethics can now not only consistently issue in a normative ethics (which is its natural *telos*) but also in a program of social action in which an attempt can be made to secure responsible values by nurturing those critical dispositions required for making intelligent moral judgment. This, of course, is the theoretical foundation of Dewey's interest in education.

Not only does the pragmatic account provide for this possibility, but Dewey characterizes philosophy itself as the actualization thereof. Philosophy is defined in *Experience and Nature* as "the rational criticism of value":

> The effort to make our desires, our strivings and our ideals (which are as natural to man as his aches and his clothes) articulate, to define them in terms of inquiry into conditions and consequences is what I have called criticism; and when this is carried on in the grand manner, we have philosophy.

As our immediate values and those of our society become problematic either because of conflict or novel situations, critical judgment is called forth; and philosophy, for Dewey, is nothing but this critical function become aware of itself and pursued deliberately and systematically.

Given this conception of philosophy, its entrance into the public arena is not only natural but necessary. Philosophy's primary responsibility is the ongoing criticism of the value structure of society so that valuation can be carried on in an increasingly critical and responsible fashion. The public character of this conception of philosophy was manifest not only in Dewey's own activism but in that of Holmes, Frankfurter, Brandeis, and others who shared some of these convictions. In classical pragmatism there was the hope that reason could give one some leverage in the realm of value and that a better society could be built.

b) *Positivism on "Facts" and "Values."* While the pragmatic position thus sketched has a certain attractive sweep about it, there is something discomforting about the circularity and blurred edges that characterize a position that so interrelates facts and values. We seem naturally to want our descriptions to be more straightforward and our evaluations to be more special. It is not surprising, then, that classical pragmatism gave way to a philosophic outlook that provided just such clarity and distinctness. For the positivistically inspired philosophies from the 1930's through the 1950's factual claims were thought to be simply descriptive and value claims to be in no way logically tied to facts. I would now like to look at some features of these theories of knowledge and valuation and their practical implications.

For the positivists "knowing" had to be a far more structured activity than it seemed to be for the pragmatists. The pragmatic account, they felt, may well have adequately captured the way in which inquiry actually goes on, but surely it had missed the philosophic point of explicating the manner in which reliable knowledge is ultimately grounded. If all knowledge was mediated as the pragmatists supposed, then no knowledge would ever have a firm foundation and we could never distinguish reality from illusion. Accordingly, the positivists set about exhibiting the foundations of empirical knowledge.

Certainly most of our beliefs about the world are justified by reference to other beliefs, but it is here argued that if there is to be any genuine knowledge at all there must be some self-authenticating instances of knowledge which epistemically ground the whole edifice. This position can be seen to involve three distinct claims: 1) there are self-authenticating, noninferential pieces of factual knowledge; 2) these privileged instances can be incorrigibly recognized as such; and 3) it is these instances which must ground other more complex knowledge claims. Moreover, it is important that these basic facts be captured in simple descriptions for their necessary incorrigibility would be compromised by any evaluative component.

The fundamental facts that this tradition turns to are the data of sense, data which can be simply and incorrigibly captured in observation sentences. Here finally we have facts which are both simple and pure, that is, which are untainted both by higher-order inferences and by evaluative stances. Herein lies the epistemological foundation of empirical knowledge and the ultimate ground of our rational understanding of the world.

Our value claims, however, are another matter. They don't seem to rest on any such foundation and thus are really of a quite different sort. They are not factual at all, but either emotive or prescriptive. When one says "this is good" or "this is right" he is merely expressing his approval or maybe making a recommendation. It would be misleading to think that there were facts which could render these valuations right or wrong, or even that valuations in general were the kinds of claims that could be right or wrong. Truth and falsity are properties of factual propositions, and evaluative propositions are of a totally different class.

This view of valuation has important practical consequences. The nexus between metaethics and normative ethics seems to have been severed. While metaethics as a rational enterprise is certainly intact, the attempt to provide rational standards for our actions in the world has been short-circuited. The notions of evidence and rational warrant seem to be inappropriate given that the realm of values is simply a matter of emotions and commands.

Even more concretely, given this view of value, one would expect philosophy in general to become quite removed from the public arena. Philosophy might be able to clarify man's moral situation logically, but it really could contribute nothing existentially. It was not reason but rhetoric that characterized normative discourse. Philosophy in this period took a speculative turn and had little to say to what Dewey termed "the problems of men."

c) *Reassertion of Pragmatic Themes.* The philosophical temper of the 1960's and the 1970's can be aptly described as a reaction against the positivistically inspired fact-value dichotomy and a return to some distinctively pragmatic themes. The normative component in factual inquiry is recognized, and in the moral order a new rationalism seems to be on the ascendancy. I would now like to look more closely at both sides of this contemporary reintegration of facts and values.

Most contemporary philosophers reject positivism's account of the way in which knowledge is grounded and actually grows. There seem to be no such things as pure observation or neutral description, so the whole foundation image of knowledge must be a myth. Theories in some sense precede observation. Intelligent observation is always under the guidance of some hypothesis which directs our attention by specifying what we are to look for, by specifying what is to count as a fact. An indispensable part is played in the business of knowing by background information already achieved. More specifically, this background provides norms which bear on how a given inquiry ought to be conducted, and even material principles which specify what kinds of things are relevant to the investigation. These norms transcend the individual inquirer and are embedded in the inquiring community of the time. The illusion of brute facticity has come from too individualistic a conception of knowing. The normative ingredient in understanding has its primary locus in the community, and it might even be said that it is the community which is really the logical subject of knowledge.

There is, of course, nothing sacrosanct about any given background theory and the norms it contains; they are fallible, and as a result understanding is always subject to radical corrigibility. It would be illusory to think that we could ever get behind this relatively *a priori* structure to get at the "facts themselves," although we do have reason to believe that even these regulative principles will undergo correction through time. But this is in no sense irrationalism. Rather, on this account, "what it is to be rational" has itself undergone modification.

This conception of rationality having been adopted, valuation does not seem to be such a terribly foreign matter. Evaluation and description are no longer diametrically opposed for we have seen that there is a necessary evaluative element even in the process of description and explanation. Moreover, on the other side of the ledger, there again seem to be two senses in which the evaluative process proper (specifically, moral judgments) can be seen to be rational.

In the first place, there is a structural similarity between the process of understanding and the process of evaluation. Just as one can speak of "the cognitive point of view" as being social in nature and involving a commitment to a certain set of rules and norms, so one can speak of "the moral point of view" as similarly structured. Certainly there is a difference between our moral notions and what we might call our descriptive notions, but the difference does not consist in the latter being rationally ordered whereas the former are not. The difference is material, and consists in the sense in which our moral notions are intimately tied up with our conception of ourselves as members of a community of ends and not simply a community of inquirers.

Secondly, there is a sense in which facts are relevant to the determination of the truth or falsity of our moral judgments. While it does seem true that no set of factual statements will entail a normative claim, nonetheless it does seem equally true that there is a wider sense of "warrant" in which factual claims can warrant normative conclusions. If this is the case, there is once again room for rational argument about normative matters and, accordingly, the reentrance of philosophy into the public arena. This would account for the public phenomena with which I began this paper.

In summary, if my reading of the contemporary scene is correct, philosophy seems to have taken a decided turn toward the concrete and toward "the problems of men" so characteristic of Deweyean pragmatism. And my thesis is that there is a rationale of a philosophical nature underlying this shift in attitude. But, of course, I am not talking about a simple return to classical pragmatism. We can never really go back again. To make this clear I was tempted to use the title "The Dialectical Development of American Philosophy." Feeling, however, that this would promise more intelligibility than I was prepared to impart (or history likely to sustain), I chose the more modest phrase "changing temper." Nonetheless, my description of the American scene may be seen by the more metaphysically flamboyant to reveal a certain dialectical structure. The change that I do see in contemporary American philosophy can be viewed as a return at a higher level of synthesis to the pragmatic perspective. This new pragmatism bears the stamp of and has profited immeasurably from the rigorous philosophizing of the intervening years.

Science and Technology

A New Age in Science and Technology?

Michael J. Crowe

ARE we now in, or entering into, a new age? Is this a revolutionary period in the history of man? This paper will consider these questions, especially as they relate to science and technology.

Consider the following statements, all of which cite evidence in support of the thesis that a new age is upon us.

I. "Eighty per cent of the scientists who have ever lived are alive today."

II. "Most of what is now known in science has been learned within living memory."

III. "The new age has dawned in mathematics; an astronomical problem which a century ago required several months from several eminent mathematicians has been solved by a contemporary mathematician using the superior methods of the present in one hour."

IV. "Not only has science changed in content; it has changed its very nature. The scientist is no longer a truth seeker; rather he is a person who devises elaborate and even artificially created hypotheses and models and of these he asks only that they work."

V. "The world did not [just] double or treble its movement in the last century . . . but, measured by any standard known to science—by horsepower, calories, volts, mass in any shape—the vibration and so-called progression of society are fully a thousand times greater now than a century ago."

VI. "A new book, telling a tale that cannot but stir the imagination, has just appeared; it tells of man voyaging, not on uncharted seas, but to the moon."

VII. "We have seen the unleashing of a force so powerful that 100,-000 men succumbed from it in a single city; it is not difficult to conceive of one-fourth of the world's population suffering the same fate."

VIII. "It was a town of red brick, or of brick that would have been red if the smoke and ashes had allowed it; but as matters stood it was a town of unnatural red and black. . . . It was a town of machinery and tall chimneys, out of which interminable serpents of smoke trailed themselves for ever and ever, and never got uncoiled. It had a black canal in it, and a river that ran purple with ill-smelling dye . . . ."

IX. "The pollution and carnage on our roads has reached ghastly proportions. In New York City alone our main means of transportation expels three million pounds of pollutative materials every day and the nation-wide death toll on our roads is at 25.5 persons killed per hundred million miles."

X. "This book unlike so many others does not consider the past or the present; rather it looks in a direction too long neglected: it studies the future."

Anyone who has read at all widely in the many recent works arguing the "new age" thesis will recognize that statements similar to the above occur very frequently as evidence in those writings. The conclusion that is drawn from them is that a new and revolutionary age is upon us. These statements will count as evidence in this paper as well but in a very different way. An excess of boldness might tempt this writer to the surprising claim that these statements cited as proof for the "new age" thesis prove in fact its *opposite*. My claim however will be more modest: I shall show that these statements *fail as evidence* for the new age thesis. But before doing this a concession and a distinction are necessary. The concession is that though statements *very similar* to the above 10 statements can be found in current "new age" literature, none of the statements is from that literature; the important reason for this will be made clear in what follows. The distinction has to do with how the significance of statements depends very largely on their contexts. The cry "There is blood on your hands!" certainly has significance if you are a lawyer, baker, or candlestick maker. But if your occupation be butchery or surgery, then the statement loses nearly all its meaning for bloody hands are the rule, not the exception, in those occupations.

Similarly the above 10 statements function as evidence only if an additional (but usually only implied) statement is joined to them. That statement is that the conditions presented in each statement are now, and *only* now, in existence. My argument shall be that no such additional statement can be accurately joined to any of the original 10 statements. Indeed I shall show that all 10 could have been made, or in many cases were made, a half century or more in the past. The statements may have then little more claim on our attention than bloody hands would have to a Macbeth who worked in a butcher shop.

Statement I is true; however it has been true since 1750 or thereabouts. As Derek Price has shown in his *Little Science, Big Science,* it could have been made with accuracy in any year for the last 220 years for in any one of those years 80 per cent of the scientists who had lived up to that year were alive in that year. While many "new age" books use statement I as evidence, so far as I know Price's book is the only one to include this all-important qualification and Professor Price includes it to show that his argument does *not* depend on this invalid use of statistics.

Statement II is derived from statement I and is thus at best no stronger than it. It is however probably weaker for the rate at which *fundamental* discoveries have occurred does not even approach the exponential curve of number of scientists *versus* time. And one would assume that statement II refers primarily to fundamental discoveries of high generality.

Statement III is not about some recent advance in computer technology; it is, rather, a paraphrase of a statement made in 1897 by Florian Cajori concerning an advance made by Gauss in the first half of the 19th century. Cajori wrote:

> In 1735 the solving of an astronomical problem, proposed by the Academy, for which several eminent mathematicians had demanded several months' time, was achieved in three days by Euler [d. 1783] with aid of improved methods of his own. . . . With still superior methods this same problem was solved by the illustrious Gauss [d. 1855] in one hour.[1]

The wonderful timesaving characteristics of recent computers, the ancestry of which may be traced back to the 17th century, should not lead us to forget that the computer is but one of many methods developed throughout history which have facilitated and quickened computation or that each of these methods has in its age evoked expressions of wonder.

Statement IV certainly represents one view, if not the dominant one, of current scientific activity; many contemporary science books surprise readers by such statements. But this view of science comes as no surprise to anyone with a knowledge of ancient science for this was the view of science taken by many ancient scientists, for example, Eudoxus in the fourth century B.C. and Ptolemy in the second century A.D. This view is then essentially as old as science and is one perennial view of the nature of scientific method.[2]

---

[1] Florian Cajori, *History of Mathematics,* as quoted in Robert Moritz, ed., *On Mathematics and Mathematicians* (New York: Dover Publications, 1942), p. 155.

[2] For detailed evidence, see my "A Prevalent and Significant Misconception

Statement V reproduces with only slight alterations a statement, referring to the 19th century, made in 1909 by Henry Adams.[3] Numerous similar statements will be found in the final chapters of that distinguished historian's *The Education of Henry Adams;* moreover it is not insignificant that Lynn White, Jr., has recently shown that the most famous metaphor from that book—the Virgin as an image of the Middle Ages contrasted with the Dynamo as an image of modern times—so understates medieval man's concern with technology that any historian, and especially one who wrote *Mont-Saint-Michel and Chartres,* should have been restless with it.[4]

Statement VI seems to refer to one of the many recent books recounting the voyage to the moon of the astronauts, perhaps Norman Mailer's *Of a Fire on the Moon.* Professor Thomas Werge has shown in his paper (included in the present collection) that certain themes in that book have their roots in early American literature. Hardly less surprising is that recent "voyage to the moon" books represent no new genre; in fact, Marjorie Hope Nicolson in her excellent *Voyages to the Moon* discussed the numerous (50 plus) books in this genre published before 1800.

Statement VII may seem to refer to atomic weaponry which did kill 100,000 persons at Hiroshima and could at some future day destroy one-fourth of the world's population; it does however refer in a stronger sense to the Black Plague which, as Boccaccio reminds us, killed 100,000 persons in Florence in 1348, and which medical historians have shown did in fact destroy one-fourth of the world's population in the 14th century. We may live in fear of massive atomic destruction but the newness in this consists not in the fear but in the source of that fear, for throughout most of recorded history men have had grounds for fearing, and have feared, widespread destruction through plagues, fires, tornadoes, earthquakes, and other phenomena.

Statement VIII is a direct and unaltered quotation, not however from a recent work, but rather from a book published in 1854 by an early critic of industrial society, Charles Dickens; his novel

---

about Science in Antiquity," *Bulletin of the Albertus Magnus Guild,* 9 (1962), 1-4.

[3] For the original statement, see Arthur M. Schlesinger, Jr., "The Velocity of History," *Newsweek,* July 6, 1970, p. 32.

[4] See Lynn White, Jr., *Machina ex Deo: Essays in the Dynamism of Western Culture* (Cambridge, Mass.: MIT Press, 1968), pp. 57-73.

Hard Times used those words to describe the conditions of Coke-
town (presumably Manchester). This passage may remind us that
though "smog" is a recent term, it names an old phenomenon.
Lynn White, Jr., notes that London in 1285 suffered from smog produced by the burning of soft coal.[5] The same point is made by
geological studies which show that the single greatest source of
present-day air pollution is volcanoes. On a more general level
Edward C. Banfield's recent *The Unheavenly City* shows us the
dangers of discussing most urban problems without the benefit of
historical perspective.[6]

Statement IX, which may seem to be about our present-day
megahorsepowered automobiles as well as the pollution and the
death rate produced by them, actually refers not to the automobile
but to the "main means of transportation" around 1900—the horse.
The three million pounds per day of pollutative materials expelled
on New York City streets consisted of horse manure (2½ million
pounds) and urine (60,000 gallons). The 25.5 deaths per hundred million miles is the National Safety Council's estimated fatality
rate for turn-of-the-century horse travel; not insignificantly, the
current fatality rate is less than one-tenth of that.[7] It is thus not
surprising that early 20th-century Americans welcomed the automobile because of its cleanliness and safety.

Statement X, parallels to which could be found in many of the
growing number of recent books on futurology, has parallels in the
past as well. Many current futurologists write in seeming ignorance
of the past of futurology. This is not however the case for Daniel
Bell who has pointed out that about half a century ago 80-some
works on futurology appeared.[8] Possibly some future historian
will trace the past of futurology.

Thus each of the above 10 statements put forth on behalf of
the "new age" thesis fails as evidence. It would be excessive to
argue that the above analysis refutes the "new age" thesis for in

---

[5] *Ibid.*, p. 78.

[6] Part of Banfield's thesis is summed up in his statement: "The plain fact
is that the overwhelming majority of city dwellers live more comfortably and
conveniently than ever before. . . . What is more, there is every reason to expect
that the general level of comfort and convenience will continue to rise at an
even more rapid rate through the foreseeable future." Edward C. Banfield, *The
Unheavenly City* (Boston: Little, Brown, 1968), pp. 3-4.

[7] This information is given in *Newsweek*, March 6, 1972, p. 69.

[8] Daniel Bell, "Introduction," in Herman Kahn and Anthony J. Wiener,
The Year 2000 (New York: Macmillan, 1967), p. xxi.

general refutation of the evidence (or part thereof) for a statement does not necessarily refute the statement. Nor is it my intention to refute the "new age" thesis; rather, my intention in the above, as well as in what follows, has been to examine this thesis, especially as it relates to science and technology, from a number of different points of view and to provide a sort of prolegomenon to a consideration of the thesis by means of a critical study of it as well as of its arguments and entailments. This may contribute to propounding the thesis on grounds less open to question, or to a rejection, partial or full, of the thesis.

What Conditions Must the "New Age" Thesis Satisfy?

Any thesis similar to the "new age" thesis must satisfy certain minimal conditions if it is to be acceptable. Certainly the thesis must be clearly and precisely stated; this entails specifying that 1) major and unprecedented changes have occurred and that 2) these changes have occurred in a relatively short time period. While these conditions are minimal, few of the proponents of the "new age" thesis meet them. We are rarely told, for example, when the "new age" begins. This can be convenient for it allows wide latitude in deciding what evidence is relevant. But this liberality may come at the price of making the thesis a truism. Truisms are invulnerable but impotent; they cannot be effectively attacked for no one doubts them nor can they tell us anything new or significant for everyone knows them. Who, for example, would deny that major changes have occurred in the recent past if by recent past is meant the period from 1850 to the present?

"New age" theorists invariably discuss major changes but they do not invariably recognize that there are different types of major changes, some of which have more or less significance for "new age" theses. Major changes are of at least three types: 1) gradual but cumulative; 2) revolutionary—as when one idea, system, or government replaces another; 3) nonrevolutionary but epoch-making. The "straw that broke the camel's back" was a change of the first type; it was part of a gradual yet cumulative process that produced a result of significance. The fact, cited by Daniel Bell, that in 1956 white-collar workers came to outnumber blue-collar workers in this country represents a change of this type.[9] The second type

---

9 Daniel Bell, "Notes on the Post-Industrial Society," in Jack D. Douglas,

of change involves a period of forceful contention between two groups, usually with some form of violence being present. The terms "French Revolution," "Copernican Revolution," and "Darwinian Revolution" are certainly appropriate, though in general the term "revolution" is overused, usually by applying it to the first or third type of major change. The third type may however go unrecognized even though such changes may at times be more significant than "revolutionary" changes. Three of the most crucial changes in 19th-century scientific thought were of the third type: atomic theory, non-Euclidean geometry, and spectrum analysis. In each of these cases a new theory arose that did not contend with a previous theory but nevertheless each theory issued in a new era.[10]

Concerning these three types of changes, it should be observed that the second—revolutionary changes—tends for better or worse to count more heavily as evidence for "unique epoch" theses. The first type, being gradual, tends to be less impressive and becomes impressive chiefly when viewed as a symbol. Thus Bell cites 1956 as a "symbolic turning point." The invisibility as well as the significance of the first type of change was noted by Paul Valéry when he stated:

> There is nothing easier than to point out the absence, from history books, of major phenomena which were imperceptible owing to the slowness of their evolution. They escape the historian's notice because no document expressly mentions them. . . .
>
> An event which takes shape over a century will not be found in any document or collection of memoirs. . . .[11]

The third type of change also tends to be less visible than the second for no highly visible period of contention surrounds its appearance. Moreover the third type of change may occur most frequently in the realm of ideas and especially in science and technology. The chief point to be made here is that "new age" theses may, by focusing too heavily on revolutionary changes, blind us to changes of possibly greater significance but less visibility—the first and third

---

ed., *The Technological Threat* (Englewood Cliffs, N.J.: Prentice Hall, 1971), p. 11.

[10] I have suggested at greater length the importance of such changes in my "Science a Century Ago" in Frederick J. Crosson, ed., *Science in Contemporary Society* (Notre Dame, Ind.: University of Notre Dame Press, 1967), pp. 122-126.

[11] As quoted in Bell, "Notes," p. 8.

types. Moreover if the first and third types are of low visibility but sometimes of great importance, it makes clear why frequent disputes occur as to whether a certain age is unique. This can also help explain why it is possible for "new ages" to be created, not by changes in themselves, but by persons arguing "new ages" into existence for various reasons. For example there is little reason to believe that major changes have a tendency to occur around century years, for instance, 1900. But there is certainly an increased tendency for persons to raise the "new age" thesis at such times. Well over 100 papers and books appeared between 1895 and 1910 surveying the development of science and technology during the 19th century and many of these writings propounded "new age" theses. Similarly we have just passed a major divide; in 1967 we had come two-thirds of the way to the 21st century and were approaching the end of the second millennium since the birth of Christ, the year 2000.

Some Dangers in and from "New Age" Theses

As man attempts to locate himself in time, to see his relationships to the past and the future, at least two pitfalls face him. He may see his era as in all ways similar to the past—there is nothing new under the sun. Such a position may lead to apathy or neglect of present concerns. But a greater danger stands at the opposite pole; so powerfully does the present bid for our attention that we all too easily succumb to what Arthur Lovejoy has called presenticentricism—seeing the present only within the context of a superficial and naive view of the past. This error can all too easily lead us to see our age as the greatest of ages, or, as is more common, as the worst. The error of presenticentricism, especially in its "worst of times" aspect, may be the great danger of the present; so at least Daniel J. Boorstin has forcefully argued. He warns that we are being victimized by a debilitating sickness of epidemic proportions and in regard to which we stubbornly refuse the only proven remedy. The disease that besets us is hypochondria; the cure is history. Boorstin suggests that our imprisonment in the present, reinforced by current "instruments of education, of information, and of 'progress' "

> . . . tempts us to a morbid preoccupation with ourselves, and so induces hypochondria. . . .
> We will not be on the way to curing our national hypochondria

until we first accept the unfashionable possibility that many of our national ills are imaginary and that others may not be as serious as we imagine. Unless we begin to believe that we won't be dead before morning, we may not be up to the daily tasks of a healthy life.[12]

The dangers in this regard are serious for we all too frequently employ a mode of thinking comparable to the train company that, upon finding that train wrecks usually most severely damaged the last car, decided henceforth to remove the last car from its trains. If we define the state of poverty as the condition of those whose incomes are in the lowest 20 per cent, then we cannot, by definition, ever solve or even progress in solving the poverty problem. The remedy proposed by Boorstin to cure such thinking is history, especially of a broadened scope. He sees history as no panacea, but he suggests that if "history cannot give us panaceas, it is the best possible cure of the yen for panaceas. And the only proven antidote for utopianism."[13]

Many of the proponents of the "new age" thesis are also futurists. The futurist, as everyone else, has a natural tendency to overestimate the brightness or the darkness of the future. Examples of the first are sufficiently rare that the two examples I have selected may be pardoned, for what they lack in suitability, they make up for in delightfulness. The first is a spoof from Elaine May and Mike Nichols who contributed to *Look* along with other celebrities their prophecy of the future by writing:

> By 1987, the world will be at peace. Those forces that have been so expensively and successfully developed for destructive purposes will have been converted toward peaceful and constructive ends. There will be no more disease, no more tyranny, no more graft, no more suspicion, no more poverty, no more war—and we are the Andrews Sisters.[14]

The second "great future" prophecy comes from Alvin Toffler's *Future Shock;* I hope it is a spoof but it occurs in the midst of a

---

[12] Daniel J. Boorstin, "A Case of Hypochondria," *Newsweek,* July 6, 1970, p. 27.

[13] *Ibid.,* p. 29. Boorstin might have added "and for antiutopianism."

[14] As quoted in William H. Honan, "They Live in the Year 2000," in Wilbert E. Moore, ed., *Technology and Social Change* (Chicago: Quadrangle Books, 1972), p. 152.

serious discussion of breeding possibilities for humans. Toffler wrote: "We will be able to create sexual super-athletes, girls with super-mammaries (and perhaps more or less than the standard two). . . ."[15]

Examples of dire prophecies are easily found, at least if John Maddox is to be believed. In an article entitled "The Doomsday Men" Maddox wrote:

> The men who used to parade in Oxford Street with sandwich boards announcing that THE END OF THE WORLD IS AT HAND! have long since been snatched away by the demands of full or relatively full employment. There are times when their place seems to have been taken by a group of writers and talkers who proclaim that the cataclysm round the corner will be brought about by the consequences of modern technology.

He blames the United States for much of the recent "Doomsday literature" and cites Toffler's *Future Shock* as a prime example. Toffler, Maddox states,

> . . . sets out in the best Puritan tradition to scare people out of their wits and then to tell them that disaster may be avoided first of all by halting "the runaway acceleration that is subjecting multitudes to the threat of future shock" and then, at greater deliberation, by setting up a variety of social institutions that make the cure seem even more dreadful than the disease.[16]

This may overstate the case, but, as Toffler notes, "Self-indulgent despair is a highly salable literary commodity today."[17]

Dangers exist not only *in* futurology, but also *from* futurology. These should be considered but only after the qualification has been made that many futurologists are cautious and balanced in their predictions and wise in looking toward future developments. Victor K. Ferkiss in his *Technological Man* has effectively warned us of some of these dangers by writing:

> Millenarian ideas have a special kind of consequence. Those who believe that vast changes are about to occur can be pardoned for paying less attention to the minor, because passing, problems of the present . . . .

---

[15] Alvin Toffler, *Future Shock* (New York: Random House, 1970), p. 201.
[16] John Maddox, "The Doomsday Men," *Encounter*, January, 1971, pp. 65, 64-65.
[17] Toffler, *op. cit.*, pp. 372-373.

Thus those who are convinced that a radical change is taking place in human society as a result of technological progress are often wont to denigrate the problems of the present, or at least to lead others to do so.

After pointing out how an overconcern with the future—or the "myth of the future"—could well direct one from such problems as racism in this country or the depressed living conditions in the Third World, he notes:

This is not to say that the myth of the future is deliberately culti-vated in order to divert attention from the day-to-day problems of the present. . . . The futurists are by and large sensitive and moral men deeply concerned at a certain level of existence with today's mundane problems. But futurism has a natural tendency to dis-orient its adherents and sympathizers, focusing their attention on what is to come (in most cases with a certain presumed degree of inevitability) rather than on what is.[18]

Another danger of the writings of the futurologists, which Ferkiss does not mention, has its source in a subtle aspect of their presenta-tions. Understanding and perceiving this danger turns on the dis-tinction between normative and descriptive statements. Statements of the form "X is Y" are usually descriptive. Thus the sentences "food tastes good" or "a car is coming" only describe a state of affairs. But compare these sentences with the formally similar but actually very different sentences: "Winstons taste good . . ." and "There is a Ford in Your Future." The latter two sentences are not primarily descriptive; their main content is normative; they tell us to purchase these items but do so in a nonintimidating manner. Rhetoricians have long known that sentences of an overtly descriptive form can appear concrete, certain, and convincing in a way that overtly normative statements cannot. This realization presumably stands behind the utopias of Plato, More, and Skinner and the antiutopias of Swift, Huxley, and Orwell.

The same principle frequently operates in futurist writings: apparently descriptive statements operate in normative ways. This is but to say that some of the statements of futurists, as well as "new age" theorists, can act as self-fulfilling prophecies. Alvin Toffler's prediction that we shall soon find ourselves suffering from "future

---

[18] Victor K. Ferkiss, *Technological Man* (New York: Braziller, 1969), pp. 26, 27.

shock" may turn out to be correct only because his seemingly descriptive statements may work normatively on his readers and induce future shock symptoms.

Effects of great significance can be produced in this way. Students of revolutions have now abandoned the view that conditions directly cause revolutions. It is now clear that for a group to revolt it need only have apparently oppressive conditions, combined with heightened expectations of better times to come. These rising expectations, if not soon fulfilled, may bring on the revolution. This is but to say that a major factor influencing man's future is his concept of the future.

Another danger associated with futurology and with the futurological aspects of "new age" theses is well known to those who have studied the history of astrology or of the Delphic oracle. Correct prophecies are more frequently remembered than those that fail and the prophet may thus receive greater credit than he deserves. Recall the French proverb: "Even a broken clock is right twice a day." We tend to forget that Simon Newcomb predicted that "Flying Machines" were impossible and that Leverrier predicted not only Neptune (found) but also Vulcan (nonexistent), and that Lord Rutherford predicted that mankind would never be able to release the energy of the atom. Looking carefully and fully at the past of futurology may save us from unrealistic expectation.

Conclusion

Are we now in, or entering into, a new age, especially in regard to science and technology? Rather than answer that large question, I have at most sketched out what an answer could and should look like. Science and technology are currently experiencing a great age as well as a not unprecedented criticism from many directions. Much of that criticism neglects a distinction that, if neglected, bodes ill for our future. Science and especially technology are frequently taken to mean the products of science and technology—from the transistor radio to the atomic bomb. But science and technology are also systems of exciting and enriching ideas that will not of themselves pollute or corrupt or dehumanize. Should our future not find a place for the vital and awe-inspiring ideas of science and technology, then our future shall be poorer for it.

But our future must find room for more than this: we must not only learn *in* science and technology but also *about* science and technology. And until the recent past little research has been directed to this area. If we cannot assess with confidence the role of science and technology in present or future society, it should not surprise us for we have not as yet been able to assess their role in any past society. The conceptual tools necessary for such analyses are scarcely advanced beyond the primitive stage and detailed research exists on only a few topics, for example, the Copernican revolution and the history and influence of the stirrup. But in the last two decades major improvements have begun to come in such areas and perhaps in some future decade a more adequate picture of our present or the present of the future may be drawn.

Mendelian Evolution and Mandalian Involution: Speculations About the Foundations of Cultural Change

Thomas J. Musial and Julian R. Pleasants

YOU must pardon our audacity in presuming to say anything of substance about the foundations of cultural change in such brief space. Our apology for undertaking such a task lies in part in our spirit of adventure, and in part in our qualified intention to be suggestive rather than comprehensive. We are not aiming at conclusive scientific or scholarly documentation. We are being speculative, as scientists and scholars are sometimes prone to be when they are away from the laboratory or library, or when they are nagged by some of the nettlesome questions they feel compelled to come to terms with as men, but which professional prudence generally forbids them to talk about in formal conference or print. We would also like to make public our belief in the deep friendship between the sciences and humanities by unabashedly talking to each other in public, proclaiming common interests in common problems, and suggesting that in collaboration we will find the best basis to our problems' solution.

Our thinking about the basis of cultural change began in a discussion of Carl Jung's *Memories, Dreams, Reflections* with three colleagues in architecture and the engineering sciences at a 1971 summer workshop in the humanities at Notre Dame. We were exploring Jung's claim that "our souls as well as our bodies are composed of individual elements which were all already present in the ranks of our ancestors," and that "the 'newness' in the individual psyche is an endlessly varied recombination of age-old components." As we will indicate later, such a claim opens up surprising possibilities in the light of the principles of Mendelian genetics and Neo-Darwinian evolution, even though it might strike many an educated person as an unsupportable claim.

Actually, Jung was trying to establish a theory about psychological evolution. He was arguing that despite man's presumed 20th-century sophistication, man is psychologically still pretty close to classical antiquity and the Middle Ages—if not, in fact, just a thin veneer of civilization away from primitivity. Jung was making a case for the historical roots of body and soul, and for the way

154

violent departures from one's past give rise to the "discontents" of civilization. He was calling attention to the psychological dangers of cultural uprootedness. He was chiding man for rushing impetuously into novelty, driven by a mounting sense of insufficiency, dissatisfaction, and restlessness. He was trying to indicate that wholesale societal reform by mere new methods or gadgets is dubious, dearly paid for, and, on the whole, grossly inadequate to satisfy a man's fundamental peace or happiness. He concluded that "inner peace and contentment depend in large measure upon whether or not the historical family which is inherent in the individual can be harmonized with the ephemeral conditions of the present."[1]

Jung's position prompted considerable discussion and created a frame of reference which we found of inestimable value in developing our position on different aspects of cultural change. We believe that what we have to say is pertinent to any discussion of cultural change and thus of general concern to all who enter into discussion on matters relating to this topic. We believe that our remarks will provide a possible basis for understanding whether our country is currently experiencing a decisive cultural change, not experiencing such a change, or whether it is about to experience such a change in the near future. Whatever one's position might be on this issue, we would like to suggest that certain models of biological change may be used for their heuristic value in understanding the very principles of cultural change. Thus we see our essay as a prolegomenon to the whole question of cultural change.

First it is necessary to have a frame of reference with respect to the use of the term culture, for there are different uses of the word and the different uses correspond to different notions of what culture is. The distinctions that we would like to make roughly correspond to the differences between the natural sciences, the social sciences, and the humanities as areas of study. It is possible to speak of *a culture,* as the natural scientists do; *cultures* as the social scientists do; and *culture* as the students and purveyors of the humanities do.

For the natural scientist, a culture is essentially an enhanced process of growth, proliferation, or increase. It is the manifestation of vigorous life; it is production, incremental development;

---

[1] C. G. Jung, *Memories, Dreams, Reflections* (New York: Vintage, 1961), pp. 235-236.

organic increase in magnitude or quantity. In this sense, the term culture is related to its fellow term "cultivate" as it involves the literal and physical husbanding of the soil or plant or animal life so that there might be an abundance of whatever organic matter is to be multiplied in a way that is most conducive to its multiplication. In this sense of the term we can speak of the culture of grass, corn, mosquitos, bees, or the cultured pearls of oysters. We can also speak of the work of Beadle and Tatum who utilized cultures of the mold *Neurospora crassa* to study the relationships between genes and enzymes, or the work of Lederberg who used cultures of the intestinal bacterium *Escherichia coli* to study the genetic constitution of one of the few bacteria in which sexual recombination has been demonstrated.

For the social scientist, culture is the interplay of human attitudes, values, customs, and institutions, as reflected in the observable behavior of a given people. In this sense, we speak of culture in the plural, and we identify African cultures, preliterate cultures, Eskimo culture, the culture of the inner city, Mediaeval culture, or the culture of Smalltown, U.S.A. Through the social sciences, we have been able to learn of countless observable and definable combinations of human attitudes, values, customs, and institutions. Insofar as each of these is definable, it is possible to speak generically about different cultures, and more specifically, about corresponding subcultures. The social sciences, however, possibly because they are descriptive rather than normative, refrain from any account of a "locus" in "the nature of human beings" which is the basis for normative value formation or any essential "givens" of man's spiritual, intellectual, social, or physical life which account for the observable behavioral consistency and diversity in human activity. Such a normative study of man is the province of the humanities and gives us our third concept of culture.

In the humanities, culture is a refined human ideal that embraces the whole nature of man. It is the legacy of those human achievements which give us a basis for understanding man's various and possible perfections. The humanist's view of culture is not a scientific knowledge to be gained, but a wisdom to be acquired. The wisdom honors facts, but within the purview of overriding values — values, moreover, which go beyond the particular beliefs, attitudes, customs, or institutions of any given person or society in any given time. In this frame of reference, language, art, religion, literature, and philosophy seek to give intelligibility, meaning, and purpose to the life of *Man,* a being with an essentially unchanging nature. Thus the poetry of Homer, the sayings of Buddha, the philosophy of Aristotle, the theology of the Church Fathers, the teachings of Mohammed, the architecture of the Gothic cathedrals, the discipline of Zen, the symphonies of Beethoven, the novels of Dostoevsky, the thoughts of Gandhi, and the essays of Ortega y Gasset furnish instances of culture as human ideals — models which serve the purposes of education by providing examples of refined or heightened achievement of mind, imagination, taste, pleasurable sensation, or style. Such models help discerning men to understand what is good, and thus how best to live a rewarding life.

It is important to speak of these three different conceptions of culture in view of the general agreement of natural scientists, social scientists, and humanists that man is an intelligent, social animal. Indeed, he lives his life in each of these modalities. Because he is intelligent, he exercises his reason and imagination in such a way as to develop a *quality* of living. In this sense, man lives in a world that is directed by his intelligence. He dreams, and hopes, and formulates ideals. He celebrates life in art and ritual. He derives moral standards. He accounts for the ultimate ground of his being in terms of religion and metaphysics — and not always as a mere abstraction, but usually in some form of living relationship with his God.

Because his daily actions take on the form of specific relationships with others, man can be studied as a social being. He works, he spends money, he marries, he organizes institutions, he goes to war. He raises a family, he provides food for his young, he participates in group customs, he develops manners (ways of doing things), and, in general, interacts in a variety of social, psychological, political, and economic ways with other men.

Because he is a biological organism, there are a number of "givens" that determine the physical limits of his abilities within which he must live. Human customs, institutions, and styles will change. In some ways, so too will ideals and values. But they can only change within the framework of man's given morphological and genetic composition.

With these distinctions in mind, we come to our more important purpose to look at certain models of biological change for their heuristic value as they suggest principles of cultural change. The first biological model that we would like to cite is known by the technical term *succession*. The principle of succession was discovered about 75 years ago at the Indiana Dunes. It is easy to describe. For many centuries the wind and waves have been adding new land to the southern shore of Lake Michigan. Because of this, one can walk back from the beach, through a dune, to a forest. As one does this, he is, in a sense, walking backward in time as he goes from what is now bare sand, to what was once bare sand a century ago, to what was bare sand two centuries ago, to what was bare sand a thousand years ago. As he walks this distance, he is aware of a definite pattern of succession: bare beach begins to sprout dune grass; scrub cherry, pussy willow, and cottonwood intrude on the dune grass; evergreens like pine and hemlock succeed the cottonwoods; oak and hickory replace the evergreens; and finally, beech trees and maples take over to produce a majestic climax forest, like that at Warren Woods. There is a principle that becomes manifestly clear in this trip from the shoreline inland. For all the stages preceding the climax state, every form of life that succeeds another form is in turn itself succeeded by still another form. In fact, it is each form's very achievement that leads to its replacement in that locality. Succession, in this technical sense, is not the same as the succession of forms which occurs during evolution, when one species becomes another species over a tremendously long period of time. In microbial succession, for example, it may take only a few hours for the first dominant species to change the environment so much that a previously unimportant species becomes dominant. Succession means new relations of importance or dominance among already existing species.

With as much literal truth as poetic image, the first colonizers, dune grass and small shrubs, are called pioneers. In the most inhospitable of soils, bare sand, they send out hungry rootlets to seek every molecule of useful mineral. They are constantly turning air and sunshine into more rootlets which can exploit these meager resources. It is their wonderful productivity itself which brings about their replacement. Their decaying leaves and roots provide a concentration of minerals, organic matter, and moisture for plants that could not grow on bare sand, but can grow better than dune grass in the environment which the dune grass has created by its pioneer virtues. The pioneers move on, as the American pioneers did, to new land, and the second stage of succession takes over where they did their work. We acknowledge the anthropomorphic nature of the language used to describe this phenomenon. We further believe this use of language is significant in that it points to correlations between human values and how they are often derived from or reflected in biological models.

Needless to say, there are cultural implications in such a model. For now, let us simply cite one which takes some of the bitterness out of the debate over what technology has done to civilization — a theme which the countercultural exponents Theodore Roszak and Charles Reich have made most of us aware of. If we regard technology as the extension, by machines and other concentrated energy sources, of the pioneer virtues, a worthy successor to a plow that broke the plains, we can see in our principle of succession that the very success of technology is the reason why it will be succeeded by another stage which utilizes its accumulation of goods, knowledge, and method to produce another kind of life style.

This doesn't mean that succession is inevitable. Vast pine forests are often kept from going to the next stage of succession, the hardwoods, by such factors as fire and logging. These acts of man or nature periodically destroy or remove the accumulations of humus that would make life better for the hardwoods than for the pines. Analogously, and speaking of culture as the social scientists do, the technological societies, by destroying their excess productivity in war, or by exporting it to countries still in the pioneer stage, could stave off the next stage of succession until the rest of the world reaches the total utilization of the technological stage. Or one country could go ahead to the stage beyond technology even while much of the world is struggling through a difficult pretechnological pioneer stage. This possibility could be a service to the rest of the world in that the advanced country could serve as an example of a future stage of succession to the less advanced, giving the rest of the world some idea of what to expect as they approach similar stages.

Succession, then, describes the process by which a genetic or cultural diversity which has *previously evolved* can bring about rapid adaptation to a changing environment. Resources which are already present in a community or in an individual but which have been latent or playing a minor role, can assume increasingly dominant roles in the life of the community or individual. And this occurs precisely because the previously dominant trait or group, by its success in altering the environment, has made the environment unsuitable for itself and more suitable for another group. In looking at cultures the way the social scientists do, to find the life style that would be dominant in a new stage of succession, we would have to look among those cultural and genetic enclaves or individuals which were *not* successful in the present stage but may possibly have the combinations needed for success in the next stage. The assumption is that people adapted to the stages of the future already exist among us.

In raising the question of whether or not we are currently experiencing any decisive cultural change, it may also be useful to be aware that our ideas of culture themselves may be unconsciously influenced by hidden biological models, models which could be helpful to our understanding, but which could also be misunderstood and misapplied. We have already pointed out the use of anthropomorphic language in describing the principle of succession. We shall also acknowledge that the very term culture goes back to a biological, agricultural analog, even though the term is now used in different senses by the biologist, the social scientist, and the humanist. From the cultivation of crops comes the root idea that man's work in controlling the environment of a living organism can greatly enhance its ability to grow and develop and multiply. Nevertheless, it is recognized that the biological potential of the organism is a given, and that man does, in a way, place himself at the service of that given, even though to a great extent he is able to put his environment to his own use. For example, when we inoculate *Staphylococcus aureus* into a culture medium, or work out the nutritional requirements of germfree mice in order to raise them as a pure culture, we are working towards a form of life and growth which may never have been realized under natural, uncontrolled conditions, but which is still very much determined by the genetic constitution of the organisms, as well as by the environment we create.

It is clear that even in the sense in which the biologist speaks of a culture, the human race is a culture, whose growth and development and multiplication are enormously enhanced by the physical and social environment which man himself creates. But American culture in an almost unique way resembles a culture in the microbiologist's sense of the term. America started like a small inoculum placed into a tube of rich medium containing few competitiors. What followed was a rapid and relatively even expansion of many different types of Americans into the available resources. This corresponds to the logarithmic growth phase of a bacterial culture, during which period they show a characteristic morphology. Similarly, American culture shows the psychological and sociological characteristics of this virtually unlimited expansion, so that growth has become the means by which we solve or postpone all problems. The demand for rapid growth has become the dominant feature of our society, determining its economic, social, political, and international policies.

This characteristically American approach was recently expressed clearly and approvingly by the distinguished analyst of American culture, Zbigniew Brzezinski. In his *Newsweek* column (March 27, 1972), attacking the politics of zero growth, he told the American people:

> . . . economic growth is about to join science and technology as the *bête noire* of our time. It is, therefore, worthwhile to ponder briefly the likely political and international consequences if zero growth were to become the dominant outlook of a country like the United States.
>
> That inequality exists in the United States is indisputable. However, what has made inequality bearable is that in the American tradition (as well as myth) it is balanced by opportunity. Opportunity requires flexibility and mobility, and these are created by growth. Growth — through inventiveness, initiative, creativity —makes it possible for an individual to rise or at least entertain the dream of rising.
>
> Those promoting zero growth as a means of advancing egalitarianism in American society have probably not considered the degree to which American capitalism might become openly coercive without further economic growth. . . .
>
> The result would be loss of liberty and opportunity, unless one assumes that without growth the system would collapse.
>
> The other alternative for America would be stagnant socialism. Equality would be attained through massive redistribution of wealth. However, it is unlikely that massive redistribution could be attained without recourse to violence — especially if there is no compensating growth. . . .
>
> In brief, zero growth is not the solution. However, the alternative to zero growth is not massive, undirected growth, but planned, purposeful growth. We do need to define for ourselves more precisely what kind of a society we wish to build, in which direction we wish the world to head, and what ecological concerns humanity

shares in common. The answer to that will be provided, in very large measure, by further economic and scientific growth, but growth geared to more deliberately defined objectives than has been the case in the past.

In a later model, we will question the effectiveness of growth, even planned growth, as the ultimate problem solver, especially when growth is defined in purely quantitative terms, with no attempt to include growth in personal maturation, interpersonal relationships, or other qualitative changes. What is alarming is that unnecessary growth does not represent mere waste which can easily be discarded, but becomes itself another problem. It represents, rather, in terms of another biological model, a cancer which can cause the death of the organism which produces it.

We do not even need to go outside the university to see the problems created by reliance on growth to solve all problems. The universities relied on endless growth to supply their faculties with security for the old, opportunity for the young, and improved compensation and facilities for all. When an end to quantitative growth appears on the horizon, we are precipitated into a crisis which seems to have no humane solution. For example, the structure of graduate education was built on an impossible rate of exponential increase in Ph.D.'s, impossible, that is, if the function of most Ph.D.'s is to produce more Ph.D.'s. For example, Notre Dame produces new Ph.D.'s at a rate (1971) which would double the number of Ph.D.'s in three years. If only half the new Ph.D.'s become producers of more Ph.D.'s, this still means a 15 per cent annual increase in academic Ph.D.'s. At that rate, Notre Dame's progeny of Ph.D.'s would in 30 years be 66 times their present number on the faculty.

Besides this emphasis on quantitative growth, other influences of biological models have left their mark on our thinking about culture. Controversies between the social scientist and the humanist over the meaning of human culture still echo the nature-nurture controversy of early evolutionists. Some of the modern controversies seem consciously or unconsciously based on some early Darwinian ideas which have since been corrected by means of Mendelian models. The term Mendelian evolution in our title, rather than Darwinian evolution, was not chosen solely for the sake of making a pun with the term Mandalian, which we borrowed from Jung's symbol for the integrated psyche, the Mandala. The rediscovery of Mendel's laws of inheritance around 1900 constituted a revolution in evolutionary thought which nonbiologists seem to have missed.

Darwin's own theories of heredity, including a blending of maternal and paternal characteristics, and pangenesis, with its inheritance of characteristics acquired by the parents, was a mechanism so fluid that it could not have sustained evolution as we know it. Genetic characteristics have, in fact, an extraordinary stability, only occasionally changed by mutation. What Mendel and his successors did was to explain the obvious diversity among individuals in terms of new combinations of very stable, though still mutable, hereditary units. The new molecular biology has reinforced this view of relative stability by referring it to the chemical stability of DNA and the *conservative* force of natural selection with regard to successful strategies. For example, in *Scientific American* (April, 1972) R.E. Dickerson provides an easily understandable demonstration of the extraordinary stability of the gene for cytochrome c in all oxygen-using organisms. The parts of this molecule which determine its energy-producing function have not changed in an estimated 1.2 billion years. They are exactly the same in microbes and man. Other parts, which are mere filler to build up the molecule to adequate size, show changes whose number seems determined by the time elapsed since the divergence of their ancestors. Thus there are no differences even of filler parts between man and the chimpanzee, but 44 differences between man and bread mold. Nevertheless the cytochromes of man and mold will react with the enzymes of either species, for there is *no* difference in their functional parts.

Thus Mendelian genetics, unlike the genetics of Lamarck or Darwin or Lysenko, establishes a fixity in man's genetic make-up which is not absolute, but is so stable relative to cultural change that it becomes a practical fixity. It was this which Jung realized when he postulated a similar fixity of psychic elements:

> Just as the body has an anatomical prehistory of millions of years, so also does the psychic system. And just as the human body today represents in each of its parts the result of this evolution, and everywhere still shows traces of its earlier stages — so the same may be said of the psyche. Consciousness began its evolution from an animal-like state which seems to us unconscious, and the same process of differentiation is repeated in every child. The psyche of the child in its preconscious state is anything but a

tabula rasa; it is already preformed in a recognizably individual way, and is, moreover, equipped with all specifically human instincts, as well as with the a priori foundations of the higher functions.[2]

In this context, Mandalian involution would be a retracing of cultural evolution within the individual psyche, discerning there the common elements which have been inherited with virtually no change except in their combinations.

It is ironical that in 1910, John Dewey, in order to free himself from any "restraint" of transcendental determining ends (Aristotle's Εἶδος), was proclaiming evolution as the end of all fixity[3] just about the time that the laws of Mendel were demonstrating the remarkable stability of genetic units despite the great diversity of their combinations. So it seems to have happened that while Dewey was removing final determining causes as principles of stability in successive generations of biological organisms, Neo-Darwinians were establishing a pragmatic basis for this fixity by applying Mendelian concepts to the evolutionary principles of Darwin. Their studies imply a rate of mutation and selection so slow in the genetic factors that affect human experience as to give no evidence of significant differences in the various ways men have experienced reality within the few thousand years of recorded history.[4] Twentieth-century cultural experience seems to confirm this inference. Men still respond to the plays of Aeschylus, Sophocles, and Euripides in basically the same way as did the theatergoers of fourth- and fifth-century B.C. Athens. In fact, this similarity of human experience over several centuries was an important factor in the empirical psychology of Sigmund Freud. Freud believed, for example, that

> If the *Oedipus Rex* is capable of moving a modern reader or play-goer no less powerfully than it moved the contemporary Greeks, the only possible explanation is that the effect of the Greek tragedy [depends] upon the peculiar nature of the material [of the play] . . . . The fate of King Oedipus moves us only because it might have been our own, because the oracle laid upon us before our birth was the very curse which rested upon him. . . .

---

[2] Jung, *op. cit.,* p. 348.

[3] John Dewey, *The Influence of Darwin on Philosophy* (New York: Henry Holt, 1910), pp. 1-19.

[4] G. G. Simpson, *Biology and Man* (New York: Harcourt, Brace and World, 1969), pp. 118-119.

As the poet brings the guilt of Oedipus to light by his investigation, he forces us to become aware of our own inner selves, in which the same impulses [of Oedipus] are still extant, even though they are suppressed. . . .[5]

While biology no longer provides any support for a metaphysical or absolute human "nature," Mendelian or Neo-Darwinian evolution provides full support for a genetic stability within the brief span of recorded history which fully justifies the humanist concern for finding, in the full range of historical time and space, resources for an understanding of what fulfills man. There is strong reason for suspecting that the more the future deviates from the present, the more likely it is to resemble some aspects of the past. There is every biological justification for the right of the humanist to judge either present or future in terms of values which men of many times and many places have found fulfilling of themselves and others.

It is at this point that we can introduce our final biological model, that of the *climax state*. Certainly we cannot set any limits to the genetic evolution of man, but it is safe to assume that genetic evolution is such a very slow process, made even slower in man by man's ability to control his environment, that for practical purposes it is unchanging, even in the flow of almost limitless genetic recombinations. Assuming that man's customs, institutions, manners, styles, indeed, his very values and ideals, must build on the relatively stable product of genetic evolution, we might question whether cultural evolution (in any sense of the term) is an endless frontier or whether it has not in fact reached a stage that resembles a climax state.

The distinguishing characteristic of the climax community (again, we speak here of the biological model) is that it is *in balance*. The producers produce no faster than the consumers consume. The climax state is a closed circle. Materials recycle within the system and energy is taken in only to the extent needed to maintain the cycles.

Has man ever culturally existed in such a state? It sounds utopian. Does he have the potentiality for such a state? A debatable point. What are the desirable combinations of diversity within the parameters of his fixed context? The answer to that

---

[5] Sigmund Freud, "The Interpretation of Dreams," *The Basic Writings of Sigmund Freud,* trans. A. A. Brill (New York: Modern Library, 1938), p. 308.

question, we believe, lies in the humanist's frame of cultural reference, but let us be discreet in saying who must assume the responsibility of answering this question. We do not mean to imply that any class of designated or self-proclaimed enlightened Grand Inquisitors are to inherit the charge of providing for the happiness of mankind by some means of manipulating masses to achieve the programmer's sense of the best values, order, and balance for society. Desirable human values and the preferable forms of social, political, economic, psychic, rational, imaginative, celebrative, loving, and spiritual (that is to say, in every respect, the good human) life will be found in the domain of the humanities, and the answers to these questions are every man's responsibility. No man is exempt from coming to terms with the great moral questions. No man is free from living within a frame of value reference, and the better he understands his values and their consequences, the better equipped he will be to meet life's complex demands. No machine, or modern gadget, or communication medium, or form of transportation, or harness on nuclear or solar power has freed him from the need for self-knowledge, or the knowledge of his life's purpose, nor has it brought an end to the succession of questions which keep man asking "why?"

Culture, as the humanist studies it, is based on the innumerable and seemingly endless variety of ways that men have viably answered these fundamental questions and demonstrated the fruits of their answers in their achievements. Some men have reflected their answers in artistic images, in forms of celebration, ritual, dance, and song. Some have shown us how to examine life rationally to make it worth living. Some have left records and testimonies of their experience of divinity. Some have furnished models of human communion with nature. Some have formulated principles by which men can live in peace with their fellow men. Some have simply provided dramatic narratives of how men act and show the various consequences when some act in one way and others act in another. All these examples are records of some form of purposeful human ordering, which, if taken together, and intelligently appraised with reference to the present, give man the basis of viable values which can in turn provide an individual ordering principle for a rewarding and self-fulfilling climax state. In other words, in the realm of the humanist's concern (which is everyone's human concern) where we find models writ large (world views) and small (personal examples) of various human ideals, we find, even amidst conflicting and ambiguous claims, the basis for wisdom — a wisdom which can guide man in the actualization of his personal or societal climax state.

The climax community is the biological model of balance and integration. The Mandala is Jung's analogous symbol on the personal level of the balanced and integrated individual. Without attempting to key on the Jungian corollary, however, it is now possible to explain the second part of the obscure title of our essay. Mandalian involution, as we use the term, designates that constantly changing (or combination and recombination) of factors which constitute purposeful order, peace, harmony, and balance, whether on the individual or societal level, whether reflected in art, or systematic analytic thought, imaginative ideals, morphological forms of nature, institutional organization, or social interaction. The Mandala is the symbol of integrated order. Involution is the principle of change, but change with reference to some pattern, or purpose, or fixity. It might involve growth or incremental development, not necessarily in a simple linear fashion, but rather in a complex pattern which can turn back upon itself as one of its etymological roots (*vol-*, to fold) indicates. It could also involve the *decreasing* of some aspect of life after it has served its purpose, as the uterus is said to involute to its former size after the end of pregnancy. Hence, as we see the phrase, mandalian involution represents balanced, harmonious individual or cultural change, guided always by some ordering principle, possibly itself one that is ever-changing.

If we now turn directly to the question of whether there is a decisive cultural change, we could answer in our frame of reference in the following way. If decisive cultural change is viewed in terms of the emergence of a new man, *Homo novus,* consisting of an essentially new genetic composition, the answer must be no. We see no evidence for such change. "Point omega from the test tube" is an interesting thought, the possibility of which has recently come into man's mental frame of reference, but to date all focus has been placed on the test tube and still too little is known about such matters as the regulative feedback mechanisms involving complicated patterns of numerous genes. Further there seems to be little attention, if any, given by those who speculate on the possibilities of genetic programming, to what characterizes "point omega."

The bosom of Abraham, the state of Nirvana, the Beatific Vision — even the universal man, or the classless society, are not subject to the criteria of operational definitions or measurable by evidence of mere empirical behavior. Besides, we are still a long way off, as Malachi Martin tells us, from discovering and validating how the memory, imagination, and other human faculties function in either behavioristic or genetic terms:

> We do not yet know how to trigger heroic behavior, self-sacrifice, denial of felt but hurtful desires; how to control the megalomania of an egoist, to stimulate the humor and wit of human conversation, the flow of ideas, respect for others, reverence for the aged and weak and young, patience under provocation, magnanimity in victory and success, or sharing with others.
> It is all very well to teach a dog to lift its paws when it has a visceral change or to instruct a child to write "I am" instead of "I is." But there is no scientifically verified way in which all men can be conditioned by behavioristic principles to forsake war, love their neighbors, or build a Taj Mahal.[6]

The difficulties of such programming are no less for the genetic manipulator than for the behaviorist. In any event, the wisdom of such a controlling value would come not from the knowledge of the scientist's laboratory, but from the humanist's value-sense of culture. And there seem to be no new dimensions to the age-old problems of man's essential meaning or the purpose of his life. We are still the sons of Noah finding our father naked and learning that he is both ennobled and victimized by this humanity — physically strong, but spiritually overwhelmed by his appetites and his difficulty controlling his will. We are still the sons of Moses standing in admiration of our father's vision, and standing in respect of his laws, but still troubled by his doubt and wrath. We are still the children of Adam, still murdering our brothers, still lying to our Gods (when our Gods still live), and still founding our paleotechnic cities, which, for all their sophistication, are still full of violent inhumanity. From both these points of view, then, the biological and the humanistic, the words of Ecclesiastes suffice:

> What has been is what will be,
>   And what has been done is what will be done,
>   And there is nothing new under the sun.

---

6 Malachi Martin, "The Scientist as Shaman," *Harper's*, March, 1972, p. 59.

But obviously there are respects in which man is always changing, minute by minute, day by day, year by year, epoch by epoch. Every moment is unique. Every experience is different. New cells constantly renewing. New life arising out of the old dying generations. The question thus becomes, "In what *general sense* is man today different from what he was last month? a generation ago? a century ago?" To answer questions of this sort requires that we define contexts and compare particulars. Does a certain class of men in 1970 exhibit more socialistic tendencies than a similar class of men in the same geographic area in 1870? Is there more evidence of otherworldly self-denial in the 13th century than in the 20th? Is there a love of natural beauty and propensity for shamanistic magic among college students in the late 1960's that may be meaningfully compared to a pragmatic and technological set of values generated three decades earlier by their parents?

These are the kinds of questions that the social sciences deal with. They are, in our frame of reference, questions of ephemeral change in man's habits and sensibilities. They are not, in our estimation, fundamental or decisive changes in the nature of man. They are, rather, like the manifestations of the particular changes which constantly go on within the climax-state forest; and like the climax-state forest, they all find their equivalents in the past. They are all instances of the ever-changing recombination of age-old factors within a general frame of reference which is, for all practical purposes, unchanging.

Our own thoughts thus force us to take some exceptions to and make some qualifications on Professor Brzezinski's criticism of the politics of zero growth. Growth of a single kind cannot go on indefinitely. There necessarily comes a time—even though some may weep about it like the Great Alexander—when there are no more worlds to conquer. This means that growth in one area must be compensated for elsewhere. For this reason we believe it is inevitable that America will change from a culture dominated by the drive for constant expansion of production to a culture based on other factors of balance. This change, for America, would be a major change in our culture as the social scientist defines it. The culture of the future will not merely be able to achieve a state of balance with the physical and biological environment as the ecological movement demands. It will involve moving to a stage of development in the individual, in society, and in international relations, in which production of goods ceases to be the dominant and controlling aspect of culture for the simple reason that the problem of production has been solved. To be endlessly productive is now counterproductive. Men will soon discover that the dominance of production is no longer necessary, and that the fruits of material production are not fully satisfying. When they see this, they will then move to the next stage of succession in which they can come to terms with other aspects of themselves, and with other types of relations to one another.

It is not necessary to say that such a change would be a change to permanent climax. Successional changes as such are changes *toward* climax, with an unbalanced excess of productivity serving as the selective force that brings about the next and more nearly balanced stage of succession. American culture has succeeded in the goals it set itself, and for that very reason it will be succeeded by a culture which can integrate the fruits of that success into a balance within and among individuals. Here we are speaking of cultural change as the social scientist defines it. But like a microbial culture in an exponential growth phase, the cultural change requires restraints, and the restraints will properly be determined by a cultural frame of reference in terms of the way the humanist defines culture.

Where do such changes begin? The first and most appropriate step in anticipation of a new American culture is taken at the level of individual action. It is not beyond the ken of most people to set their own house in order. In fact, to fail in this responsibility in mild form is neurotic; to fail completely is sheer madness. Despite man's myriad inconsistencies and fragmented knowledge, the character of civilized man—indeed, whatever it is that we mean by human culture—is reflected in the way individuals order their experience, their knowledge, and their means and style of living. Work toward the order of a viable future cultural climax state can and must begin for every man in his own life.

To be sure, this is not saying anything new. The principle of ordered living is one of the oldest concepts in man's historical cultural traditions, and it is hard to think of a time when it has not been in evidence. What is new is our awareness of how principles found in the biological model of the climax state correlate with and can be applied to forms of personal and cultural change. Ordered living, we discover in our new frame of reference, is no less valid for our time and the foreseeable future than it was for our ancestors thousands of years ago. The Greeks of the fourth century B.C., for example, held the concept of balance, measure, and harmony to be inseparable from their ideals of human excellence and virtue. The good man and the happy man was the whole man, the well-rounded man, the man with equally developed and properly integrated body, spirit, and mind, living in harmony with his society and his natural environment. The principle of self-regulation which was both rigorous and flexible, and which took into consideration changing circumstances and foreseeable consequences, was called reason, the distinguishing mark of man's intelligence. Through its power, man was able to prevent things from getting out of balance, both personally and socially. We can conjecture on the basis of our frame of reference that the efficacy of reason and an ordered life will, in the years to come, give further testimony to the basic similarity between future human experience and that of men 2,500 years ago, despite the countless differences among individual men over this long period of time.

It thus seems to make sense to say, in conclusion, that the quality of human living for the future depends, as it has in the past, on a knowledge of the physical nature of man and the world, a knowledge of the particular facts of current human attitudes, customs, and institutions, and a reliance on man's reason and good will to regulate these factors in the innumerable ways which demonstrate viable human values in practice. We believe these all-important values can be found recorded in the humanistic traditions of man's cultural past in both the Eastern and Western worlds and we believe the stability of future cultures will reflect them, in new combinations, in ways analogous to the principles of permanence and change found throughout generations of biological organisms.

Putting one's life in order is no small task. It is a project which is truly a life-long endeavor. Some men never succeed. Others never even take up the challenge. A new *politics* of a new climax state suggests staggering difficulties, and we are not now about to say what the prerequisites are for its success. But we are sure that we would all rest a bit easier at night if we knew that each of us had done just one more thing during the day to set our own hearts at peace.

Technology and Social Change

William I. Davisson

WE live in a world of constant change. Western society as opposed to Eastern society has always been characterized by change, though perhaps today Eastern societies such as China and Japan are changing faster than we of the West.

Our folklore in America pictures the "new" world that Rip van Winkle found when he awakened. Every day we listen for the news. What's new in the world? We have a *news*paper. We have newscasters on the media. We greet each other with, "What's new?" Our scientists set out for New Worlds to conquer. We have New Math and Art Nouveau. We change washing machine models every year. We change dress and hair styles. In most cases anything 100 years old is fit only for discard. We tear down our old buildings and move to the suburbs. Things change so fast we don't have time or the inclination or the ability to evaluate whether it was really necessary to have a new style of car or washing machine or a new design for the detergent box. We are driven by maximizing of profits, by being efficient, and by moving people and things.

I propose to examine here the idea of change and our technological society. In short, how and why does society change? Does man allow society to change? Do people evaluate change or does technology today cause people to change? What of the quality of men's lives, man's environment, and the future of man himself?

Technology has caused change. Man has not properly evaluated that change because of several factors, primarily lack of information feedback and the influence of the delivery system. I intend, then, to discuss these three areas:

1. Technology: the process of applying the arts and the sciences to the process of the production and use of goods and services.
2. Delivery System: methods by which technological processes and phenomena are used in the production of goods and services.
3. Information Feedback: the observation of the effect of technology and technological change on the processes of production, and the subsequent evaluation thereof.

I will also look briefly at three areas that show the effect of technology on society:

172

1. Automobiles and air pollution.
2. Economic growth and environmental pollution.
3. The computer—tool for a viable life?

I have come to the conclusion that technological change becomes autonomous as a result of the requirements of the delivery system. My response to the problem is that each man must deliberately extend his interest and competence to many areas and be willing to make judgments about the way he lives and the things he uses or chooses not to use. He must come to grips with those things which motivate him in the short run. He must be able to encounter his society and evaluate it with its technology or he will be its slave.

Technology

I assume that man must survive physically. He must make a living in his society. After that he may hope for higher things. Thus the facts of the production of goods and services, and the ways in which goods and services are produced, have a basic effect on all the members of the society.

Most societies are judged to be "civilized" or "primitive" by the sophistication of their productive systems and the number of people engaging in activities other than direct agricultural production. The more civilized the society the more people who do not work directly at food production, but keep records, fight wars, or engage in politics.

At any point in history when man has a new idea or invention and applies it to a specific function or process in order to use it we call it technology. The man who first saw the round-shaped stone and recognized it as possibly useful had the idea, or made the *invention*. Until the stone was actually used as a hammer or an ax it was just an idea. Once used, the shaped stone became useful and therefore became part of man's capital equipment, or production assets. The knowledge of how to use the capital equipment becomes part of man's intellectual assets.

Technology is not the new idea. Technology is the knowledge of how to use the new idea, and in fact the use of it for a specific task.

Man has always had some form of technology. Before he invented and used the stone hammer he must have used his hand as a tool to pound or hit. After man invented and employed the stone hammer he invented or learned how to use metal. He used bronze (copper plus tin). Then he learned to make and use iron. As each new invention became a part of the man's intellectual equipment— or his culture—the man changed a bit, as did his society. The first change was small. For example, using the old bronze tools the man's arm was stronger than the capability of the tool or weapon. The tool or weapon was a weak link in the chain of activities of producing something or killing something or somebody. With the change in technology from bronze to iron using the same tool, the weak link was transferred to the man's arm. There was little change in the tool but vast changes in the possible fighting techniques.

The use of a new idea, technique, or process requires that man change his usual way of doing a task. He must usually change his behavior patterns and relations with others in his society in order to use the invention. Thus social change often accompanies, or is the result of, or is clearly associated with, technological change. Rarely can one use new ideas or new processes or new tools in doing something and do the task in the same old way.

The employment of technology has served to satisfy man's wants and needs. In the medieval period Clairvaux Abbey in France was concerned with saving time and effort in producing the necessities of life in order that more time and effort could be spent in meditation and prayer. Certainly a noble motive. The most modern technology of the time was used to mechanize all tasks formerly done by hand. Manufacture or making by hand was in a sense deemed inefficient. The Cistercian regulations recommended that monasteries be built near rivers that could supply power. The following description of Clairvaux Abbey (quoted in *A History of Technology* II [Oxford: Clarendon Press, 1956], p. 650) gives some idea of this mechanization:

> The river enters the abbey as much as the wall acting as a check allows. It gushes first into the corn-mill where it is very actively employed in grinding the grain under the weight of the wheels and in shaking the fine sieve which separates flour from bran. Thence it flows into the next building, and fills the boiler in which it is heated to prepare beer for the monks' drinking, should the vine's fruitfulness not reward the vintner's labour. But the river has not yet finished its work, for it is now drawn into the fulling-machines following the corn-mill. In the mill it has prepared the brothers' food and its duty is now to serve in making their clothing.

This the river does not withhold, nor does it refuse any task asked of it. Thus it raises and lowers alternately the heavy hammers and mallets, or to be more exact, the wooden feet of the fulling-machines. When by swirling at great speed it has made all these wheels revolve swiftly it issues foaming and looking as if it had ground itself. Now the river enters the tannery where it devotes much care and labour to preparing the necessary materials for the monks' footwear; then it divides into many small branches and, in its busy course, passes through the various departments, seeking everywhere for those who require its services for any purpose whatsoever, whether for cooking, rotating, crushing, watering, washing, or grinding, always offering its help and never refusing. At last, to earn full thanks and to leave nothing undone, it carries away the refuse and leaves all clean.

Bertrand Gille, archivist of the Archives Nationales of Paris, notes that most early abbeys had an extensive water system of this type.

The point is that technology served to satisfy man's wants and needs. The monks thought they wanted meditation so they brought the powers of "science" to bear on the particular production problem. The harnessing of the water caused their social relations to change. It bought time and released effort for satisfaction of the monks' material needs. If the monks had not used the power technology to grind grain they would have had to grind it by hand. They simply exchanged one form of technology for another.

Technology has always existed. Man used his hand as a tool before he used a stone or a bronze ax or an iron hammer or a laser ray. Technology is merely the application of a way of doing something.

Delivery System

The next thing to look at is the delivery system, which is the method by which technological processes and phenomena are used in the production of goods and services.

The monks decided they needed time for meditation. That was their goal or objective. They had a new idea, or used someone else's idea, in harnessing the water to do their work, thus buying time and saving physical effort. They had to decide how to make the machines work for them. The delivery system is the actual processes of forcing the water to work for the monks.

Benjamin Franklin had an idea about the presence of electricity. He used it only to the extent of flying his kite in an electrical storm. His delivery system, to make a key light up, was the wet string. Thomas Edison invented the electric light. Man has since employed the technological phenomenon of electric power in a number of uses. The vast array of generating stations and electric conduction wires are a far cry from Franklin's kite. Getting the power from the source to a desired place in a usable form constitutes the delivery system.

The use of the horse harnessed to a buggy with wheels constituted a kind of delivery system from ancient times. Until the 20th century man could fairly easily understand the delivery system. Its workings were not so complex that he couldn't see each step in the process. However, it may have been more complex than one today might imagine. Before the invention of the rigid horse collar in the 11th century the horse collar was a soft choke collar. It literally choked the horse because his windpipe was closed when he pulled on the wagon. The medieval peasant in northern Europe invented and used a rigid collar which allowed the horse to push with his shoulders and not pull and cut off his wind. It took centuries for the improvement of that delivery system, although to us it seems fairly obvious.

Sometime in the 19th century the relation between the user doing a job and the technique of doing it became obscured by the delivery systems. One effect of this appears to have been the specialization of function in industry. A man had to take a lifetime to learn how to care for one aspect of the delivery system with its necessary technology. He could not come to grips with the technological phenomenon itself.

A man who has taken a lifetime to learn how to care for one aspect of a delivery system with its necessary technology may not be able to come to grips with the technological phenomenon itself. A man might build parts for generators in a Grand Coulee Dam but not understand the transmission of electricity over hundreds of miles, nor would he understand the process involved in the delivery of electric power from a river to an electric toothbrush. The man may not understand the nature of electricity itself.

Information Feedback

This brings us to the next point: information feedback. The man might spend his lifetime making parts for generators and never come to grips with the technological phenomenon of electricity itself.

Then too the capital and human investment in a given delivery system may well preclude changing it. For example: the man possessing the technical knowledge to make generators is in a poor position to evaluate whether it is efficient, profitable, or desirable to dam up the streams or whether one should burn coal to obtain electricity. In fact one may ask whether it is necessary or desirable to keep factories running day and night producing more electric toothbrushes.

So there are in fact two decisions that must be made each time someone is to accomplish something in our economic society. First, a decision is made (a value judgment) that the job is worth doing. Second, a decision must be made about how the job is to be done—that is, by hand, using a machine, what machine, how, by what power source, and so on. Therein lies a terrible possibility for tragedy, particularly for a society that is acclimated to machines and to change. People in a society such as ours are apt to fall into a trap: something will be done because it is technologically possible to do it. The proponents of the supersonic jet would answer that it has to be done. However, those who defeated the bill to continue work on the jets were perhaps facing the philosophical question noted above.

Our present society has come to the point where the delivery system dominates the information feedback and evaluation because the technology, the investment in time and money, and the motivation for profit dominate our thought. There is a delay of a generation or more from the decision to make things (because we have the technology available) to asking if the things are worth making. At this point the user, the job, the society, and all else are dominated by the delivery system. Technological changes are apt to occur, and do occur, because they are compatible with or necessary to the more efficient operation of the delivery system.

Although the present fate of the supersonic jet may be an exception to the rule or perhaps an instance of information feedback and evaluation catching up with technology, the automobile reveals an opposite story.

Automobiles and Air Pollution

Ralph Nader has done much to force the issue of pollution controls and safety in automobiles. Nader, however, is caught in the delivery system-information feedback lag. He assumes that automatic technological change implies that as the technology to make safer, less polluting cars is available, that same technology will be applied to making safer cars that pollute less.

Nader does not evaluate the whole point of the automobile, which is to move a mass of people and goods hither and yon. He is not even asking that it be done efficiently. Assuming it is desirable and necessary to move masses of people and goods from place to place, what is the most efficient and safest way to move them? Certainly not by single-unit, gas-burning cars, not even by electric cars. Mass and rapid transit may well be the safest, fastest, least polluting, and most efficient way to move people and goods.

Whatever the answer, the decision should be made at the human level, not the technological level.

In the present instance the direct relation between the user and the job to be done is lost. The delivery system—that is, the automobile and the processes of producing the automobile—tends to overwhelm and to dominate the technology, the user, and the job itself. The job may be done because it is technologically possible to do it, not because the job is necessary. Cars, as devices for moving people, may be made safer and less polluting, but not because cars are the best ways for moving people but because the industry can make safer cars that pollute less. The social and political ramifications of an entrenched system are significant. The automobile industry was the one single industry aided by President Nixon in his policy of the "Freeze" and subsequent "Phase II."

My thesis here is that the connection between the doer and the job becomes obscured by the delivery system. Technology and to an extent society are now operating at least once removed from people and their decisions and their actions. The delivery systems now dominate all else.

One might now ask, what of the information feedback? How has it been lost by the majority of Americans today who certainly seem to give Nader and Nixon their ear?

Earlier I defined information feedback as the observation of the effect of technology and technological change on the processes of production, and the subsequent evaluation thereof. In ancient societies there appears to have been a more direct and a more intimate relationship between the production problem and the technological solution. When the first club or staff was sharpened or when the first shaped stone was used as a hammer is not precisely known. Neither is it precisely known when the first pointed staff was hardened in a fire after it was sharpened. We know only that it was done. We postulate with some reason that the first time it was done, the act was done by the person who directly would use the staff or pointed stick. The need to use the thing involved several (if dimly separated) points:

1. The ability to recognize the need for some tool or weapon to do something.
2. The ability to abstract from a possible type of tool to the specific use.
3. The ability to recognize the tool in its natural state or the ability to make the tool (both perhaps accidental).
4. The ability to use the tool.
5. The capability of modifying traditional methods of action in order to be able to use the new tool. Ancient Egypt rejected iron technology in favor of the existing but more primitive bronze technology.

Since this whole process is a trial and error process, it involves considerable effort and feedback to the user about the nature and impact of the new tool or technique. Since the user of the new tool, weapon, or process is in ignorance of its success or failure until it is used, it must be used before it may be evaluated. It is only by a continual trial and error method that the proper use may be determined for any new technological phenomenon.

The innovator has the new tool or process in hand. He uses it. He observes the effect of its first use. If the first use has less than the desired effect, the attempt may (or may not) be made again. In the heat of battle or the danger of the hunt, or in the anxiety of building something, the feedback information may be long obscured. If the innovation is to be successfully used, or intelligently discarded as not relevant, the feedback must occur; the evaluation must occur. The process may seem to involve a clarity when outlined, but in actual practice such clarity is rare. Many have died because of improper use of a new tool, weapon, or process. The feedback was not observed or noted. A sharpened stick may be inappropriate for killing an elephant, no matter how sharp the stick.

We cannot evade technology. We can, however, evade making the observations and the evaluation that provide the feedback that will allow intelligent decisions about the type and magnitude of technology that is suitable to a particular job.

Economic Growth and Environmental Pollution

The American economy has long been on a vast economic growth cycle. The resources of the country have been sacrificed to the goal of economic growth. The human activity has found its most rewarding aspects — both monetarily and morally — in promoting economic growth. In many instances, even such things as the Nobel Peace Prizes have been awarded to those scientists and social scientists who have sought after and attained methods of promoting and fostering economic growth. Certainly the goal of all productive activity as well as the aim of most governmental policy until about 1930 has been tuned to help attain the goal of economic growth. Technological innovations that have most profoundly affected the nature of our economy and our society have been those that have promoted economic growth. The goal of all this has been to give to people more wealth so that they could purchase more things. The emphasis has been on increasing the output of industry and at the same time lowering the cost of goods to the consumer. If this was not possible, then the effort was made to demonstrate that the higher priced goods were "better" or of higher quality.

Sometime after 1930 another idea began to acquire new force in America, namely that perhaps other things were as important or even more important than economic growth. For a long time that idea remained dormant. Eventually, however, the idea took root in some portion of the American conscience and appeared as a quest for the control of "pollution" and the creation of a "clean environment," however defined. Eventually it became clear that what was meant by a clean environment referred to physical pollution of the air, atmosphere, and water by industrial activities and by the actions of people.

Social action groups (or political action groups) were formed and, in the American tradition, someone passed a law. *There.* Now, clean up the environment. There were only two problems encountered in finding the solution.

First: an institutional problem. America is a "sort of" free enterprise society, based on business and industrial activity and the profit motive. Money is the incentive to action—rather, profit is the incentive. To clean up the environment would require great amounts of capital outlay for which no specific monetary return could be envisioned. General Motors will be happy to put an exhaust control device on a car and charge the consumer a price that includes 30 per cent profit before taxes. The copper companies in Arizona are not nearly so willing to undertake the capital outlay to remove sulphuric acid from the smelter exhausts because they can see no way of recouping the cost. Based on a specific free enterprise profit calculation, some companies may shut down rather than clean up the industrial exhaust into the air.

Second: a problem that may be more important than the institutional problem. One of the cries of industry has been that the technology required to accomplish pollution control is simply not presently available. In the case of one device for control of automobile exhaust pollution, the cost was about $750 initial cost and about $120 every six months thereafter. Given the concept and cost of an automobile, this is probably not a financially feasible device, even assuming an acute problem of pollution of the environment.

The point is that the American economic society has been on a "growth binge," convinced that economic growth can solve any and all problems. This has clearly been reflected in the nature of the technological innovations that have appeared as inventions and been adopted into the production process. Our society is characterized by a technology that has promoted mass production and growth. Since, historically, our society has not placed emphasis on conservation and pollution control, we have not developed a technology or a technological capability that can handle mass-produced capital and consumer goods efficiently and with a clean environment.

When the industrialist notes that the technology is not presently available to produce the clean atmosphere and water desired by law (not necessarily by society, but by law), he is correct. Furthermore, the consumer in our society is not willing to pay the price, either in money or inconvenience, that pollution control would require.

The total feedback (and evaluation) within American economic society always has been designed to develop a technology compatible with the goal of economic growth.

Now there is the first beginning of a feedback that something is not right, that something else is required, that the growth of technology is inadequate to solve all of our problems. However, the user or member of society has expressed little dissatisfaction with the technology or with the goals of our society until now. There is no magic wand that can make either the new embryonic goals or the new technology instantly available. There are no instant utopias. The feedback has been missing and/or is a generation delayed. The generation today that is not satisfied with the ability to produce at the cost of pollution is not the generation that has created the basic technology of our present economic society.

If the present feedback is transformed from dissatisfaction into economic action, the technology required to produce and to provide a clean environment may become available within the life span of the next generation, because we may apply the potential of the arts and the sciences to the problem.

American economic society is today in the position of the primitive man with the hand ax. He may or may not be vaguely dissatisfied with the stone hand ax that he has, but he does not release it or throw it away because he has nothing better to replace it with. Further, the hand ax is comfortable, convenient, and useful within the limits of the user's experience. However, the essential ingredient for change is present if only one person is dissatisfied with the hand ax.

The Computer—Tool for a Viable Life?

A new stage of technology, rather a new phase of technological progress, has appeared on the American scene since 1945. It has appeared in the form of a computer. A computer is a machine that can perform various types of operations on symbols and can remember the answer. A symbol may be any numeric digit, alphabetic letter, or other configuration or combination thereof. A computer operates by means of an internally stored program as compared with a cash register that performs operations on numeric symbols but in response to an external program — that is, the operator manipulating the controls.

When first developed the computer was used primarily by statisticians, or scientists, or others who use numbers. Thus the computer attained a reputation of being only a scientific machine. Since it attained the reputation of being a scientific machine, most people felt that they could safely ignore the computer. The economist remained concerned with his models of reality, in conformity to the compartmentalizing of our society, without realizing that the computer, using simulation techniques, is perhaps the premier device on which economics or other models may be developed and studied. The artist, secure in the feeling that there were no aesthetic considerations involved, ignored the whole thing. The scientist, who developed the machine in the first place, continued developing it, refining it, and using it as a numeric symbol manipulator.

Here was a machine that could perform operations on a myriad of types of symbols at hundreds of thousands of calculations per second. Further, it could store the anwers in its own memory. The computer has been improved so that now it can read 1,000 cards per minute where 10 years ago it could read only 250 cards per minute. The machine can now print paper at the rate of 1,100 lines per minute where 10 years ago it could only print at the rate of 150 lines per minute. The technological advances in computers have concentrated on the delivery system of the computer, its input, its paper output, its manipulation of data, and its intermediate storage devices.

The question has not been asked whether the piece of paper is the relevant central focus for the work that such a magnificent machine could do. Western and American society has been organized about pieces of paper for centuries. We create them, file them, lose them, and then spend most of our time looking for them. What most people want is not the paper but the answer. With the computer and its memory devices paper is not necessary. However, the total development of the computer has been based on the ubiquitous piece of paper. The technological development of the computer has been based on the assumption that the piece of paper is the premier way of getting an answer. Alternative ways of getting output from the computer have either been academic toys or are just now receiving some attention. It is interesting to note that only recently, after the computer began to be more than a scientific machine and came into some sort of general business and academic use, has the piece of paper not been the central focus of the computer. Airline reservations, for instance, want an answer, not a piece of paper.

Conclusions

With the complexity of society and the general attitude of social and vocational isolation desired by most Americans, the feedback that ought to be present in our economic society does not in fact manifest itself. Even when it does it may be late by a generation or two. Thus technological change becomes autonomous, and becomes the product of the change required by the delivery system. Technological change becomes dispensed like model changes on an automobile assembly line. Each change is different, but they are all the same.

My only response to the problem of breaking the hold of the delivery system as I see it is that it is not sufficient for a person to be competent and successful in his own field. If he is competent only in one field he will be either part of the delivery system, or will be unable to evaluate or affect the technology itself. Man must make a living in our society, but it is no longer sufficient to be merely a competent artist or physicist, economist, politician, or humanist. Nor can man be the universally educated man. Man must, however, deliberately extend his competence and his interests into the various areas of our society, and must be prepared to make a value judgment on them. Man cannot escape into a hole, for the tool used in digging the hole (even if only fingers) demonstrates the degree of technological advance and the culture of the society. The economist must extend from economics to computers to history. The physicist from physics to art to politics. Man cannot be universally educated, but he must be able to encounter his society sufficiently to make judgments about it and its technology or he will be mastered by it.

Arts and Media

From Counterculture to Anticulture*

Donald P. Costello

THREE films circumscribe the counterculture of the last decade.
These three films have as their subject the counterculture, and
they themselves became cultural events. *Woodstock, Easy
Rider,* and *A Clockwork Orange*: they define, warn, and predict.

Woodstock (the event) and *Woodstock* (the film, which became the event for millions of the young) defined the counterculture of the 1960's. Of course, that definition did not *begin*
the phenomenon of a youth culture that runs counter. Nor was
Woodstock the first description of it. Anthony Burgess wrote his
counterculture novel *A Clockwork Orange* over 10 years ago, and
he has told us in a June 8, 1972, *Rolling Stone* article that he planned the book nearly 30 years ago. The droogs in that novel were
some version of Teddy Boys or greasers or hipsters projected into
an apocalyptic future: "The work merely describes certain tendencies I observed in Anglo-American society in 1961 (and even
earlier)." Some of those tendencies, and several others, were exposed by the counterculture itself in *Easy Rider,* just before *Woodstock.* But *Woodstock* purified and refined the counterculture—and
successfully made it self-conscious, mythologized it. And thus
defined it.

The young of the 60's had contended that their culture was
based not on exploitation but on love, not on violence but on
peace, not on restraints but on freedom. *Woodstock* showed them
that that was true. Their culture was communicated from one to
the other not by mind and words but by sights and sounds. Sensations, feelings, intuitions, spontaneity reigned. To receive the
message of the culture, then, required not sharpening the reason
but expanding the consciousness.

Woodstock is perhaps the most verbally inarticulate film ever
made. We hear conversations and interviews, but they are grunts,
mumbles, you-knows, and exclamations. Words are indirect; the
culture of the film seeks a more direct means of communication.

---

* This essay on counterculture films was written as a part of the Notre
Dame symposium on American culture; it has also appeared in *Commonweal,*
July 14, 1972.

The young of *Woodstock* communicate by their music and, in the skinny-dipping scene that won the film its "R," by their free and glistening bodies, ringed lightly with laughter, while the sound track contrasts the snipped and turgid voices of the townspeople, their words heavy with suspicion. The charming interview with the porto-san man stands out in our memory precisely because this humble old servant and admirer of the counterculture reveals himself through his medium and ours, words.

But the point of the film, the fact of it, is both the fact it records and the fact is re-created in thousands of movie theaters for those too young, too poor, too far away, too busy to have been an original citizen of the Woodstock Nation. Michael Wadleigh knew what he was about. His was not a film for observers but participants. The motion picture is the art form of the young precisely because it can do what *Woodstock* did: exploiting sights and sounds to a hyperrealism, it can create myth. The place Woodstock could not have been as visually and sonically perfect — loud, clear, selective, now ordered, now chaotic — as was this film which brought us into communal participation. No one could not hear it, God knows. No one could not see it, from arrival through cleanup. Accidents are made part of a pattern, are made inevitable: we prepare for the rain, we are uncertain and fearful as the rain begins, we exult in the joy of the mud in the rain's aftermath. Sights and sounds become one, reenforcing and building. The voices of Crosby, Stills and Nash, their instruments, their harmonies, blend on the sound track just as their images blend, harmonized, counterpointed, on the screen. Wadleigh underlines the frenetic quality of the sounds of Ten Years After with those seemingly uncontrolled images which snap from positive to negative, which spin into reverse images. If we had no drugs to give us extra eyes, to turn on and to sharpen the lights, the film gave them to us, especially by expanding the visual surfaces through multiplying the image and through dynamically varying the sizes and shapes of framed and unframed pictures. It was an initiation rite of sights and sounds, expanding both the consciousness and the self-consciousness of the young, uniting them in spite of real time and space distances into a community of illusion, into a culture aware of itself, aware of its superiority, aware that it is counter, a Nation apart.

Easy Rider had been made just a bit earlier by members of

the counterculture for other members of the counterculture, and it was a warning. The critics misunderstood the film because they saw only its self-consciousness and thought it was also self-pitying. The cultists deep into the counterculture misunderstood it because they would not accept its warning that the values of the counterculture were becoming indistinguishable from the values of the mainstream.

Peter Fonda and Dennis Hopper show the new American Myth repeating the failures of the old American Myth. The new American pioneer, searching for freedom, rides not a stagecoach but a motorcycle, travels not West but East. Other travelers on the same road are not on horses or mules, but on jets and in Rolls Royces. But distances are covered: state lines are crossed, bridges—from here to there—flash by, the road goes on. The ability to move seems a refutation of static lives. The dream of freedom in this film is clearly an *American* dream. It is dreamed by a classic pair of comrade heroes, wearing a beautiful cloak of cool, weighted down by red, white, and blue, by stars and by stripes, and by names-titles-labels: "Captain America," who is also "Wyatt" (Earp), accompanied by "Billy" (the Kid). But the quest is not now—was it ever?—ideal; it is mercantile: The American Dream—both old and new—has become simply middle class. The new heroes are exploiters, buyers and sellers, who stuff the American flag with money and who are heading for rich retirement in Florida. *En route* they are haunted by the American past, which echoes only death: they continually pass graveyards; they sit and expand their own current consciousness on an old mound of Indian bones; a final stop in their trip is a bad trip in a graveyard just outside a slave market.

Can the new American be free of the death-ridden mercantile-based old America? Captain America has two chances to choose freedom: First, at the ranch where the naturalness of the horse is clearly contrasted with the ugliness of the motorcycle wheel, and where the simple satisfactions of domestic and diverse and fertile beauty allow the rancher, in Captain America's words, to "do your own thing in your own time." Second, at the commune where *Woodstock* values struggle for permanence, where Captain America sees a nonmercantile religious peace and unity, where the body is free and beautiful, not sold or violated, and where he can predict, "They're going to make it."

But Captain America and Billy do not choose the peace-free-dom-love values of either the old-style rancher or the new-style commune. Billy speaks the words of their choice: "You go for the big money, man—and then you're free." George rides along with Captain America and Billy because he thinks that they represent freedom. George is aware that "we're all in the same cage," and he thinks that the movement of these new pioneers represents an escape. But Captain America and Billy carry George only to his violent death. Captain America and Billy learn nothing from George's death on the road to Mardi Gras. They travel on, across America.

They choose the mainstream American values: they take their money on to New Orleans at the time of Mardi Gras, the celebration that moves inexorably into the season of death, to the site of the old slave market and whorehouse where the flash-forward predicts Captain America's death in flames. In the self-discovery scene, Captain America's words "We blew it" are clear in meaning; and they are a warning for a counterculture that can't really be counter if it accepts the values of the dominant culture into which it enslaves itself.

The dialog says that the dominant culture is afraid of Wyatt and Billy because they are free. Money-slaves always hate those who are free. But *Easy Rider* questions whether the new Americans are free. Are they blowing their freedom, are they, after all, not the stuff of counterrevolution, but merely a sold-out generation? An easy rider is a pimp who lives off a whore-slave: Is the new generation made up of pimps who live off dope-slaves, whose ride is easy, without commitment, whose enslavement to easy money and instant pleasure means that when real values—of the past or the present—are there to be chosen, the only reply can be "We blew it"?

Stanley Kubrick takes the values of *Woodstock,* the prophetic warning of *Easy Rider,* and reduces them to the ashes of the future. If *Easy Rider* was prophetic, *A Clockwork Orange* may be apoca-lyptic. And it has become no less a cultural event than those other films, obviously striking sensitive chords in the movie public which is a young public. The representatives of the counterculture are now the droogs who do not hold to the values defined in *Woodstock,* but to their reverse; they do not have the ability to choose the old-style values or the new-style values that the characters in

Easy Rider consciously passed by. They are conditioned to other values, or to none at all. Value choice no longer exists. The impossibility of choice becomes the theme of the film. The droogs are not shown as choosing creatures, but seem conditioned by their society—apathetic, private, drug-laden—into behavior of violence, sex, and hatred, into anticulture. But the alternative, the Ludovico Technique of reconditioning, espoused by the law-and-order party, is equally anticultural because it, even more directly, eliminates human choice. "When a man cannot choose, he ceases to be a man," contends the Chaplain.

In the future society of extremes which Kubrick posits, man does not exist within recognizable human values. Peace has become totally replaced by violence. Freedom exists for no one, the victims or the victimizers. Love has been totally replaced by sex; a body is not any longer free or revered, but the subject of obscene graffiti and the object only of violence, a sickness to be cured. Kubrick caricatures, exaggerates, mocks, makes varyingly mad, all of his characters and events. Critics have complained that the victims are as unpleasant as the victimizers. Precisely. In this brilliant *reductio ad absurdum,* everything is indeed reduced and everything indeed becomes absurd. Even the style of the film is mocking: terrible humor undercuts the terrible violence. The artist's stance toward his material is ice cold, uninvolved, primitive, dehumanized. All is juxtaposition, seemingly unguided; and we are left to sort out our own emotions and reactions as best we can. The violence and sex are exaggerated into stylized nonrealism: flying exits through the window two at a time in a better-than-any-Western style; slow-motion gore; fast-action sexual romps; a pop art explosion at the moment of the murder. In such an extreme world of the nonchoosing and nonhuman, no culture—mainstream or counter—can exist.

Clearly no communal culture, no passing on of values, remains in the future world of *A Clockwork Orange.* The rococo concert hall—now called "The Derelict Casino"—is deserted, decaying, dusty; it is no longer the site for the Rossini playing on the sound track but for the gang-bang being performed on the stage. Sometime after *Easy Rider,* the last picture show closed, not only in dim Texas towns, but throughout the modern world. Everyone has become, in the words of *A Clockwork Orange,* "a victim of the modern age." Culture has retreated. People have locked their doors against other people: "I never open the door to strangers after dark." They sit in chairs that look like wombs and eggs. Culture is anticulture because it has become private.

Communication is gone. "Oh brothers" is a verbal tag in a world totally devoid of brotherhood. The fascinating Anthony Burgess Nadsat, which in the medium of the novel rendered great respect to language because it allowed the reader the leisure to figure out and to savor the Russianisms, the coined words, the puns, the word-games, becomes in the quicker and nonreversible medium of the motion picture the primary symbol for the non-communication of nonculture. In case we *might* be able to figure out the meanings of the words, or remember them from the book, Kubrick has them spoken in a Cockney that begs for subtitles, has them shouted, screeched, mumbled, in huge echoing rooms, under blaring music. The Minister of the Interior gives us a key: "But enough of words. Actions speak louder than. Action now. Observe all." The counterculture's cry for the nonverbal has been heeded.

Verbal communication has so disintegrated in *A Clockwork Orange* that noncommunal music—private, on discs, cassettes, tapes—is the only art that remains; and it is stripped of human resonance—any type of music fitting any mood: Elgar in a prison corridor, "Singin' in the Rain" during rape and beating, Beethoven during the cutting of friends.

Despite the predictions in *Woodstock,* the departure of the articulate has not been accompanied by an arrival of the spontaneously good. The droogs don't effectively communicate even with one another, except by slashes and blows. Expanded consciousness has not resulted in humanly value-laden sights and sensations. On the contrary. In Kubrick's film the colors are primary, unsubtle. The landscape is vandalized, garbage-ridden. The taste in artifacts is totally pop and crude and vulgar: phallic lollipops; nude white plastic women bent into tables; huge plastic nipples as milk dispensers; a bloated phallic sculpture, now a dirty joke, now a work of art, now a murder weapon.

Words, music, artifacts are all disconnected from the human, from the value-carrying. And so, of course, has mind departed. The irrational tendency of the counterculture defined so clearly in *Woodstock* has triumphed in *A Clockwork Orange.* Alex the narrator tells us, "I was thinking all the time . . . thinking was for the gloopy ones," and so he gives up thinking and at that moment attacks his friends, his "brothers."

In spite of its futuristic settings, does *A Clockwork Orange* really deal with the future? Or has the future become the present? Burgess, writing in *Rolling Stone,* has his opinion: "The age of violence and scientific conditioning it depicts is already here." Another counterculture story, running alongside ours, would seem to agree with Burgess: the "festival" films—from *Monterey Pop* to *Woodstock* to *Gimme Shelter*—clearly tell a story of apocalypse, with the death at Altamont somehow eerily present in the happy days of Jimi Hendrix and Janis Joplin at Monterey. But that is a different story, even though the ending may be the same. The story of *Woodstock, Easy Rider,* and *A Clockwork Orange*—the three best films of the counterculture—is a story that deals with values of the past, of the present, and of the future, a story that takes us from documentary, to fiction, to . . . is it, let us hope, fantasy? Or is it not?

A Decade in the House of Irresponsibility

Thomas S. Fern

STUART HAMPSHIRE has used the term "irresponsibility" to describe or set apart creative activity of an artistic sort from a code of behavior as it is defined and practiced by society.[1] This code is a product of the society's value system and establishes what is or is not responsible behavior.

His point is that values are held and shared by members of a society and are considered useful and desirable for the group as a whole. Most people feel some responsibility to perpetuate these values; consequently various structures—political, financial, social—exist to ensure their application and uniformity. A supporter of these values acts responsibly, then, to the extent that he lives by the code.

On the other hand, says Hampshire, *avant-garde* artistic behavior is usually not recognized by society as being useful or resulting in a useful product or even furthering the goals of the group. The artist is seen as a unique type, atypical, and if not a direct threat to the establishment, certainly an annoyance. Distrust arises because the artist deals with forms that baffle the public and defy description. He manipulates materials and media in strange ways and at times he seems to attack the very values that society holds dear.

In addition, art styles in the last 10 years have changed at a record-setting pace; and while one has never known what the next new form will look like, the rapidity of change today magnifies this kind of confusion. So the average citizen is frustrated by modern art and exasperated by its unconventionality. He is unwilling or psychologically incapable of purchasing original works of art and unhappy when his tax money is used to support the arts. The house of irresponsibility, then, from this point of view, is peopled with those who move counter to society in some part of their lives. Prominent among the irresponsible, of course, are the artists.

From an artist's point of view, the word irresponsibility does not have a pejorative sense because it pictures rather accurately, albeit

---

[1] In a lecture at the University of Notre Dame, "Art, Politics and Repression," March 17, 1972.

dramatically, an essential condition of the creative act. This kind of irresponsibility places the artist, as artist, beyond the tyranny of tradition and the restrictions of a nonartistic society.

From the vantage point of the removed position, reached perhaps because of his unconcern or dislike for established patterns of living, doing and thinking, the artist gains some independence. Such freedom makes it easier for him to experiment with new materials and modern technology, to seek an artistic application of such materials and to assess their expressive potential. It also helps him to turn a fresh eye onto man's thoughts, beliefs, taboos, and behavior, or whatever interests him, and to reflect on his observations. Ultimately the artist's task is to bring these two activities together.

The artist's function in this light is hardly irresponsible; instead, it poses an unusual set of challenges. The artist recognizes his otherness relative to his contemporaries but at the same time realizes he must remain so to uncover the right form. In one sense he gains freedom by moving counter to the current but in doing so acquires a different set of burdens and pressures. In this position, which should be called one of "creative insecurity," the artist experiences his alienation and his own kind of frustration on several levels. His art will probably be ignored by the majority and denounced or ridiculed by some of the "cultured" elite. Even if he acquires a following, their numbers will not be legion but more like that of a platoon or squad. Similarly his idea or what is called content when incorporated into the art form is apt to go unnoticed. At present the public is predisposed to dismiss the work of the artist as a kind of leisure-time play that results in a product of little significance or with little seriousness behind it. Other indictments note his lack of respect for traditional concepts of beauty and his willingness to do silly things. He is said to assault the eye of the beholder and the intelligence of the people and to make a mockery of good taste. In addition he attacks critics and challenges museum directors and most aspects of the art system. He is seen as a kind of maverick and is rarely one of society's heroes.

If that set of burdens isn't enough, the creative act itself imposes its own kind of anxiety. From his position outside the conventional art world, he experiments, analyzes, arranges, and rearranges his elements or manipulates new ones in a process for which there is no predetermined sequence or direction. The artist is in that frustrating position of looking for a form but not knowing in advance what it looks like or exactly how to find it.

When form and content finally blend to his satisfaction the work is deemed complete, and at that point he realizes that this is the form he was seeking. It is a moment of elation and release.

So with this picture of the professional artist and his relationship to society in view, let's look at some of the products of artistic irresponsibility over the last 10 years. First a quick overview of the major innovations and then some opinions about an emerging new art.

The decade has brought on dramatic changes in the art world, not only changes in style but significant changes in materials, the art object, and the role of the artist. In 1962, Pop Art had pushed into the foreground, elbowing past Abstract Expressionism that had dominated the art world during the 1950's to capture the attention of the critics and the press. The newcomers, Andy Warhol, Claes Oldenburg, Roy Lichtenstein, and others, couldn't have been more brash or flamboyant or more surprising. Close behind followed the color field painters, Morris Louis, Kenneth Noland, Larry Poons, retaining some of the qualities of Abstract Expressionism but leaning more to hard-edge painting rather than what is called action painting.

About this time Robert Rauschenberg, Louise Nevelson, and Lee Bontecou exhibited some startling works made of old junk and other refuse of our civilization. These examples have been classed as Assemblage or Combines but are actually three-dimensional constructions. Other artists like Allan Kaprow turned their attention to what has come to be called the Happening. Outwardly, the Happening is a nearly spontaneous event involving participants and props (often perishable material) in a preselected setting but without prestaging or control.

Other artists called Minimalists focused on monumental structures of the utmost simplicity—the cube, for example. They carefully avoided recognizable subject matter or literary inferences in their work and concentrated on the architectonic qualities of their forms, presented forcefully. Sculpture was made kinetic in the period 1962-72 by means of motors or magnetic fields. In one case of planned obsolescence, Jean Tinguely's motorized sculpture not only moved across the ground but was wired with dynamite and programmed to destroy itself, which it did.

From the Happening it was a short step to Conceptual Art where, in brief, the things, the action, and the sequence of these is imagined or pictured in the mind's eye. There need not be an art object in conceptual art, other than what one can imagine; however, verbal descriptions or instructions to introduce the concept are standard fare.

A wide range of commercial products found their place in the art world during the last decade. Among these are neon and fluorescent lighting, electronic devices and controls, bulldozers and other earth-moving machines, photosensitive emulsions for transferring photographs to almost any surface, and so on.

There have been many changes but the ones mentioned will suffice to illustrate the range of new interests among artists today. The preponderance of wholly new materials indicates a major revolution is under way, one that may relegate the process of traditional painting and sculpture to the attic.

In looking at these changes, a number of trends emerge to suggest art is undergoing a significant change and beginning to play a different role. Again new materials and processes figure importantly here.

Until the last 10 years the art media were, for the most part, quite standardized and fell into either two-dimensional or three-dimensional categories. Painting and sculpture are typical of this tradition.

There are generic properties to painting that are evident regardless of whether an example is a watercolor or an enormous fresco or an easel-size oil on canvas. Similarly, the characteristics of sculpture are evident no matter what subject matter is presented or what material it is made of. The changes that have occurred in painting prior to 1962 and going back hundreds of years have been chiefly that of style. While new kinds of paint (oil in the 15th century, acrylic polymer in 1957) and improved surfaces on which to paint were introduced during this period and represent technological advancements, the process and product of painting did not change. Each age left its stylistic mark as did the significant artists but such change hasn't upset the generic qualities of painting. Painting, no matter what style, remains a closed form, separated, even isolated, from the wall on which it hangs, the room in which it is displayed, and removed from the viewer. A painting is really a very private affair, the product of a very private act, by one individual. It may be hung in different museums, owned by different collectors, and outlive generations of viewers without losing its internal and singular form.

Experiments with new materials—objects, stuff, or anything that is not normally used in an art context—occurred long before the decade being reviewed but neither caught the interest of most artists nor challenged the traditional role of art until recently. Picasso is credited with the first collage when he pasted a small piece of paper in the center of a drawing in 1908. Later he and other cubists perfected *papier collé,* or collage, as an art form.

The Dadaists, during World War I, experimented with commercial objects. For example, see Marcel Duchamp's "ready-mades": a urinal titled *Fountain,* a bottle rack, and a bicycle wheel. The Dadaists were the real innovators of this century but their contribution wasn't fully appreciated at the time it was made.

The Constructivists tried new materials during the period between the two World Wars, creating sculpture out of metal and plastic. However, their material remained subservient to the art form. That is, the intrinsic nature or appearance of the material is concealed or at least restrained for the sake of a carefully designed work of art. Art history is a factor here because the Constructivists perpetuated the primacy and preciousness of the work of art. They, as well as we, were taught what a work of art should look like and they merely used a new material while retaining the classical generic properties. Thus the antiart lesson of Dadaism was either not understood or ignored in the 1920's and 30's.

During the years 1940-1960 a few artists like Julio Gonzalez, Alexander Calder, and David Smith constructed in steel and iron but, in general, the tradition of art and the look of the art object were maintained.

The Materialists of our decade, for that is how I label them, select the most everyday materials that are around us and assert them as art. In this act they are philosophically like Duchamp and the Dadaists. Rauschenberg seems to be the first in this category. His now-famous combine painting, *Monogram* (1959), incorporates a stuffed ram encased in an automobile tire and his *The Bed* (1955) is actually a sheet, a rumpled quilt, and pillow, made up as a cot-sized bed with cover turned down. The ordinariness of this subject is destroyed by mounting it vertically and splashing the whole assemblage with paint. While Rauschenberg's two shocking innovations were built before our decade they were not widely known until the 60's and represent the beginning of a new art. During the 60's large numbers of artists dropped the traditional materials and searched for new. John Chamberlain assembled the crumpled parts of cars into free-standing monuments to man's ability to manufacture and to destroy. Cesar employed a junk-yard compressing machine to squash an entire yellow Buick into a nearly solid oblong measuring 59½ by 30¾ by 24⅞ inches. This last work is in the collection of the Museum of Modern Art.

Bontecou constructed in canvas and steel what look like festering and dingy landscapes seen from an aerial view. The shapes resemble the casual order of farmland and fields pockmarked with yawning crater-like eruptions. The canvas is gray and grimy and still bears stenciled words and trademarks—reminders perhaps of its industrial origin. Some critics liken Bontecou's constructions to various anatomical openings of the human body but I prefer the ecological protest point of view.

In the 1960's Nevelson assembled another kind of found object: wooden remnants of old buildings that look like newel posts, decorative moldings, balusters, table legs, and a variety of shapes cut from lumber. Such things are neatly arranged inside wooden boxes and the boxes themselves stacked or grouped to form whole walls or a kind of contemporary reredos. The whole construction is painted in one color, which is usually black or a dark gray but sometimes white or gold.

This group of Materialists—Rauschenberg, Chamberlain, Cesar, Bontecou, and Nevelson—are alike in that they work with objects and things that once functioned in society in practical ways. The automobiles of Cesar and Chamberlain and the architectural elements of Nevelson originally had their aesthetic dimensions too but, in general, the material used by the Materialists comes from the commercial side of our civilization and retains its industrial character even when recycled by the artists.

One of the changes effected by this group is a move away from that kind of illusionism that conceals the character of the physical material of a work of art. When looking at a painting, one loses sight of the pigment and canvas (the physical properties of painting) and is caught up in an apparition. Similarly, sculpture materials can be submerged or made less important than the subject

depicted so that one may note, say, the softness of flesh while knowing that the work is made in bronze or stone.

But with the Materialists the integrity of the original material
is maintained at the same time that it takes on new properties that
contribute to the art form. In such cases, part of the art experience
arises from the viewer's awareness of the former function of the
materials and objects as well as their new contribution to the work
of art. Out of this awareness comes a significant change in the
function of the work of art.

The work of art takes a step away from the overrefined or
essentially elitist position it has maintained for centuries and moves
toward one of more relevancy. The Dadaists initiated this some 50
years earlier, not specifically for reasons of improved communication or understanding but more as a protest against the stuffiness of
official art and the art world at that time. Today's artist is not
reacting to a conservative art scene but chooses contemporary
materials, sensing perhaps their appropriateness for that new form
he needs as well as their potential content.

In a way, the work of the Materialists becomes more public and
less private because the spectator or viewer not only identifies the
physical properties in the work of art, but sees how they were
formed. Being familiar with their background it is easier to relate
to the art form and he is better able to imagine how the work was
formed. In these circumstances the gulf between form and content
is considerably lessened, making the import of the work of art more
accessible to more people. So, in essence, the new art of the
Materialists is more genuinely rooted in today's society and appears
to be making significant comments about it. In this case the irresponsible posture of the artist seems to have resulted in a social
good.

While the Materialists that I have identified are making a
significant contribution to the new, they remain conservative when
compared to other artists of the 1962-72 era. A work by Rauschenberg or Nevelson is still an art object and generically within the tradition of art forms. These objects can be bought and sold, exhibited
in galleries, and are again tangible evidence of an individual's creative art. Another group of artists, using nonartistic materials, began
a series of works that challenged the necessity of the art object
itself. Their stance seems to best embrace the spirit of Duchamp's
antiart concept.

Kaprow experimented with the Happening, a one-time event, or sometimes a sequence of events involving people, an environment, and props. A Happening has a plan but no rehearsals and a minimum of outside direction. It is an event that happens as spontaneously as possible and in that way comes closer to being like life itself. In some ways it is like theater. There is a performance of people in a setting, except that only the participants are likely to know or experience it. One of Kaprow's Happenings or sequence of Happenings occurred recently in Los Angeles. He arranged for several truckloads of 200-pound blocks of ice to be delivered to as many different sites in and around the city on successive days. Some went to residential neighborhoods, others to commercial areas. In some instances special police permission was secured in advance.

Kaprow and his friends would then stack the blocks into walls or simple geometric piles. At some locations crowds gathered, at others there were only a few observers. In any case, all were invited to join in the activity. The crew answered questions in a general way and avoided explanations or a rationale for the goings-on. The typical first question was "What in the world are you doing?" The answer was usually a noncommittal "Stacking ice." The next question "What for?" would bring a low-key response of "To see what it will look like" or something like that. Passersby did participate and when they suggested changes in the shape of the pile, they were tried. It is said that one young man who happened to be driving by on his way to work stopped and spent the rest of the day on the event. He even suggested the walls would look nicer if lighted from within, and in his enthusiasm purchased red warning flares for that purpose.

Generally speaking, this is a fairly typical Kaprow Happening. It does not produce an art object that lasts or that is marketable or even of traditional beauty. As a matter of fact, the object is unimportant or, in some cases, nonexistent. Instead there is a shared experience of productivity for no practical purpose other than its own occurrence. In this respect the participants are more or less free to follow inclinations, hunches, or, in other words, to become part of a creative experience. Each person's part may be as free, inventive, or artistic as he is capable of or as he desires it to be. The value of the Happening, as its name implies, is in the action of doing or sharing an aesthetic act even though it is essentially unplanned.

The Happening is one more long step toward a public art and at the same time a step away from the traditional importance of an art object. Its own process is public in that it may happen anywhere and that many people are responsible for and share in the aesthetic experience. Reflection on the event reinforces its social nature rather than its form. *Process,* here, supplants the object as the work of art.

Another variation of nonart or antiart in today's art scene is found in certain earthworks and what has come to be called Process Art. Robert Smithson has been working back and forth between these two with his use of earthen materials. For example, Smithson will collect samples of dirt and rocks from selected sites and display them in rather unusual boxes or bins. Accompanying the boxes of earth and displayed as part of the exhibition are maps and careful descriptions of the location of the site as well as the geological nature of the place and the material found there. One views the boxes and information but senses a dimension other than geology.

In a sense this is like a conceptual happening. Instead of taking part in an event, as a participant in a Kaprow Happening would, an observer of a Smithson site-nonsite infers the relationship between the two. He spans the distance or closes the gap between the two locations. He experiences the unusual time-space relationship between the display in a gallery and the original site plus comprehending that Smithson went to the trouble to survey the site, remove some of its material, display it, and plan elaborate descriptions of the place and the substances found there. Furthermore, the viewer is aware that this entire operation has no practical purpose but was done for the sake of its own process and its own internal, chiefly conceptual, form. As such it takes its place as art and offers an aesthetic dimension or thrill.

A Smithson piece differs from the public display of stones used in the Memorial Library mural at Notre Dame although they have similarities. One might ask, if the one is art, is not the other also? That is a fair question because both display similar materials from distant sites as well as information about their basic properties. The Library display, however, exists to furnish information about the material in the mural. It is secondary to the mural and, while interesting, not necessary for appreciation of the mural as art. The Library display is instructional and intended as such. The relationships drawn by a viewer of the Notre Dame display are concerned with the identification of the different kinds of stone and their properties, locating their place in the mural, and noting the different parts of the world from which they came. The mental process, here, yields information without the poetic or aesthetic dimension of the Smithson operation and thus does not achieve the status of art. In other words, the art quality is tied to artistic intent which in these two cases is or is not evident.

Another contemporary art that differs from either Kaprow's or Smithson's but shares similar qualities is Christo's wrappings. Christo wraps buildings, public monuments, and rather large portions of landscapes in canvas or plastic, tied with rope. As one wag put it, Christo is an undercover agent . . . his bag is bagging things.[2] About 1968, Christo wrapped the facade of Chicago's Museum of Contemporary Art much as one would casually cover furniture for storage or a set of suitcases on the luggage rack with canvas and rope. The ropes lace around the outside of the wrapping and appear to hold the canvas in place. It is not a neat package as packaging goes; in fact, the ropes are usually in disarray and the wind billows and slaps the canvas. In this instance the wrapping completely covered the Contemporary Museum, including the entrance, and was really quite foreboding. That is, when approaching the museum with the intention of going inside, Christo's wrapping is a startling deterrent that brings one to an abrupt halt. From that moment of realization it takes considerable nerve to walk up the steps and pull the flap aside in order to push open the door.

The package not only conceals the architecture of the museum and its identifying characteristics but seals it off from the world. In fact one isn't really sure what is under the wrappings which, visually at least, make that structure something extraordinary. When confronting a Christo there is also something of the mystery and anticipation one experiences when receiving a package in the mail. What's inside? Who sent it? And so on. To carry the analogy further, the excitement continues during the opening of the package in the one instance and entering the package in the other.

Like the site-nonsite operation, artistic intent is present in a Christo wrapping even though there is no practical aspect to the process. Both of these new art movements have visual elements

---

[2] "Etcetera," *The Art Gallery Magazine,* December, 1969, p. 171.

which are more like signs than art objects because they are not complete art forms. They point to the conceptual nature of this kind of art. Interestingly, such art is difficult to contain in a museum or gallery but not difficult to imagine, contemplate, and perceive.

For the final step along this path that has been leading to a really new kind of art, consider now what is called Conceptual Art. In its pure state, Conceptual Art is without a tangible art object, although it came to that point gradually. The growing importance of conceptualization in art is evident in Cesar's *Yellow Buick* and more so in Happenings and Process Art. In these movements, however, only part of the art experience is evident in concrete form. The interested observer is forced to react to the sign that's given and to relate to the process that it points to. In the 1960's each of these styles we've looked at moves further into Conceptual Art.

The conceptual artist, on the other hand, does away with the form, art object, or sign whenever possible. In its place he poses a situation that doesn't exist but conceivably could. For example, one artist proposed a kinetic sculpture piece as a time-space mailing to six consecutive locations set on a straight line between a West Coast city and one on the East Coast. The line defined the trajectory and direction of the sculpture (a package) moving to the east while registered mail return receipts (one for each of the six stops along the way) were moving westward. The action involves a public means of communication and artistic volition alone separates it from thousands of similar acts every day. One's imagination can grasp the rhythm of this event, the scale of it relative to the continent, and perhaps embellish the act with one's own ideas about postal service.

In the same genre another artist noted that computerized traffic systems capable of ascertaining traffic jams before they occur and instantaneously controlling stop lights and vehicle directions to avert the snarl will be a reality in the near future. For his conceptual art piece he proposed arbitrary control of the computerized system for one huge metropolitan choreography of vehicular movement. Imagine how you might design such an action.

A variation of the above proposed computerizing all the lights in tall office buildings and then programming configurations, transitions, and linear accelerations by means of lighted and/or darkened windows up and down the buildings as well as horizontally and from building to building.

There are hundreds of examples of Conceptual Art but these should suffice to make my point that a new kind of art has appeared during the last decade. It is one that has shown less and less dependence on the art object and eventually has eliminated it altogether. In its place it substitutes process, real or imagined or both, as the essence of a new aesthetic experience.

The new art embraces nonart materials and other ordinary things. For that reason it achieves a structural relationship with the environment of here and now or, in other words, the new art is a more public art. It contains a quality of realism that has not been seen since primitive art, when art was more intimately a part of life. The new art acquires more of this public or universal dimension as it becomes involved with everyday life and events.

Instead of a painting within a frame or a sculpture on a pedestal, a situation where man stands outside art and its reality, the new art is composed of elements that almost everyone is familiar with and can manipulate to some degree in his own way. Hence the new art has the potential of reaching a larger audience and engaging larger numbers of people in its own creation.

The final word in this context suggests that what is irresponsibility to some becomes discovery for others. The artist as rebel is not only a critic of existing systems but is in a position to effect change. And while not all such rebellions are fruitful, the ones delineated above can be seen as having social as well as artistic significance because they have become a more intimate part of today's culture and have the potential of involving larger numbers of people directly in the creative act.

The Blurred Image: Some Reflections on the Mass Media in the 1960's

Thomas Stritch

MOST of the new developments in the mass media during the 1960's turned out to be unfulfilled promises, for good or ill. A partial list is suggestive:

1. The tapering off of the underground press.
2. The inconclusive, still smoldering Agnew controversy.
3. The decline of the mass magazine.
4. The rise of pornography as a mass medium.
5. The gradual eclipse of McLuhan and his theories.
6. The ambiguous influence of TV in politics following the excitement of the Kennedy-Nixon debates.
7. The blunted impact of the big reports: Kerner, Eisenhower, Pornography, and the Surgeon-General's report on violence.
8. The failure of educational TV to get up a full head of steam.
9. The failure of commercial TV to develop new, innovative, and imaginative programs.
10. The technological promises unfulfilled: the electronic newspaper and magazine, TV cassettes, CATV's slow march, home video tapes, 3-D TV, and so on, along with the persistence of raised-type printing, radio, comic strips, newsboys, and much else often proclaimed obsolete.

Despite inevitable overlapping, it is convenient to divide the foregoing into print and broadcasting.

Print

During the 60's the underground press sprang up, rolled and roared, and now seems beginning to run down. Like the university newspapers it so much resembles, it doesn't have any built-in stability, and when stability does begin to show, as with *The Village Voice,* the radicalism fades.[1] Not always, and not altogether: in

---

[1] See Jesse Kornbluth, "The Underground Press and How It Went," in William M. Hammel, ed., *The Popular Arts in America* (New York: Harcourt, Brace, Jovanovich, 1972); also J. Kirk Sale, "You've Come A Long Way, Baby, But You Got Stuck There," in Francis and Ludmila Voelker, eds., *Mass Media* (New York: Harcourt, Brace, Jovanovich, 1972).

New York and Los Angeles especially there's lots still going. But the fire and mischief that animated papers like *The Berkeley Barb* and *Good Times,* both now defunct, are not only dimmed but seem faintly embarrassing, like a college caper reviewed after 30 years.

Part of the reason for the change is change in the established press the underground press fought so fiercely. Journals like *The New York Review of Books* and *New York* magazine both float successfully somewhere between the old underground and the changed establishment. As usual, the establishment accommodated the new wave more readily than the radicals could envision; Norman Mailer, I. F. Stone, and the Henthoffs have themselves become established figures, if not precisely in an establishment, and the battleground for the fight between Mailer and the protagonists of Women's Liberation was staid old *Harper's,* not the underground press. Things got mixed up. *Playboy* hired the editor of the highbrow *Kenyon Review,* Robie McCauley, to be its fiction editor, college instructors assign *Rolling Stone* as required reading, and the callipygous fixations of Kenneth Tynan in *Oh! Calcutta!* become commonplace not only in *Life* but in college lit mags. In such a world, what's underground?

No matter; the underground press has left its mark. Perhaps its most enduring influence is the new attitude of those who write for the established press. The same spirit that sparked the underground press also sparked that portion of it which criticizes the established press, like *The Chicago Journalism Review.* This touched a responsive chord in many a city room. Staffers on the big city dailies supported the critical press with articles and tips, and often organized in clubs or informal meetings where attitudes toward editors and publishers were hashed over, policy made and sometimes successfully pursued. As a result there is more consultation in most big-paper city rooms now, and this means that the reporter has more voice in running newspapers. Actual democracy is probably impossible, within the movement as well as on the newspaper; witness the recent counterconvention (counter to the establishment's Newspaper Publishers' convention) staged by New York's critical review of journalism, *MORE.*[2] But Tom Wicker, Nicholas von Hoffmann, Anthony Lewis, and their peers are insisting more and more not only on more consultation about news and news

---

[2] See "The Enemy Within," *Newsweek,* May 8, 1972, p. 61.

emphasis, but outright expression of opinion in news columns.

This trend is connected to the peculiar role of the American press, especially in Washington, as a kind of branch of government. The practice, so skillfully developed by Franklin D. Roosevelt, of using Washington correspondents to send up trial balloons in their columns to get public response to some planned move has gone on apace. This participation in government itself may have encouraged the publication of the Pentagon papers and similar leaks of official government documents. In any case the American press, again especially in Washington, has developed a hubris unknown elsewhere, and newsmen and newspapers an almost diplomatic immunity.

Not much of this is new, merely overt. The plaints of a long line of chairmen of the Democratic National Committee that the press is overwhelmingly Republican miss the point. To be sure, the owners are, but rarely are they so deeply committed as to attempt to force newsmen and photographers to hew to their line, which leaves them only with the notoriously unread editorials. Most reporters and photographers and editors are Democrats, and they give the Democratic candidates far subtler and stronger support than overt endorsement—favorable pictures, intelligent omissions, and eye-catching positioning. Indeed, the best public relations available to any public figure is his own ability to inspire such support—FDR, Greta Garbo, Harry Truman, Judy Garland, Mae West, John Lindsay, Adlai Stevenson, Lindbergh in his early days, Babe Ruth, and Dag Hammarskjöld are good examples among hundreds. And where newsmen gather, in Washington permanently, Cape Kennedy occasionally, Saigon or Paris, or at their conventions, often these attitudes take on an ideological tinge—although it never embraces the whole cadre. As with the United States Senate, the bonds of professionalism are stronger than those of ideology.

Critics of the press, underground, academic, anywhere, seem congenitally unable to understand this. The underground press charges that the daily press by and large exists only to defend and support the social and economic *status quo;* that it's hostile to the aspirations of the minorities and fails to report their activities; that it squelches news harmful to important business and political interests and plays up the crimes of the hopeless and the despairing. To this let's add the widely circulated charge by Edith Efron in her recent book, *The News Twisters,* that the network news programs during the 1968 presidential campaign were outrageously biased, by a factor of 10, against Richard Nixon.[3] Both these charges, from opposite ends of the opinion spectrum, ignore what critics of journalism from presidents of the United States to presidents of garden clubs consistently have ignored: what goes into a page or a time-segment of news is based on a professional judgment of what news is and upon what Paul Weaver, in a perceptive article on Miss Efron's book, calls "traditional and distinctively journalistic models."[4] It may be, as Professor Weaver argues, that these journalistic models and judgments are too narrowly conceived; in any case, as he observes, only the professionals themselves can raise the standards. Yet they are constantly striving to do so; few professionals are as self-critical as newsmen. Moreover, judgments about what is news and how to present it are affected far more by events than by criticism. Agnew's charges, substantially the same as Miss Efron's, have, like hers, caused few changes in television news broadcasting, but the shocked and horrified response of professional newsmen in all the media to the riots of the late 60's caused plenty. More news about blacks and more black newsmen are the obvious results of professional standards made more aware of and more sensitive to the plight of the minorities. The repeated contention of black leaders that the press is, because of its structure, unable to tell the black story truly is of a piece with their other charges about economic and social power.[5] But almost certainly qualified black men are the only applicants in the spring of 1972 sure to get jobs in the media, and this has been true roughly since the riots of the 60's.

Take it by and large, then, American journalism, both print and broadcast, is run not by owners, not by revolutionaries, not by fat cats or advertisers, but by professionals in the trade. And, by and large, these professionals are animated by some sense of good service to the community as viewed through their professionalism, and still a good measure of the reformism that has always charac-

---

[3] Edith Efron, *The News Twisters* (Los Angeles: Nash, 1971).

[4] Paul Weaver, "Is Television News Biased?," *The Public Interest,* 26 (Winter, 1972), 66. I disagree with Professor Weaver about television's political power, however, as will be apparent later on in this essay.

[5] A good though comparatively temperate example is the one by Lerone Bennett, Jr., "The White Media," in Charles U. Daly, ed., *The Media and the Cities* (Chicago: University of Chicago Center for Policy Study, 1968).

terized, as the underside of its cynicism, a large segment of the profession.

This cast of mind is rather old-fashioned as befits an old-fashioned industry. Despite the growth of chains the press is still largely family-owned. It has embraced no major technological change since photography. Its unions are still largely old-fashioned craft unions, around 30 for a major publisher to deal with; its research and development not only minor for a great industry, but largely limited to smaller papers with fewer and milder unions to deal with. The underground press could never have made it without bypassing the unions with newly developed inexpensive offset printing; similarly, at the other end of the scale, no great American daily is technologically as advanced as those in the Soviet Union and other places, like Cairo.

This technological bind has played a major role in the trend toward the local monopoly paper—one paper, or at least one printing and advertising setup, to a city. Such critics as the late A. J. Liebling and Stanford Professor William L. Rivers are afraid that this trend will make the daily press bland, plastic, and homogenized. However, there is something to be said for this situation. If it is well-managed and well-edited, the monopoly paper can afford to be more independent and objective than competitive papers, and it does not feel obliged to espouse causes or beat them to death for a competitive edge. It can more readily admit mistakes and more easily refuse deals. If the paper is locally owned responsibility is visible and vulnerable. The record of competing papers in the United States in the past, despite the nostalgic sighs, is by no means reassuring: most of the excesses of journalism, sensationalism, crude political partisanship, criminal associations arising from advertising, and circulation wars, came from tough competition. Similarly, the fear that a monopoly position will result in too much power seems empirically ill-grounded: so far it hasn't happened. There are plenty of checks from the broadcast media, and above all from public opinion.

And, of course, from magazines and other sources: *The New Yorker* continued its long tradition of casting a wary eye at the daily press with Edward Jay Epstein's remarkable articles demolishing the claims of the Black Panthers to manic police persecution, paperbacks began to appear all over the place devoted to mass communication, and in high schools courses in communication blossomed along with bell-bottoms. The press, which has often called itself the watchdog of freedom, has got plenty of watchdogs dogging the watchdogs.

And the press continues to grow. With fewer papers, total circulation is up, reflecting perhaps no more than the population increase. Magazines show an opposite trend. The 60's saw the great mass media magazines being displaced by national television: *Look* is dead, *Life* and most of the big-circulation women's magazines are in poor health. It seems clear that the kind of national advertising that made these huge successes now goes to television, while special audience magazines still get attentive and productive advertising readership. The big successes in magazine publishing are mostly aimed at special audiences however large, like *Psychology Today* and *The National Geographic*.

Their formulas—focused special advertising, informal personal tone, leisurely nonfiction, lots of comment, and so on—raise doubts about whether the magazine field can be called mass media. The typical successful American magazine is not a household word; it's *The Journal of the American Medical Association*. There are hundreds of these immensely profitable business journals. They are profitable because their readers need the specialized goods advertised and the specialized information of their articles. It seems safe to say they will continue so long as the clienteles they serve do. And there are hundreds more magazines without profitable advertising kept going by the interests of the groups they serve, from fraternal lodges and churches to cockfighters and sports car fans.

Even more specialized is the pornography publication. Edges of pornography show up, of course, even in college texts, and *Life*'s ambition to show the American nude as well as clothed is realized in all sorts of publications. But the growth of "adult" bookstores all over the country indicates that the pornography issue is not unlike that of marijuana: wide usage has not yet settled into accepted custom and law. Quite possibly, as Marshall McLuhan says, both are essential parts of the youth culture.

Broadcasting

Set beside broadcasting, no part of the press looks like a mass medium, not even *Reader's Digest* and TV's handmaiden, *TV Guide*. The circulations of these biggest American magazines, hovering around 17 million, wouldn't sustain a prime time TV show past 13 weeks. Television has succeeded radio as *the* mass medium in the Western world, especially in the United States. "Just as the printing press democratized learning, so the television set has democratized experience," says Daniel Boorstin.[6] It's a neat formulation. The invention of the steam rotary press in the 1830's made the penny press possible. Highbrows were shocked at its vulgarity, and it defended its mission to inform and educate the great mass with an almost religious zeal. But it couldn't touch the illiterate, and education, however widely interpreted, is still far short of experience.

What are the nature and effects of this experience? Boorstin goes on to say that the television experience *privatizes,* atomizes each individual even within a family that owns plural TV sets, and by making everything pictured makes it also immediate, thereby helping to destroy a sense of history, continuity, and community.[7] In this, as in much else, he is at odds with television's best-known oracle, Marshall McLuhan, who contends that the television experience helps turn the world into the "Global Village," makes experience shared and creates a new sensibility especially among the young generation who grew up on it.[8]

McLuhan generated a good deal of excitement during the 60's; it is hard to recall a parallel case of a pundit becoming an industry, like a pop singer or an athlete. If that excitement is now beginning to ebb, it is still worth noting that his books make the most plausible case for a new sensibility, quite possibly generated, as he maintains, by electronic communications.[9] This contention, along with the rest of the McLuhan credo, is both sweeping and prophetic; McLuhan asserts his insights without benefit of demonstration, albeit with immense offbeat erudition.

What is refreshing about him, as about the French writer who is in some ways his counterpart, Jacques Ellul, is viewing modern

---

[6] Daniel J. Boorstin, "Television," *Life,* Sept. 10, 1971, p. 36.

[7] These same effects were attributed to modern urbanism in pretelevision days in a seminal article by Louis Wirth, "Urbanism as a Way of Life," *American Journal of Sociology,* XLIV (July, 1938), 1-24. It would be interesting to know whether Professor Boorstin regards television as a natural development of modern urbanism, or as playing a larger role in this syndrome.

[8] Compare Marshall McLuhan, *Understanding Media* (New York: McGraw-Hill, 1964), with Daniel J. Boorstin, *The Image* (New York: Atheneum, 1962).

[9] The most readable presentation of the basic McLuhan ideas is in "An Interview with Marshall McLuhan," *Playboy,* March, 1969, p. 53 ff.

communications as pervasive.[10] Both know better than to believe that making announcers talk better will make people talk better, or that putting opera and ballet on television will improve the cultural level, or that participatory TV discussion, the pet project of such naive liberals as Nat Henthoff, will make any difference in race relations or anything else. They understand that the case lies far deeper than such things, that what count are modalities, structures, attitudes which seep into us because of our technology rather than this dab of content or that exhortation to betterment. They are valuable if only to show how wide of the point most criticisms of television are, from Agnew to Minow to Toynbee.

Yet McLuhan claims too much for television, it seems to me. McLuhan's insight into small things, like attitudes toward clothes and cars and nudity and radio, is often brilliant, but in larger matters he sometimes works into eyebrow-raising science fiction, like his idea that speech will erode away into some sort of ESP communication à la *2001,* or his comic-book theory of history. Take his comments on the current American political scene. Along with many others McLuhan believes that it was Kennedy's television image that enabled him to win over Nixon in 1960. I can't see how, in anything that close, anyone can say which of the many possible determinants was decisive. McLuhan claims that it was Nixon's adjusting his TV image, in ways described in *The Selling of the President,* that enabled him to win in 1968. I don't believe it. If so, how did Johnson win so decisively in the intervening election, with what was admittedly a poor television image? And what about the elections of 1970? Here for the first time television was used up to the hilt in state elections for United States senator. The results are inconclusive. Television is a factor in political campaigns, along with many others. It is not a decisive factor. Party organization, issues, personal exposure, public sentiment not developed by television but by real events like busing, housing, and the usual social demands and needs also count. To judge from the 1970 record, which I regard as more instructive than 1960 or 1968 because there were more diverse offices sought and candidates for them, the television political image cannot be manipulated or created at will, and its political power *per se* is largely a mirage. This is not to say that television isn't a powerful

---

[10] Jacques Ellul, *Propaganda,* trans. Konrad Kellen and Jean Lerner (New York: Knopf, 1965).

medium for political purposes; it is to note that control of the medium is as chancy and as subject to miscalculation and the public nay as any other human affair. So too for the McLuhan contentions about dictators. Of course radio was skillfully used by Hitler and Nasser, and of course Castro airs his charisma through television. But even in such totalitarian systems as theirs, I wonder if the charisma doesn't come first and the impact through the media second.

I have the same doubts about television and violence, television and the urban riots of the 60's, and television and education.

The Kerner Report (official title: *Report of the National Advisory Commission on Civil Disorders*) partially absolves the communications media from the natural suspicion that their coverage made the riots worse, sparked others elsewhere, and generally were inflammatory. The considerable literature on this subject, chiefly periodical, seems to confirm this general absolution; the facts are about what one would expect: that where coverage was intelligent and sensible, the media helped cool the riots, and where it wasn't helped heat them; and above all that the media got a great deal better at riot coverage as time went on. Most good newsmen, both print and broadcast, had already done most of the things that lay within their power the commission recommended before the report got into print. So, too, the police. It may be a sad commentary on our society that in the 70's we know more about controlling riots than we did in the 60's, but it is not necessarily a sad commentary on the police and the media newsmen.

The staff report of the Eisenhower Commission (official title: National Commission on the Causes and Prevention of Violence), entitled *Mass Media and Violence,* endorses the recommendations of the Kerner Commission but goes much farther in tieing up violence shown on television with violent behavior. Like most staff reports this is a very uneven book, with some excellent chapters like I. W. Cole's on journalism education, but the part about TV and violence, especially the work of Professors Siegel and Catton, is to me unconvincing. As Professor James Q. Wilson has pointed out, the evidence from the social sciences on this controversial subject is far from conclusive; such as there is suggests that TV watching doesn't spark any violence in normal people, old or young; and that the ardor of those who insist that it does arises from moral considerations rather than from the conclusions of social science. Moreover, Professor Wilson points out that the Commission on Violence recommended banning violence from children's television programs while the Commission on Pornography wants to legalize everything and let the kids take their chances.[11] Despite their ponderous and expensive panoply, these commissions, it would appear, rely less on the dubious findings of their science than upon their reactions to whose liberalism is being gored.

This is not to recommend that television's program makers should be turned loose to do whatever best sells their cereals. It is rather to point out the complexity of the issues, to suggest that some of the staff investigators consult philosophers and theologians as well as social scientists, and to raise doubts about the value of the reports of government commissions.[12] Violence itself is one of the most baffling aspects of contemporary life. One can still make a good case for there being less of it than is generally supposed from the scary FBI statistics and the public fascination with it in legend, film, and literature—as Daniel Bell did during the 1950's.[13] Murders are less frequent, prison population is down. And yet there is violence in the very air. People are afraid. One hears again and again stories of muggings and assaults and other crimes against the person. Crowd behavior erupts into violence more commonly than before, it seems. It is possible that student and youth crowd behavior is less violent thus far in the 70's because the kids saw how swiftly the scene of love at Woodstock could turn into the scene of terror at Altamont—and how cynically the media exploited both. Is this fear, this quickening of the nerves against expected violence where'er you walk, the result of reporting violence on the media? It is hard to think such reports haven't spurred airplane hijackings. Is the hatred of the Vietnam war the result of having it in one's living room on television, as McLuhan contends? And if so, then why doesn't showing domestic violence discourage further assaults? Do pictures and films of bad automobile accidents discourage reckless driving? Or does anything of this sort simply make no difference? The plain fact is that nobody knows the answer to any of these. All we know is that the media provide

---

[11] James Q. Wilson, "Violence, Pornography, and Social Science," *The Public Interest,* 22 (Winter, 1971), 45-61.

[12] This goes also for the Surgeon General's Report on Violence and the Media, the first volume of which has just appeared.

[13] Daniel Bell, *The End of Ideology* (Glencoe, Ill.: Free Press, 1960).

instant information about the whole world, if we want it. But
we don't know whether that makes us brothers à la McLuhan,
or strangers à la Boorstin.

The story of television in education is similarly inconclusive.
Closed circuit television instruction has not developed as fast as
its early enthusiasts thought it would. This doesn't mean it's no
good, though; education in general hasn't developed as much as
predicted. Older teachers especially are very conservative people,
and school organization and instructional materials are pretty much
the same now as they were 20 years ago, in striking contrast to
the subjects taught. However, education by television is part of
the much larger subject of educational technology, beyond the
scope of this paper, though once again it seems safe to say that its
progress is slow and its promised blessings mixed.

The more than 200 noncommercial television stations in the
United States can scarcely be said to constitute a mass medium
at the moment. Along with a very few of the more than 2,000 FM
stations they bring what little sustenance the cultivated user of
the electronic media gets. It is pathetically little. Most of the best
things come from Britain. Lots of time is wasted doing what
television can't do well, like symphony and opera and ballet. Some
of the discussion programs are pretty good, but much of the daily
fare of these stations is so poor that much as I want something
better on my TV set and FM radio I wouldn't and don't support
most of what we now have.

Which raises the baffling question about quality entertainment
programming on television, both commercial and noncommercial.
Commercial television is so commercial, so tuned in to the huge
mass audience and advertising dollars, that it can't even keep the
Cavett talk show going. The shows with the big ratings are themselves so formularized, so calculated and carpentered that freshness
wears off rapidly in torrents of imitation, for examples, *Laugh-In,*
the Lucy shows, and the more recent *All in the Family.* Moreover,
the network program makers are so sure of their carefully researched
formulas that the flavor of the creative individual has no chance—
gone, apparently forever, are the days of a Pat Weaver or a Robert
Saudek. Everything seeks the level of the bland and folksy least
common denominator, even the local news programs, which are just
about all the station-originated programming there is.

The Federal Communications Commission thought local and

regional programming would burgeon if encouraged. So they encouraged, requiring all sets to be manufactured to receive UHF signals with their more limited range than the established VHF ones. They also forced stations to lay off the networks for one hour a day of prime time, and they opened up the FM markets. Never were the calculations of bureaucrats so wide of their hopes. The result of all these moves in terms of better programming is close to nil. So, back to reruns and movies.

Survey after survey shows the American listener likes his TV the way it is. He doesn't care that the British Broadcasting Corporation maintains five symphonies and the Japanese three. There is nothing sinister in the network policies, though one could wish they could give a little here and there. They are simply giving the customer what he wants.

But the customer is at the dead level of society. Unfortunately there isn't much for the minority audience of any sort. *The Wall Street Journal* for April 5, 1972, tells the sad story of a Washington, D.C., good music radio station which feels it must switch from a classical format to contemporary music. Its fanatically loyal audience is simply not large enough for it to attract advertisers. And, as the *Journal* article goes on to point out, the same story can be repeated again and again, even with university FM stations. FM good music stations, because of the small investment required, represent the best hope for diversified programming for all sorts of minority audiences. If little diversity has happened there, what chance is there for the far more expensive TV stations?

There is some hope that a fourth network can be built. The Ford Foundation has primed the pump by contributing around $150 million for public television. If Congress appropriates enough, National Educational Television may become a real force for better television. So also if profits from cable television are used to originate programs for minority audiences.

Cable television, checked in the big cities by the FCC, is coming on very slowly to the mass markets. To judge by its performance where it has been operating for some time, it's not going to break up the mass audience or challenge mass taste. All the predictions of the 60's about technological developments in the media themselves promoting the satisfaction of minority interests and tastes simply haven't happened. Home video hasn't amounted to anything, and if it should, won't it be much like home movies? Cassettes were supposed to be the big breakthrough against the monopoly of the networks. Buy or rent the cassette program of your choice and play it on your TV set. It's too early to say yet—Sears has gone big into cassettes, but CBS, a pioneer, is out—but my feeling is that people probably won't, except for pornography, which is a likely cassette trade. The electronic newspaper, which shows you just the parts of the paper you want, or the electronic magazines, where you choose the articles you want, or the electronic shopping service, where you summon store and market on the TV screen and shop by picture—none of these predictions have happened though technically all are ready. I sense that the temper of our society at the present wants television for entertainment rather than such services as these.

Why is it, I wonder, if that is true, that entertainment television so rarely edges into art? Other mass media often do, films, comic strips, and jazz, to name a few. Is there something about the medium that discourages art—perhaps that small screen, which grinds everything down to minisize?[14] As Joanne Woodward says, there are no stars on TV; its people seem more like domestic pets than heroes or supermen. Or is it that we just haven't found the key to using it properly?

There is a bright side to these melancholy reflections on the poor quality of television. It is that if it isn't important it probably can't be powerful. There is, it seems to me, a syndrome of enduring myths about the mass media, which goes something like this: any medium which reaches that many people has got to be powerful; if television can sell soap it can also sell democracy; the greater the audience the more powerful the impact; television because it is the great mass medium of all time can have great power for good or for ill; serious drama, serious discussion, serious debate should have an important place in television programming; and so on. But what if none of these is, under the conditions of ordinary everyday life, true? What if television is merely pervasive, like basketball and knitting, and like them, not really important at all in things that matter—the formation and development of religious and political beliefs, ethics, philosophical attitudes, family and community living? What if television is more toy than monster?

---

[14] The frequent prediction of big-screen, 3-D, and stereoscopic TV so far hasn't come through. See Dennis Gabor, *Innovations: Scientific, Technological, and Social* (London: Oxford University Press, 1970), p. 56.

This view can be derived from what the most respectable social scientists have to tell us about the nature and effects of the mass media.[15] Actually, that isn't very much. Although often challenged since then, the formulations by Berelson, Schramm, Klapper, and others made largely during the 1950's still stand up: that mass media reinforce rather than originate attitudes, that they are largely powerless to change strongly held beliefs, and that they reflect rather than lead society. Against this view, which really says this is all we can prove as things are, there is the mounting sense that the media do matter more than this. The tension between these two views is likely to be healthy for the media, oddly subject to very little criticism outside their own ranks. Maybe we're too close to television to be intelligently critical of it; film criticism in the United States began to be generally worth reading only when the films ceased to be *the* mass medium. Maybe McLuhan is right in thinking that the television experience provides strong though unutterable social bonds. Perhaps we ought to hope so. We need them. But the experience of the 60's doesn't confirm this hope.

---

[15] An excellent brief statement is that of Bernard Berelson, "The Great Debate on Cultural Democracy," in Donald N. Barrett, ed., *Values in America* (Notre Dame, Ind.: University of Notre Dame Press, 1961).

The Literature of Reduction

Ronald Weber

"Literature is now in the process of telling us how little it means."

I

"**I**T CONSPIRED to convince the McGraw-Hill Book Company that I was in communication with Howard Hughes, and in fact I was not." With that it was over. Looking back, a brief fling for Clifford Irving: the whopping advance for an "autobiography" of Hughes, certain to become the book of the year; then the day-by-day disclosures on front pages and evening newscasts that it was all a hoax; the *Time* cover story ("Con Man of the Year") with color portrait by Elmyr de Hory, the art-forger subject of Irving's prophetic book *Fake!;* the slide from media sight in favor of Nixon in China and politicians on the primary stump; finally the terse confession in Manhattan District Court. A very brief fling—though at the time, the late winter of 1972, the Hughes-Irving story seemed to run on endlessly, and of course isn't over yet. The legal tangle goes on and rumor is that Irving is coming out with a book about the *other* book—which, we now guess, might have been the point all along.

But if we haven't yet heard the last of Irving the story is sufficiently behind us that we can consider him in a different light: not as celebrated fraud but as a literary figure of a symptomatic sort. Thinking back on the Irving affair one detects a compelling rightness about it, a sense in which it was a nutty but not wholly inappropriate low-comic parody of a recent drift of thought in high-serious literary culture; one gets the feeling that the author of faked autobiography of a famous rich recluse may not only be the con man of the year but, given a certain critical persuasion, the writing man as well. To put it another way, thinking back one begins to fancy that the distance on the literary landscape from, say, John Barth to Clifford Irving is not as lengthy as might be thought—or wished. Which is not to question Barth's high standing as a novelist, nor casually blur distinctions between serious writing and the most crass commercialism, but only to suggest that by following out some currently fashionable attitudes of the new criticism (not the New

220

Criticism—just the latest variety) a representative work of the time might as easily be thought to be Irving's faked autobiography as *Giles Goat-Boy.*[1] A perverse notion of course, rather in the manner of the literature of reduction itself. If left standing it's only in the hope of glimpsing with passing reference to the Irving affair something of the reductive way we came to talk about literature, fiction especially, during the 1960's, a period in which we generally were concerned with jettisoning accumulated cultural baggage.

II

I mention Barth because of his well-known essay, "The Literature of Exhaustion," in which he tells us that literature has reached a certain kind of dead end in our time.[2] He doesn't so much have in mind the novel-is-dead idea that is heavily with us as related and more pertinent feelings (since the novel obviously persists though, as the new criticism holds, the *age* of the novel may be past) about the "exhaustion of certain possibilities," the "used-upness of certain forms" with which the modern literary imagination must contend. Fictional tones, narrative devices, whole structures of the imagination associated with the novel seem to the modern sensibility to have been exploited to the point of exhaustion—used and abused to the extent that they can no longer carry new perception, fresh feeling— and as a consequence simply are not available to the serious writer. Partly Barth seems to suspect that the whole enterprise of the novel has reached such a point of development that it can only be carried forward as sterile repetition; clearly there is no point in the writer attempting in the present what has been done to full perfection in the past. But short of this pessimistic conclusion, the problem is one of adjusting fictional techniques to a new situation, one in which the writer feels the *near* impossibility of writing original fiction yet continues to write.

---

[1] As far as representative works go, an even better example might be Irving's rumored *The Book About the Book,* unfortunately (for Irving) already scooped by *Hoax: The Inside Story of the Howard Hughes-Clifford Irving Affair,* published by Viking and advertised as *"This* is The Book About *That* Book." Note the narrowed distance between the hack style of book selling and the involuted aestheticism of some of the new criticism.

[2] John Barth, "The Literature of Exhaustion," in Marcus Klein, ed., *The American Novel Since World War II* (New York: Fawcett, 1969), pp. 267-279.

As Barth portrays him the modern writer, finding himself in such a dilemma, must first bring himself to full awareness of what his predecessors have been up to in areas of technique. This means that he not only take on the task of succeeding the great modernist experimenters (Joyce, Kafka) but those who have already succeeded them (Beckett); no small task. But with his technical equipment thoroughly modernized the up-to-date writer theoretically is freed to reexplore the familiar literary territory abandoned by the 20th-century masters, freed to rediscover old interests in grammar and punctuation, characterization and plot, theme and meaning; theoretically, as Barth illustrates the possibility, Chartres cathedral wouldn't necessarily be an embarrassment if designed today if the designer were someone "quite aware of where we've been and where we are."

Theoretically—but in fact unlikely. The literary situation in which Barth finally locates us is one in which the composition of genuinely refurbished works of literature, let alone genuinely original ones, appears increasingly difficult, perhaps impossible. Brooding in the background of Barth's appreciation of fully up-to-date techniques is the feeling that narrative literature may already have reached the end of its historic period, finished off by *Finnegans Wake* or changed social-class conditions or competition with film, so that while it may be possible for the modern writer (to switch the image from the cathedral builder) aware of Beckett to rediscover and reinvent Henry James without embarrassment, it's more likely he will write criticism, turn to journalism, make a film, or do nothing. Or, which brings us to Barth's real point, still hooked on fiction, he will write about his inability or unwillingness to rediscover and reinvent James; which is to say that in some individual fashion he will follow the metafictional paths marked out by such contemporaries as Vladimir Nabokov and especially Jorge Luis Borges.

The great vogue of Borges among writers like Barth and for the new criticism generally stems from the fact that in poems and stories he turns the "felt ultimacies of our time into material and means for his work," that he "confronts an intellectual dead end and employs it against itself to accomplish new human work." In other words, Borges strikes Barth as uniquely modern because he has written original fiction whose implicit point is the unlikelihood of such fiction in our day. Borges' Chinese boxes—stories within stories in the shape of pedantic commentaries on imaginary texts, curious collaborations with obscure writers to correct real or invented historical errors, studied anecdotes of a mythic Argentine past—take their form and tone from our sense of the exhaustion of the possibility of fresh literary effects and in so doing manage to create just such effects. In further explaining his admiration for Borges, Barth offers a similar description of his own work: *The Sot-Weed Factor* and *Giles Goat-Boy* are "novels which imitate the form of the Novel, by an author who imitates the role of Author." He half-seriously acknowledges that this may sound unpleasantly decadent but adds that there is a sense in which the fiction writer always has approached his work through pretense and parody (Fielding parodying Richardson, etc.)—and decadent or not, this is the way the modern writer *must* approach his work if he hopes to be a figure of his time.

To repeat: Barth says the writer must always turn the felt ultimacies of the day into material and means for his art, and one of the felt ultimacies of our day, turned to brilliant account by Borges, is the sense of the exhaustion of inherited literary forms. I have no quarrel with this view, nor with the appreciation of Borges' illuminary role in modern fiction; if fiction writing is akin to making magic, the pulling of fat rabbits from silk hats, Borges' particular trick is that he appears to omit the hat—and does so in a time when the audience is restless with the whole act. It may be, too, as Barth says, that Borges' stories have the added pleasure of disturbing us in an odd metaphysical way and of reminding us of the "fictitious aspect of our own existence" (though this may be more a sample of the high style of the new criticism than of what we find attractive in Borges). But I want to offer the obvious remark that while many old novelistic devices indeed seem thoroughly shopworn in our time, Barth's sense of a near-total exhaustion of traditional forms of fiction is far from new and, more important, far from widespread.

Joyce and Kafka, among others, long ago discovered that writing could be more than the carrying of mirrors along the roadway, and that the novel could be used to describe primarily itself as well as experience or reality. But as Roger Shattuck has pointed out, the early modernists, like "savvy con men," worked alone. Some of their latter-day successors, on the other hand, seem bent on dogmatically dominating the field by setting it down that the modern

novel "does not express, it explores, and what it explores is itself."[3]
That's one function of course, a rich and compelling one with a
tradition of its own, but there are others, less introspective and self-
consciously literary but no less legitimate and certainly no less
modern.

Though we seem to assume otherwise, it has yet to be effectively
demonstrated that the traditional modes and mannerisms of Balzac,
Dickens, and James, or Saul Bellow, John Updike, and William
Styron, are really outmoded and inferior. The usual assertion is that
the true creative thrust of the time is to be found among novelists
given to experimentation and the discovery of new forms rather
than with those who maintain in one way or another the naturalistic
tradition; but the view is too narrow, obscuring too much of the
varied complexity of what Lawrence called the bright book of life.
The truth is that the novel has multiple functions: to entertain, to
satirize, to describe new sensibilities, to record life, to improve life.[4]
And it remains as true now as in the past that fictional methods are
never interesting enough in themselves and only become so when
fused with the writer's full absorption in the life he imagines.

To come back to Barth, what he asks us most to admire about
Borges is his ingenious solution to a technical problem—the exhaustion of inherited literary forms. In turn what he suggests we
most admire in his own work is his stylish invention of himself as a
Borgesian technician—an author imitating the role of author and
writing a novel imitating the form of the novel. With both Borges
and Barth we are left with the impression that inward-turning
technical ingenuity in a diminished literary environment is the sole
remaining resource of serious fiction. It just isn't so.

III

Here we might well turn back to Clifford Irving and *his* solution
to the exhaustion of literary forms. But before that a look at two
other aspects of the way we now talk about literature, writing as
words and writing as performance.

William Gass, a gifted writer and an engaging spokesman for

---

[3] From Alain Robbe-Grillet's *For a New Novel: Essays on Fiction* (New
York: Grove Press, 1965), a basic manifesto of the new criticism.

[4] The terms are John Fowles', "Notes on an Unfinished Novel," in Thomas
McCormack, ed., *Afterwords: Novelists on Their Novels* (New York: Harper
& Row, 1969), pp. 160-175.

the central place of language in modern writing, tells us straight out that "literature is language, that stories and the places and the people in them are merely made of words as chairs are made of smoothed sticks and sometimes of cloth or metal tubes."[5] One would hardly wish to argue this view yet the effect of the realization that novels are made of words, merely words, is, Gass insists, shocking: "It's as though you had discovered that your wife were made of rubber: the bliss of all those years, the fears . . . . from sponge." But the shock is therapeutic in that it can rid us of the flabby illusion that fiction is something other than words, that it's history or sociology or psychology; that it's character or time or event; that it's, silliest of all, like life. By insisting that there is nothing in fiction save words the writer is freed to wring pure effects from his medium and so become, in Gass' phrase, a "true lie-minded man," a fictionalist yet one who knows the fiction serves the wonders of language, not the reverse. One who knows that the "novelist's words are not notes which he is begging the reader to play, as if his novel needed something more done to it in order to leap into existence"; one who knows, finally, that words are not windows through which something else may be glimpsed but opaque and sufficient entities.

Gass appreciates full well the heavy demands his intensely linguistic fiction makes on the reader; of his novel *Omensetter's Luck* he has said: "It was written to *not* have readers, while still deserving them." However private and essentially poetic, the position is the one he prefers and from which he does his best work (which *does* deserve readers), and while making an ardent critical case for it he sees and accepts the human limits. Other voices of the new criticism, lacking Gass' reluctant balance, turn his passion for style into a simplistic explanation of all that is new in contemporary writing. Warren Tallman finds that the chief difference between the older American writing and the new "is that between writing considered as a means to an end, sentences used as corridors leading to further rooms, and writing considered as an end in itself."[6] And the effect of writing so considered? "When it is accepted as such the first sentence becomes an arrival, a foot set in the word world. The chief elements of this world are not earth, air, fire and

---

[5] William H. Gass, *Fiction and the Figures of Life* (New York: Vintage, 1972).

[6] Warren Tallman, "The Writing Life," in Donald M. Allen and Robert Creeley, eds., *New American Story* (New York: Grove Press, 1965), pp. 1-12.

water (and certainly not wisdom, truth, reality and morality) but
sight, sound, sense and syntax." Richard Kostelanetz rightly ties
the undeniably greater attention to language in recent fiction to the
decline of realism as a literary mode and the consequent effort to
stake out for fiction (as against the visual media and other verbal
forms) its own unique territory, prose style.[7] But he goes from this
useful enough insight to the generalization that "without a special,
heightened language, no piece of fiction is truly interesting as
literature."

Again, it just isn't so. Like Tallman, Kostelanetz turns a development—and one that belongs to the whole modernist tradition
rather than the present moment—as well as personal taste into a
definition that goes a modest way toward accounting for the work
of Barth, Gass, Thomas Pynchon, John Hawkes, Robert Coover,
and Donald Barthelme, but has little bearing on that of such contemporaries as Bellow, Styron, Updike, Bernard Malamud, John
Cheever, Ralph Ellison, Walker Percy, Eudora Welty, J. F. Powers,
and Joyce Carol Oates, to name off a few. Quite simply, there are
levels of interest in modern fiction that don't have much to do with
the creation of a special, heightened language, and there are approaches to writing that don't consider words an end in themselves.
To hold otherwise is to settle for modish critical statements that
have only partial use in thinking about the broad range of recent
writing; it's also to think of writing in the self-conscious, enclosed,
virtuoso terms that Barth suggests as appropriate to an age of exhaustion. It's to fasten critical attention on tools, methods, and the
triumphs of technique, to think of literature—fiction, at any rate—
as nearing the end of its allotted time and out of that last-gasp
necessity turned in upon itself, upon its own forms and primary
means, no longer responsive to or controlled by the pressure of its
old stimulus: the sense of the actual, or as Philip Roth has put it,
"the tug of reality, its mystery and magnetism."[8]

---

[7] Richard Kostelanetz, "The American Short Story Today," *12 from the Sixties* (New York: Dell, 1967), pp. 9-21.

[8] The writers who appear in the collection with Tallman's essay illustrate Roth's view as much as the notion that in new fiction writing is considered an end in itself. In a biographical notes and statements section one of them says that "Novels are about people, for people." Another says he writes because of an "obsession for 'framing' life" and adds: "Art slows life down, injects meaning into it, orders the horrible, brutal chaos." Very old-fashioned stuff.

IV

To deeply concern ourselves with technique, with inward-turning invention and the glitter of metaphor, is to deeply concern ourselves with the technician. If certain literary forms seem worn out
in our time, the writer himself clearly isn't—isn't yet; his presence
can still command us, his skills still draw our applause. If we rid
ourselves of all that is stodgily old-fashioned or dumbly naive in our
conception of modern literature what remains for us is the true lie-
minded man himself, the writer at work.

Which brings us to a more formidable example of the new
criticism, Richard Poirier's recent collection of essays *The Performing Self*.[9] The work calls attention to what Poirier sees as a sadly
neglected aspect of literary study, an awareness of literature as a
phenomenon of performance; his insistent purpose is "to reclaim
the energy of human performance, especially in writing, from the
humanistic and liberal traditions that have all but smothered it."
He points out that for the author an event, real or imagined, exists
only in the shape he is able to give it in the writing, and so it is the
writer's private performance—rendered in "pacing, economies,
juxtapositions, aggregations of tone, the whole conduct of the
shaping presence"—that is of primary importance to him and that
always exists in "perpetually tensed antagonism" with the public
presentation of the finished work. Poirier quotes Robert Frost to the
effect that in poetry the whole thing "is performance and prowess
and feats of association" and that regardless, say, of the agony that
might be expressed in a poem, or the agony experienced in writing
it, what the writer always wants to communicate is "what a *hell* of
a good time" he had in the making. Before it's anything else then—
from the writer's standpoint *more* than it's anything else—the
literary work is an act, a composition, a performance, and it's
Poirier's position that it's with such performance and the writer's
tough self-knowledge of himself as a performer (competing tooth
and nail against other performers, other modes of performance, and
most of all against his sense of his own mortality) that literary study
must begin to concern itself.

Poirier's focus on the writer as a performing self—with illustra-

---

[9] Richard Poirier, *The Performing Self: Compositions and Decompositions
in the Languages of Contemporary Life* (New York: Oxford University Press,
1971).

tions drawn from Andrew Marvell, Thoreau, and James, Frost, Borges, Barth, Pynchon, and Norman Mailer—is illuminating in ways I can't do full justice to here and indeed suggests fresh ways of thinking about literature. There is no doubt that literary study takes on new dimensions of interest when we begin to ask the most elementary and therefore the hardest questions about a work: "what must it have felt like to do this—not mean anything, but to do it." Poirier quotes Frost confiding to a fellow poet: "My whole anxiety is for myself as a performer. Am I any good? That's what I'd like to know and all I need to know." To grasp what Frost means is to get hold of a revealing insight into the calculating (Poirier offers the word "brutal") self-absorption that is a necessary part of the creative imagination—that in a sense *is* the creative imagination. All the same, such a call for an awareness of the writer as a performer within his work can tempt us to so exclusively concern ourselves with acts of performance, with prowess and feats of association and a heightened sensitivity to the inner rewards of craft, that we dismiss as relatively unimportant what in fact has been performed.

As readers we can cast ourselves into Frost's anxiety for himself as a performer but can never fully share it; his assessment of himself as a performer may be all he needs to know but never all we need to know. We insist in asking other questions about a work since we must in a fundamental sense remain outside it, members of the world into which it is issued and in which it becomes a quite different performance from that experienced by the writer. We can never wholly share the hell of a good time he had in making the work any more than he can wholly share the hell of a good time we may have in reading it; just as we may have scant understanding of his "brutal" calculations so too he may have only the most general notion of what he has wrought and is ultimately responsible for.

James had an appropriate bridge-building metaphor for the tension between the writer's concern for himself in the motions of performance and the audience's concern with the finished product:

> The bridge spans the stream after the fact, in apparently complete independence of these properties, the principal grace of the original design. *They* were an illusion, for the necessary hour; but the span itself, whether of a single arch or of many, seems by the oddest chance in the world to be a reality; since actually the rueful builder, passing under it, sees figures and hears sounds above: he makes

out, with his heart in his throat, that it bears and is positively being "used."[10]

The "they"—the original design and acts of the builder—are only an "illusion" in relation to the apparent solidity of the bridge itself; they cannot be left out of account in any full consideration of the bridge. It's with these details of building, the "principal grace" of the workmanship, that we must begin the study. But begin—surely not end. For the traveler it remains that the crucial fact about the bridge is that it "bears" and is capable of being "used"; to fail to take into account this "reality," as James called it, is to ignore the basic independence of the finished construction. To paraphrase a comment of Flannery O'Connor, the more complete the bridge the less important it is who built it or why.

A conventional view of course, one that keeps the critical focus on the objects of performance. But the new criticism is inclined to have none of it; in full flight from the finished object, it reverses attention and concentrates on the performer and *his* engagement with the performance. In the process another thing stripped away is any fundamental concern with whether the performance is cast in fiction of nonfiction, poem or play, history or criticism. The essential thing is the style of the performer, and only as circumstances of genre enhance his performance—an original performance in fiction enhanced by the high modern odds against it—is genre itself worth particular note. Another way to make this point is to maintain, as Poirier does, that all writing is equally fictional and so measurable on the same scale; to "talk or to write is to fictionalize" and to write novels, plays, and poems is merely to "refictionalize." Further, claims for fiction as a unique literary mode are obviously unsupportable in such an obviously fictional time, a time when "creative" writers of any hue pale before the likes of "Rusk and McNamara and Kissinger, the mothers of invention, 'reporting' on the war in Vietnam."

While differences of genre are supposedly unimportant in the new criticism, it's here, with ironic reference to reporting, that we may have the most uniquely contemporary performances of all. To

---

[10] The passage is quoted by Poirier as illustration of the constant antagonism between acts of performance and the thing performed—which is just my point. Poirier knows that the recognition of such tension is needed for a full understanding of any literary work, but in emphasizing literary "doing" as an escape from the problems and pretensions of literary "meaning" he seems to me to frequently lose sight of it.

make Borgesian literature out of the exhaustion of fictional possibilities is a neat trick, but to make an original literature out of the
mind-numbing nonfiction fictions (to hold for the moment to the
insistence on the fictional basis of all writing) that assail us is all
the more impressive as performance. If Borges is a representative
figure on the one hand, Mailer is his counterpart on the other, and
although Poirier doesn't distinguish between them in terms of forms
employed he favors Mailer as the more interesting (an all-purpose
distinguishing term when discussing the performing self) since his
engagements with language are more broadly political than narrowly literary and so closer to what we sense as the core of the time.
Mailer is a contender for language and literary performance not
only against used-up literary forms but against all forms and
mediums of expression that presume to represent our reality. "More
than anyone else of his time," says Poirier, "Mailer is implicated, in
every sense of that word, in the way we live now," and in his recent
work he has grappled so directly and personally with that manner of
life that it has become impossible to tell where the living performance ends and the writing performance begins.

The current literary interest in reporting—and Mailer's particular success with it in books like *The Armies of the Night* and *Of a
Fire on the Moon*—is linked to the new criticism's romance with
technique and feats of technical prowess (Truman Capote called *In
Cold Blood* a breakthrough to a new form, the "nonfiction novel";
Tom Wolfe claims to be a founding father of the "new journalism"), but this is not Poirier's emphasis. Instead, he recalls Mailer's
remark that the first art work in the artist is the shaping of his own
personality and marvels at the massive intellectual and verbal energy
with which he has dominated—in the sense of realizing himself as
a dominant presence at each event—the Pentagon march, the Chicago convention, even the moon landing. If writing is performance
Mailer is hands down our leading performer and as such a chief
exhibit of the new criticism—and not because of notable acts of
self-conscious invention, as with Barth and Borges, or poetic concern with the language of prose, as with Gass, but because he has
become his own pure performance, indistinguishable from it, stage,
characters, and audience rolled into one.[11]

---

[11] Although Mailer is a favorite of the new criticism he is hardly a per-
suasive example of many of its deepest concerns. As a novelist he is generally
conventional both in technique and style and seemingly unconcerned with the
exhaustion of old forms or the creation of a special language. His literary

V

Which brings us back to Clifford Irving, another nonfiction performer of note.

In portraying Borges' inventive response to literary exhaustion Barth mentions that someone once vexedly accused *him* of inventing Borges. One wonders; but who—Barth, Borges, Mailer—who could have invented Irving and his invention? A minor Hemingwayesque novelist before, Irving somehow (the insight courtesy of *Time*) transferred all his old-style fictional ambitions to the new nonfiction and "finally performed an act of daring imagination." "Through *his* Howard Hughes, through all of his minutely conjured secret rendezvous, through the forgeries, Irving, in some perhaps sleazily refractory way, entered a world of fabulation in which he was simultaneously living and creating high adventure." Without the corporate attribution one might think this some advocate of the new criticism calling attention to a spellbinding new literary performer who had topped even Borges in "daring imagination," even Mailer in melding "living and creating" into amazing new work.

Only one thing might beat it. Seeing how right and fitting it is for the age of literary reduction to have written his celebrated non-confessions of Hughes as a way of contriving material for his own true confessions, Irving might realize that working it up into another book would only be an anticlimax. His real triumph and ultimate art would be to conclude that his story, as a genuine life contrivance and exquisite put-down of mere literary "refictionalizing," didn't require the inking of a single line. Pure reduction is nothingness. At that inspired point he might be considered by the new criticism to have entered, with Beckett, beyond exhaustion and into silence.[12]

VI

Some years ago Norman Podhoretz, defending Mailer's maligned "existential" novel *Barbary Shore,* pointed out that to write naturalistic fiction one had to believe that "society is what it seems

---

roots are directly and dramatically in life, as evidenced by his recent journalism, and he has none of the inventive and abstract aestheticism that usually attracts the new criticism. For Mailer's relation to an old and central tradition in American literature see Thomas Werge's essay in this collection.

[12] Barth: ". . . for Beckett, at this point in his career, to cease to create altogether would be fairly meaningful: his crowning work, his 'last word.' "

to be and that it reveals the truth about itself in the personalities it throws up, the buildings it builds, the habits and manners it fosters; all the writer need do is describe these faithfully . . . and truth will be served."[13] But Mailer's point in the novel was just the opposite: American society wasn't what it seemed to be; it seemed to be prosperous, purposeful, and sure of itself when in fact it was empty, confused, and in the grip of invisible forces it neither recognized nor controlled. The only hope of making literary sense of such a society was through the indirect means Mailer had chosen, for "invisible forces" can't be described but can only be "talked about abstractly and pictured allegorically."

Podhoretz' account of American society and its effect on literary form may not make *Barbary Shore* a better novel but it has become a commonplace point of departure for thinking about new experimental writing. We tell ourselves that such work is forced to separate itself from the naturalistic conventions and to operate through fable and fantasy, poetry and symbol, parody and black humor (or through the abandonment of fiction entirely in favor of personal styles of journalism) if it's to discover a fitting literary manner for the way the world is now. We tell ourselves that such work is seeking literature's dramatic truth at a time when society is sunk in confusion and deceit and old, familiar methods of literary photography simply will no longer do. Art must continually seek its time, and if the effort today seems more demanding and the forms of invention more outrageous because our break with the past is more severe, it's still understandable enough—and we counsel ourselves to be open to the fresh and the strange, however thin and boring it may strike us in the effort to be ingenious, however showy and vain in the effort to be rigorously honest, and to be wary of resisting the new because it doesn't resemble the mediocrity of the past.

But the new criticism perceives literary problems far more troublesome than finding alternatives to naturalism given the chimerical state of our society. For one thing, it detects a fundamental unease with the very notion of narrative literature. As the argument has it, the problem is that few of us really can believe anymore in narration, in the process of telling stories; which is to

---

[13] Norman Podhoretz, "Norman Mailer: The Embattled Vision," *Doings and Undoings: The Fifties and After in American Writing* (New York: Noonday, 1964), pp. 179-204.

say that few of us can believe anymore in what has always been a ruling principle of the novelist's art. Richard Gilman, a central figure in the new criticism, tells us that narrative "is precisely the element in fiction which coerces it and degrades it into being a mere alternative to life, *like* life, only better of course (or a serviceable nightmare), a way out, a recompense, a blueprint, a lesson."[14] The curse of narrative, its better-than-life and essentially escapist quality, is its assumption of rationality and control. A narrative has a beginning and an ending and something between; it moves from point to point, from causes to effects, a development heading toward a conclusion. And the conclusion isn't just the last event but in one way or another an explanation. The tale, Lionel Trilling has said, is never "told by an idiot but by a rational consciousness which perceives in things the processes that are their reason and which derives from this perception a principle of conduct, a way of living among things."[15] The narrative presupposes a controlling narrator, someone arranging, managing, counseling, bringing order from confusion if only the order of simplification; the sound and fury of narrative always signifies something.

And that's the rub, narrative's both naive and presumptuous sense of an ordered world. Trilling raises the question: "Can we, in this day and age, submit to a mode of explanation so primitive, so flagrantly Aristotelian?" The new criticism says no—and so seeks out writers who evade, obscure, and ideally abandon the narrative principle, writers who struggle, as Gilman puts it, against the "untruthfulness of storytelling."

Yet the problems go even deeper. Narrative is not only suspect in our time because it tends toward significance (so do other forms of telling though they as well experience the pinch of the moment: tell what?), but quite apart from this it brings into play what James called the blessed faculty of wonder. Narrative traditionally has sought to cast a spell over the reader, to draw him out of himself into a word world of other people, other places; it has sought removal from the self, a magic transportation of consciousness. And it's this, narrative's manipulation of the reader through absorption, that draws forth the sharpest modern skepticism, as Trilling recog-

---

[14] Richard Gilman, *The Confusion of Realms* (New York: Random House, 1969).

[15] Lionel Trilling, "Authenticity and the Modern Unconscious," *Commentary,* September, 1971, pp. 39-50.

nizes when he says (discussing the critical position of Walter Benjamin) that "there is something inauthentic for our time in being held spellbound, momentarily forgetful of oneself, concerned with the fate of a person who is not oneself but who also, by reason of the spell that is being cast, is oneself, his conduct and his destiny bearing upon the reader's own."

Inauthentic. That's the root problem the new criticism finds with inherited literary approaches—they are inauthentic for our time; and so the task becomes one of erecting an argument for a kind of literature that is authentic, one that doesn't presume to tell us anything, and certainly one that doesn't presume to exercise such primitive authority over the reader as to induce in him a sense of wonder or concerns that range beyond his own, but instead keeps him at arm's length from the work, in his own realm of reality. Technique and invention are to be celebrated as sufficient literary ends, as are language and the writer's concern with himself as a performer, doing but not meaning; in each case interest is required of the reader but not absorption. And reductive statements about literature become necessary to set it in properly honest perspective in relation to the inflated literary-humanistic claims of the past. Thus Gilman: "For most of us writing is at best a minor act within civilized society, one of its attributes, a divertissement, a sort of skill in putting into formal verbal modes what we already know or sense, a change of pace or an enlivenment, and no true source of prophecy, discovery or power." And thus the new criticism's attraction to the literature of self-parody which draws its spirit from a self-conscious mocking of the forms and aims of literature. Such work, says Poirier, "proposes not the rewards so much as the limits of its own procedures; it shapes itself around its own dissolvents; it calls into question not any particular literary structure so much as the enterprise, the activity itself of creating any literary form, of empowering an idea with a style." So much for traditional literary hopes in our time.

VII

Throughout I've been offering a response of sorts to the reductions of the new criticism based on taste, on old notions of what literature is and does, and on the plain fact that there is more variety, including more traditionalism, in contemporary writing than such critical talk might lead one to think. And I've suggested, in the perverse spirit of the literature of self-parody, that Clifford Irving isn't an inappropriate figure to come forward in a period of literary diminishment; if literature is now in the process of telling us how little it means, as Poirier says, Irving would seem to be an intriguing case in point. Other responses could be set out as well, all equally familiar. Against the emphasis on literature as language rather than character or event Bellow's belief that a "work of fiction consists of a series of moments during which we are willingly engrossed in the experiences of others"; against the up-to-date technicians his suspicion that it is writers who most despair of existence who make the most of the art of the novel; against writing as performance the classic view of the writer as one always subordinated to his art, judging himself, as Flannery O'Connor said, with "a stranger's eye and a stranger's severity," for in this view "No art is sunk in the self, but rather, in art the self becomes self-forgetful in order to meet the demands of the thing seen and the thing being made"; against the modern mistrust of the storyteller's sleight of hand Miss O'Connor's belief in the dramatically rendered tale as a means of experiencing in a special and intensely concrete way the mystery of existence, a mystery that is in fact a plunge into reality at such depth that "it requires considerable courage at any time, in any country, not to turn away from the storyteller."[16]

All of which may sound more entrenched on the matter than I really feel and may only serve to extend the polarized situation in which literature now finds itself, splitting the field between the innovators and the traditionalists, the up-to-date and the old-fashioned, thereby obscuring the varied rewards to be found in present writing. It may also obscure a point I want to make clear: that despite these and other objections that might be raised against it, the new criticism effectively gets hold of a deep unease that now surrounds our response to literature. Trilling is surely onto something when he questions the authenticity of literature for modern man. Writers at all points on the spectrum of attitudes find severe erosions of literary faith. Bellow laments that, awash in a new self-centered egalitarianism, we now refuse all authority, including that of the artist: "As Protestantism denied the power of priests, We deny the power of these priest-substitutes, the artists, who wish to

---

[16] Saul Bellow, "The Sealed Treasure," in Theodore Solotaroff, ed., *Writers and Issues* (New York: Signet, 1969), pp. 214-219; Flannery O'Connor, *Mystery and Manners* (New York: Noonday, 1969).

cast a magical spell over Us and to invest their work with sacredness. There is no such sacredness now." Iris Murdoch, noting the
fallen status of writers and artists in general, describes "a deep crisis
of confidence in the very idea of art as the making of completed
statements" about life or the world. People today instinctively mistrust all claims to completeness and so "want to challenge the completeness of the art object itself as a way of challenging the authority
of the statement it appears to be making. Traditional art is seen as
far too grand, and is *then* seen as a half-truth." Leslie Epstein is
even more despairing: "The only arts with a chance to survive are
those which have devoted themselves to being inartistic—to destroying illusions, or obliterating the gap between character and bystander, annihilating point of view. Literature has no place in the
scheme."[17]

Despite plenty of instances of rhetorical overkill, the reductions
of the new criticism indeed reflect the diminished position of contemporary literature, the feeling, as a cynical critic suggests in a
Kurt Vonnegut novel, that the function of the novel in modern
society may only be to provide touches of color in rooms with all-
white walls. The situation in literature is of course simply an aspect
of the diminished situation in which all the arts, traditionally considered, now find themselves. All the arts have experienced in one
way or another a cultural radicalism that has attacked content and
meaning and emphasized style and form; all have seen a shift of
critical attention from the independent work to the manner of the
artist, from the completed object to the process of its making; all
have been influenced by a democratization of culture in which
distinctions between "high" and "low" and "serious" and "pop"
appear less and less meaningful; all have experienced a rejection of
art's general claim to convey a truth higher than that perceived by
ordinary intellection. All the arts, in short, are now telling us how
little they mean—and this in the hope of emerging in a more
authentic pose, reduced yet honest, less assuming yet more self-
aware.

Death-of-art attitudes in literature and the arts as a whole (in
turn mirrors of what Daniel Moynihan has dubbed our present

---

[17] Saul Bellow, "Culture Now: Some Animadversions, Some Laughs,"
Modern Occasions, I (Winter, 1971), 162-178; Iris Murdoch, *The New York
Review of Books,* June 15, 1972, pp. 3-6; Leslie Epstein's remarks appear in
a symposium on the writer's situation, *New American Review 10* (New York:
Signet, 1970), pp. 204-208.

"culture of disparagement") may yield the promised phoenix-like rebirth, or at least something fresh and stimulating and even enlightening, but on the basis of present evidence I'm inclined to doubt it. Other possibilities, somewhat more probable, are that they represent temporary stances of little lasting importance or, the contrary and darker view, that they indeed are important, that they are likely to have great effect, and what that effect will amount to is a sharp loss. Along those lines a remark borrowed from William Gass may be suggestive: from some ashes no bird rises. The time is given to the contemplation of last things, to apocalyptic thoughts and ideological burials, and it may not be literary adjustment we are set upon so much as abandonment, the whole inflated, elitist, used-up tradition at last junked, enduring only as a plaything of an insatiable entertainment industry or a lingering base for the truly authentic expositions of the new criticism. Perhaps only a petulant thought, itself suggested by apocalyptic attitudes that find chaos in the necessary motions of change. We have to keep reminding ourselves that literary order is always provisional, that in writing there can be no orthodoxy for the kind of work that most deeply interests the serious writer is always work that hasn't been written; yet as long as some old human needs continue to be felt—to touch the heart's truth, to experience a consciousness alive to joy, pain, and time, to see inwardly—the creative task would seem to be to manage change without utter destruction. As Bellow (a distinctly anti-apocalyptic writer) keeps reminding us, the forms of literature wear out but the mystery of mankind doesn't.

Not that the best contemporary writers have really thought otherwise. One of the weighty burdens the new criticism labors under is that it can locate few good examples and almost no pure ones of the kind of work it finds most fitting for the time. The most talented writers around, some of the most experimental included, continue to indicate by their practice (whatever they might find themselves saying) that fiction can't wholly be separated from lived experience, that to confuse art with life is a basic fallacy but that it's an equal mistake to deny their abiding interrelation.[18] However

---

[18] For an elaboration of this view and a general rejection of the new criticism see Philip Rahv's caustic review of *The Confusion of Realms, The New York Review of Books,* June 4, 1970, pp. 57-59. For views generally similar to this and to those of mine sketched above see, in the same publication, reviews of current fiction by John Weightman, June 1, 1972, pp. 6-10, and Roger Sale, May 4, 1972, pp. 3-6.

battered, the dream of Stephen Dedalus persists: to re-create life
from life. One of the deep ironies of the time, as Daniel Bell has
noted, is that with all the turbulence of the 1960's and talk about
originality there have been almost no noteworthy revolutions in
aesthetic form or style.[19] For the most part writers keep on telling
stories, creating characters, offering significations; there have been
important adjustments of course: a scaling down of large ambition,
a muting of claims, a lessened interest in the intricate artifice or the
evidently well made and a consequent increase in fun-and-games
attitudes toward language and fictional event; in the strains of
experimental and naturalistic writing and various combinations
thereof the sense of literary diminishment is heavily in the air, leading to a common admission of gloom. But it remains that the
literature of reduction—Clifford Irving aside—is still largely a
critical literature, written by critics for critics and legislating a
program for work yet to be written. As such it's probably a sensitive enough reflector of literary uncertainty and maybe a portent
of things to come but a thin description of the actual state of affairs
in serious writing.

19 Daniel Bell, "Sensibility in the 60's," *Commentary,* June, 1971, pp. 63-73.